TIME'S CHARIOT

SIR JOHN POLLOCK, *Bart.*

LONDON

JOHN MURRAY, ALBEMARLE STREET, W.

First Edition . . . *1950*

1629

Made and Printed in Great Britain by Butler & Tanner Ltd., Frome and London

But at my back I always hear
Time's wingèd chariot hurrying near.

ANDREW MARVELL

If a man should find credible what I have
here set down, then let him believe it ; if
not, then let it not further hold his attention.

CLAUDIUS ÆLIANUS : *Varia Historia*

. . . vivre à reculons, pour respirer encore
du printemps.

BÉRANGER

CONTENTS

LIST OF ILLUSTRATIONS

PREFACE

THIS book is not the story of my life, on the improbable supposition that my life has a story worth telling. Nor is it a family history. But there are things about my family that may be worth recording before they are clean forgotten, and I have in the course of a life now fairly long met many remarkable people and seen the world perhaps from a standpoint not accessible to everybody.

Mr. Somerset Maugham has said that only a very few books are worth a second reading. Since a good number of his own are worth that, and more, he has the right to an opinion on the subject. I cannot hope that the present work will escape so just a condemnation ; but I trust stuff may be found in it to justify one reading. The material in the chapter *And Two Great Friends* is reprinted by kind permission of the editor of the *Contemporary Review*.

J. P.

June 1950

CHAPTER I

1880 AND ALL THAT

I MADE my bow in this world about six o'clock on the morning of one Boxing Day. My mother, a woman of original character and much resolution, had anticipated the custom of a later date and, instead of reclining on a day-bed, the proper English word for the more fashionably named chaise-longue, while awaiting her time, went about her business and pleasure until the end. Nowadays it is no uncommon sight to see young women, far advanced in pregnancy, out shopping or amusing themselves. There was a day when these would have been the same thing; but since the second World War and the advent of pitiless Socialist restrictions, so many of them unnecessary save to justify the existence of Socialists and their myriad minor bureaucrats, there has come into being a vital difference between a woman's amusement and that grim business, for men as well as for women, shopping. The twentieth century saw greater latitude in the conduct of expectant mothers. One lady was actually delivered in the office of a West End theatre, hastily converted into a bedroom; in her enthusiasm for Lewis Waller, a handsome Jewish actor, whose popularity was such that a club of his admirers was formed with the name " The All-for-Wallerites ", she had run things rather too fine. And a Spanish Infanta was taken with the pains of labour during a show by Grock, that clown of genius. But in the heyday of Victorian England cosseting and cushioning was thought the right rule for a woman about to produce a baby; and it was across this rule that my mother cut with her usual good sense and perfect simplicity. So on Christmas Day she went to a dinner-party, that now almost forgotten event of cardinal importance in the social life of seventy years ago and, being of real importance, more formal, longer, and more exhausting than people who meet round a table in the volatile modern style can readily imagine. First, unless you were rich enough to keep a carriage, which not many moderately placed upper-middle-class people could afford, and certainly very few youngish married pairs like my parents, the invited couple went to their destination in that jolting, stuffy, dirty contraption known as a four-wheeler, or more colloquially, a growler. The convenience of a nice-looking carriage to be hired for the evening had not yet been born. When it did come, London owed it to the invention of Mr., afterwards Lord Courtauld Thomson, who started The London Coupé Company. Even so in a growler drove out to dinner Lord Cranborne—he who was to become famous as the Marquess of Salisbury and modern England's best Foreign Minister ; and Lady Cranborne, as she entered the drawing-room of their hosts, made a display of picking out of her gown wisps of straw adhering to it from the floor of the growler. Most ladies examined their trains and extracted any possible straws in the room set apart for their uncloaking before going upstairs. But Lady Cranborne took care to do the deed in the drawing-room after being announced, so as to impress on the assembled company the odious stinginess of her father-in-law who would not run to the expense of a brougham for his heir. Next, after your mounting an often steep and narrow staircase and being solemnly admitted to accompaniment of the butler's dignified voice, ensued a long wait filled with formal conversation till all the guests were assembled when, dinner being announced, you paired off according to orders and descended again solemnly arm in arm to the business of the evening. In the case of a narrow staircase, much adroitness was required on the part of the gentleman to seem to keep on the same step as the lady on his arm, while in reality balancing himself one step above or one below. Gentlemen used to take their opera hats up to the drawing-room with them and after the procession downstairs, as they passed from the hall into the dining-room, handed them to the butler who deftly tucked them away much as Nelson's boatswain dealt with the swords of the captured French officers after the Battle of the Nile. I had this ceremony impressed upon my mind by the delight always caused me as my uncle Walter Herries Pollock flicked his opera hat out like a jack-in-the-box into my face over the banisters at my father's, when at the age of four or so I was allowed to stand on the stairs with my sister, a few steps above the drawing-room landing and watch the guests go down.

Dinner would then be at 7.15 for 7.30, and I vividly remember the change made in my world when the hour for it was put on first by a quarter, then by half an hour. At 7.45 for 8 it stuck for many years and, when invitations began to be sent out for 8 o'clock, people would excuse the innovation by saying mysteriously : " You know, the Queen always dines at 8." Which may or may not have been true.

A business, dinner of those days really was. The long menus of our ancestors have been too often described for them to be worth repeating. But it may be noted that there were always two soups, which the butler followed round with a whisper : " Sherry or r'Ock, sir ? ", fish, two roasts, poultry or game, and two very solid sweets, trifle being among the most approved. In season, this simple repast, for simple it was then in comparison with, say, City banquets, often began with oysters : in season too it always ended with piles of fruit, served from one of those silver, in part filigree, monstrosities known as *épergnes*. Vegetables were much what you are given at Simpson's today, where, so long as English fare survived the assault of finally victorious austerity, English fare it was. My mother once shocked a celebrated physician sitting next her by refusing the cabbage. He rebuked her in these words : " My dear lady, you don't know what you are refusing—bottled sunshine ! Bottled sunshine ! " Although the definition seems to contain a preview of the as yet unsuspected vitamin, its application to the national " greens " was wholly fallacious, for nothing can ever have contained less of any nutritive principle than English cabbage, " plain-boiled ", and the water containing its vital juice poured down the sink.

After her Christmas dinner then, at which of course in honour of the season of the year the poultry served would be turkey and the sweets a flaming plum pudding and mince pies, my mother returned home having enjoyed herself thoroughly and being taken with the pains of labour in the small hours was delivered of me by the light of oil lamp and candle, still the only illumination of bedrooms though there was already gas in passages and on the staircase. On such occasions doctors and midwives had to be fetched on foot, unless a providential cab were met in the street, nor is it surprising that in cases of difficulty or of accident supervening childbed and infantile mortality was far higher than in an age dowered with telephones and motorcars, to say nothing of nursing-homes that later became the almost normal place of delivery for thousands of women. Gas had reached the rest of the house early in the 1880's or earlier. Until the invention of the incandescent mantle, gaslight in a bedroom was apt to give off an unpleasant smell and was thought unwholesome. The first dining-room to be lit by gas was, I believe, that of the Athenæum ; this was in 1830 and was considered an astonishing innovation, as indeed it was, and the original gas chandeliers (a shocking misuse of a word, but there seems to be no other) are there to this day, long since converted for electricity, " to tell you ", as Calverley writes in his parody of Macaulay, " if I lie ".

My mother's doctor was named Hames, a ruddy-faced and slightly reddish-haired man, with a large, drooping moustache, a brilliant diagnostician to whom no trouble was too great in his patients' interests. When the so-called " Russian " influenza, forerunner of the equally miscalled " Spanish " variety of 1918, first struck London, my parents, my grandmother, my sister, our nurse, the housemaid, and the parlourmaid were all in bed with it at once and the cook, who took it first, barely recovering. Hames came every day, sometimes twice, and managed to see that we were all properly fed, washed, and tended. So doubtless did he minister to the needs of many another household. Patients under the National Health Service may think themselves lucky indeed if the doctors to whose lot they fall today serve them with a tenth of that devotion. Actually Hames was a F.R.C.S., that is a surgeon, but he was one of the best general practitioners I have ever seen. When he brought me into the world he must have been pretty young, for he went on for over twenty-five years being our medical attendant. I was already grown up when he took into partnership Harry Huxley, Professor T. H. Huxley's handsome and cheery younger son, a great favourite with the ladies. It was only when I was told by an acquaintance who had had occasion to consult Hames in that capacity that I discovered him, whom I had known all my life as a first-rate family doctor, to be in addition a well-known consultant and one of the best London specialists on venereal disease.

My father was so much flustered by the circumstances of my birth that he entered the date wrongly on the birth certificate.

GEORGINA HARRIET DEFFELL (LADY POLLOCK)

My mother in youth. An amateur portrait

No doubt it was he who in the dark of Boxing morning walked to fetch Hames and the monthly nurse. To walk for several miles through the London streets was not, as I shall show later, a thing to upset my father in the least, whether by day or by night. But he got the day of the month wrong. My mother evidently did not turn a hair at my arriving somewhat unexpectedly. She had a singularly imperturbable nature. Once she was in Italy with a party of friends, all devoted to one another but all exhausted by a long excursion, hungry, thirsty, and having just learned that by an infuriating chance they had missed an important connexion. A lively quarrel was on the point of breaking out when my mother exclaimed : " Oh ! Isn't that the nightingale ? " It may not have been, but the mere name of the bird uttered in my mother's ringing, yet sweet, voice brought back the company to normal sense and spirits. If she added a laugh, she would have been very hard to resist. Her laugh was exceptional, unique, I think, in my experience. Nor in mine alone ; for once A. B. Walkley, *The Times* dramatic critic, wrote in a notice which, though personally unknown to my mother, he cut out and sent to her : " I was sitting in the stalls behind a lady whose laugh would have made her fortune, had she been on the stage."

My mother was three parts a Scotswoman. Her father, John Deffell, a Calcutta merchant unluckily carried off still young by a fever when engaged in the fascinating but dangerous commercial exploit of " pyramiding ", had for mother a Mackenzie, whose mother in turn, on the testimony of my grandfather's sister, to me " Aunt Charlotte ", was a Macpherson and daughter of Macpherson of Cluny, Prince Charles Edward's celebrated supporter and subject of a chapter in *Kidnapped*. My Aunt Charlotte was a character such as it would be impossible to find nowadays. She lived, a spinster, to be ninety-five, flanked by beautiful Persian cats, fine eighteenth-century furniture, and a portrait of her Mackenzie mother. She had never been out of England but read, and spoke fairly well, French, Italian, and German. She had the distinction of having been jilted for a richer girl by Cardinal Manning who had married and was a widower before he took Orders in the Church of Rome ; and in youth she had been presented to the Duke of Wellington. Somewhat strangely, the chief impression made on her by the great

duke was that " he was a little man—a very little man, my dear ".
This is by the way, but few people today appear to know that the
victor of Waterloo was never in his lifetime called " the Iron
Duke ", the sobriquet frequently tacked on to him by modern
writers. The name was that of a ship, one of the first iron ships
to be made, christened *The Duke of Wellington*, and her name
contracted by the popular instinct to *The Iron Duke*. My Aunt
Charlotte had a charming Peninsular anecdote from an uncle
who had fought under Wellington. Before the campaign that
led up to Vittoria the army lay at Cadiz longer than many of
Wellington's officers thought prudent. It was rumoured that
their Chief was enamoured of a Spanish beauty. Wellington was
notoriously inflammable, but never let such affairs interfere with
his military judgment. And if he had an inamorata in Cadiz,
he was not the only one. The Spanish ladies were not niggardly
of favours shown to their English allies. This was my Aunt
Charlotte's contribution to the incident :—the voluptuous curves
of the beauties of Cadiz, when seen from the front, were known
as *entusiasmo* ; the equally provocative view from the opposite
direction, as *patriotismo*.

The Deffells came from round Bristol and by their name must
have descended from some de Fel (the capital F being then
normally rendered by a double small ff) settled on the Welsh
borders by Edward I. John Deffell married Letitia Hill, the
eldest daughter of David Hill of Edinburgh, captain of an East
Indiaman. David Hill's wife was Letitia Macnaghten, granddaughter of that Sir Stuart Macnaghten who by marriage at the
age of eighty saved his clan from extinction and had over ninety
grandchildren. He lived to see his two eldest sons come of age.
In those days a captain in the service of John Company was a
person of consequence. Not only had he charge of all the souls,
goods, and livestock carried in the great windjammer on that
long sea trek round the Cape of Good Hope, round Ceylon, and
up to the unwholesome delta of the Ganges, teeming with wealth
and malaria ; but, besides a share in the Company's profit on the
voyage, he had reserved for his special use a portion of the hold
and was authorised to devote this to trading on his own. David
Hill was a man of some parts. As a youngster he was intimate
with Wilkie, who painted his friend in one of those early portraits

far superior to the paintings of crofter life by which Wilkie rose to popularity. When Hill died he left £30,000, worth in our money ten times as much, to be distributed between his numerous daughters, three of whom lived unmarried to a good age, while a fourth became the wife of yet another servant of the East India Company : she had lived so long in the East that, on retiring to childless widowhood in London, she always kept the blinds of her drawing-room pulled halfway down, as though the fierce Indian sun had pursued her to Dorset Square. To say that David Hill's money was worth ten times that of the third generation after him is if anything an understatement. Miss Crawley in *Vanity Fair*, accounted a rich woman, had £80,000 that, at interest current then, would produce for her £4,000 a year. To have £4,000 a year to spend when modern taxation is taken into account, a man must now have £300,000 or so capital. Nor is this all. Rents are at least four times higher now, and the cost of food, drink, and service of all kinds higher still. The buying value of the £ sterling is therefore at least fifteen times less in the mid-twentieth century than in the 1820's and 1830's.

Like the respectable Edinburgh family they were, the Hills belonged to the Church of Scotland. They were extremely pious and of course very Low Church. But they were liberal minded enough. Before they left Scotland after the manner of good Scots to colonise her southern neighbour, the Hill girls had known Madeleine Smith whose beauty was as famous as her trial for having, as charged against her, poisoned her lover. A verdict of " not proven ", that excellent opening granted to juries by Scottish law, was given ; but the Hills stoutly maintained Madeleine's innocence and refused to desert her. They came off well too in a further test of liberalism. This was when my mother became engaged to marry my father, who made no pretence whatever to religious orthodoxy. If in the 1870's it required firmness of character in a man to take his stand with Darwin, Huxley, and Tyndall, how much more was needed for a bevy of Scotswomen, to whom the Bible contained all the philosophy needed for salvation, to accept as husband for their only daughter and niece a man, not only from a notoriously literary, artistic, and even theatrical family, things strongly suspect to the Low Church mind, but one dealing in totally non-biblical speculation, quite

7

contrary even to the tenets of revealed religion ? It reflects real credit on these good ladies, for good they were in every sense of the word, that they did accept Fred Pollock and that there was never the semblance of dispute between him and them. My father, on his side, behaved very well, not attempting to interfere with Mrs. Deffell's teaching of the catechism to his children and, so long as she lived and could come down to them, always himself conducting family prayers, according to the established ritual of the time, in the dining-room before breakfast. Among his many merits was a broadmindedness that cost him nothing to practise, so naturally did it come to him. At the time of his marriage he was a friend from Cambridge days of Canon Llewellyn Davies, the vicar of the Marylebone Church to which my grandmother led us on Sundays, and remained throughout his life on good terms with priests of all religions, however little he subscribed to their dogmas. How my mother, brought up in an atmosphere of strict religious views, reconciled her conscience with marriage to one who, not to put too fine a point on it, was an infidel, I do not know ; but it is certain that living with my father soon mellowed and softened the ideas inculcated in her in childhood. It would have been good for Scotland had her sons and daughters at the time of the Reformation been touched with more of the latitudinarian spirit that the Hill family brought with them from Edinburgh.

My mother never paraded her Scottish origin or even probably thought much about it. Nevertheless, Scots she was by blood. Among her cousins was Lord Macnaghten (he became a law lord much later), accepted chief of a clan that had been riven for generations into warring factions ; through his mother Edward Macnaghten was a grandson of my Pollock great-grandfather, so that the families were linked in two ways. Another cousin was Melville Macnaghten, who was to become head of the C.I.D. I suspect it was part of Melville Macnaghten's technique to put off chatterers at dinner-parties (" Oh, do tell me, Sir Melville, how *do* detectives detect criminals ? ") that he devised an answer still often quoted, but too often seriously : " A detective's best friends are Inspector Chance and Sergeant Luck." My mother was also related by marriage to C. P. Scott, the well-known owner and editor of the *Manchester Guardian*, and (jumping

LETITIA DEFFELL

From a painting by Sir William Richmond, R.A.

to another country), to the Comte de Lalaing, minister of the Court to Leopold I of Belgium. During Melville Macnaghten's tenure of office at Scotland Yard, the third Commissioner was Sir Alexander Bruce. His son, Kenneth Bruce, to become colonel in the Gordon Highlanders, and I sat next one another for years on benches at Eton, while the third of our party, always ahead of us and ending up as Captain of the Oppidans, was Harry Mc-Laren now Lord Aberconway, who later married Melville Macnaghten's daughter, my second cousin. My whole early life therefore was passed in an atmosphere strongly tinged with Scottish influence, the more so as my mother, as was very natural in her, had chosen for nurse a Highland girl, with the charmingly native name of Jessie Shiach and lovely copper hair. When I reflect that my father's great-grandfather was pure Scots, and that his mother too was from the Border family of Herries, I think it strange that not until I was grown up did I realise the force of this influence. Charles Boyd, one of Lord Milner's celebrated " nursery ", whence came too John Buchan and Lord Lothian, one of our most successful ambassadors to Washington, once at the Savile Club heard me say something disrespectful of Scots. " How dare you say that ? " he cried, bristling like a proper champion from north of the Tweed. " You are one of us yourself ! " I am not sure that in his excitement he did not say " yoursel' ". In that moment I realised that I was nearly three parts a Scot and understood why Scottish tales and songs and the music of the pipes had always a fascination for me. Odd as some people find it in men, though never in horses, blood will tell.

My mother's northern origin had doubtless a part in her independence of character. Among other instances of this was her surprising habit of riding on the top of a bus. To those who know alone the motorbus with its covered top deck and easy access by a winding stair this may not seem much. Buses of the 1880's were a very different proposition, as a Western American would say. To begin with there was no cover at all. This had the advantage that you could really see your surroundings, a feat barely possible from the top deck of a modern motorbus. Then the seats were not placed across the bus as now, when you face forwards, but consisted of a single bench running the length of the bus and divided longitudinally by a hard back against which

passengers lent, spine to spine, looking out upon the houses .
between which the bus passed. This bench was known as the
" knifeboard " from its resemblance to that article of domestic
utility kept in the cubby hole of a Victorian house where boots
were also cleaned, generally by a little wizened man who slept out
and was not therefore one of the household servants but known as
" the odd man ". He also cleaned and sharpened the knives on
the real knifeboard, an object driven out of use by a knife-cleaning
machine that did the same office for half a dozen knives at once
by the turning of a handle, itself to vanish on the happy advent of
stainless steel. Cleaning old-fashioned steel knives was a messy
and wearisome business. The " knifeboard " of the bus went out
on the invention of the so-called garden seats, planted on top of
the bus so that two people could sit on side by side in fair comfort
and look in the direction in which the bus was going. This was
in the second half of the 'eighties. A further refinement was to
provide the garden seats with movable tarpaulin aprons, so that
the passenger could protect his or her nether limbs from the rain
—it was not discomfort of the wet, but the greater speed of the
motorbus that made a roof for the top deck essential—although
he must do for his head and shoulders as best he could. An
amusing drawing in *Punch* of the 'nineties by Reginald Cleaver
portrayed the horror of a young lady, whose voluminous skirt her
near-sighted neighbour mistook for the apron and draped round
his own knees. Access to the knifeboard was originally by a per-
pendicular ladder modified, while I was still at my private school,
into something like a rudimentary stair. Males alone, and an
occasional schoolgirl, climbed to sit on the knifeboard. Ladies
never. It was far too unladylike ; it was not done. Ladies
never—except my mother. She cared little for what was done or
not done, and often, if she was accompanying me, would trip up
that awkward stepladder rather than stair and settle herself on the
knifeboard. Such advanced conduct was looked at a good deal
askance by the elder generation. Sometimes her peculiar ideas
touched on matters of health. Fresh air was beginning to have
its way by day, but at night the greater part of the population of
Great Britain still shut windows tight. My mother insisted on
those in her nursery being well opened, despite the lament of
Jessie Shiach : " Oh, but the night air must be foul, me leddy ! "

My father's oldest living uncle and eldest of my grandfather's younger brothers was admitted soon after my birth to see the new baby. He held a book in his hand and looking at me said to my mother : " Ah, Georgie, that's your baby ; this is Fred's." The book was my father's *Spinoza*, recently published. Uncle George, as he was always known to my generation, although in reality our great-uncle, was what Arnold Bennett would have described as " a card ". Precision concerning the closeness of his relationship to my father and grandfather is needed, for my great-grandfather, Lord Chief Baron Pollock, had twenty-two children and family relationships were apt to be complicated. Once at a dinner-party after the ladies had left the men alone to port, coffee, and cigars, and the elders gathered round their host at the top of the table, while the younger men drifted to its other end, one of the latter whispered to his neighbour : " You see that old josser there. He's got twenty-two children." " Twenty-two legitimate children," put in from a distance the L.C.B., who had remarkably sharp ears, with much relish.

My mother never quite forgave my Uncle George his remark about *Spinoza* and me. But he was one of the kindest of men and certainly did not mean it nastily. Mental excitement was the breath of life to him and a philosophical achievement or a new mechanical device roused his enthusiasm to the point that he sometimes forgot his surroundings completely. One day when so rapt he was walking from his home at Hanworth to the railway station, and was nearly cut down by a small shunting engine dawdling along the line as he crossed it. Uncle George sprang back in time and struck the engine a smart rap with his umbrella, calling out to the driver : " That, sir, will teach you how to run your engine when a gentleman wants to cross the line ! " George Frederick Pollock, to give him his full name, senior Master of the King's Bench and Queen's Remembrancer, in which office he succeeded his elder brother, my grandfather, inherited a bent for science from their father who had been Senior Wrangler at Cambridge and was reputed a mathematician to be reckoned with. Uncle George was a friend of Faraday, Owen, and Lockyer and was consulted by the John Murray of his day about the publication of *The Origin of Species* which Darwin had offered to Murray. The latter decided to publish but in a small edition and with misgiving : the Darwinian theory, he said, was as absurd as if one were to contemplate a fruitful union between a poker and a rabbit. George Pollock differed. He thought Darwin's book as a whole beyond the comprehension of any living man of science, but advised Murray to bring out an initial edition of a thousand copies because, he wrote : " Mr. Darwin has so brilliantly surmounted the formidable obstacles which he has been honest enough to put in his own path." Subsequent events proved my Uncle George's judgment to be well grounded. He was also a brilliant watch and clock maker, a practical plumber, a first-rate bicycle mechanic, and rode a bicycle till he was eighty-four years old. He died in 1915 ten days off his ninety-fourth birthday. In the evening of his life motorcars came in ; so keen was his interest in their internals that it was impossible to get him off the subject. But all things mechanical touched him closely. His younger brother General Sir Richard Pollock, who died, a mere seventy-two, in 1899, was cremated at Woking. It happened that a new system of shooting the coffin into the furnace-room—on the switchback principle, I think—had recently been installed at the crematorium. This took Uncle George's fancy so much that, after seeing his brother disposed of, he stayed behind to witness the two following cremations and make sure how the contraption worked. Uncle George's sister Mary, born in 1820 a year before him, died in 1913. An impressive family gathering was to be seen at the church at Hanworth, Uncle George, nearly the sole survivor of the Lord Chief Baron's first family, being its centre and the cynosure of all eyes. He and his sister had been devoted to each other : never a week passed but he visited her at Twicken-ham, generally by bicycle so long as he could mount one. He was very bowed at the graveside and, as the service proceeded, seemed to sink lower and lower towards the ground. When the last rites were over he stood, peering down at the coffin, so that his sons, nephews, and nieces, and great-nephews and great-nieces, wondered whether he was not going to collapse on top of it. But after a little he turned round and walked away, tottered rather, along one of the churchyard paths. Would he collapse there, instead of into the grave ? I happened to be nearest him as he passed and, obeying a general signal, followed at his elbow to render what assistance I could. From a totter, Uncle George's step turned to a firmer stump ; he pulled himself up inch by inch to something near his normal height and, as he turned a corner of the church, clapped his top-hat on his head.   There is no other word for it : he clapped his hat on.   No vain lament was here, no sentimental nonsense.   Then with a glint of triumph, almost of glee, in his eye Uncle George cried blithely : " I always said I'd outlive her.   And I have !   I have ! "   Of such stuff were the Victorians made.

The prolific progeny of early nineteenth-century families that makes us gasp was sinking to more manageable proportions by the middle of Queen Victoria's reign.   Thus the Lord Chief Baron as aforesaid had two-and-twenty children, " legitimate children " to quote him again.   He had two wives.   His ninth child, Sir Charles Pollock, known as " the last of the Barons ", with three wives, had sixteen.   But my Uncle George had no more than eight, and my grandfather three.   Economic pressure was one reason for the disappearance of gigantic families.   Money lost value rapidly owing to the discovery of goldfields in California and Australia ;   and incomes did not rise in proportion to the fall.   Pitt had said that anyone with ten thousand a year had the right to a peerage.   Nowadays it does not matter two straws whether a peer has money or not.   But down pretty well to the end of the nineteenth century a peer was expected to be able to " support ", as it was said, his peerage, that is to say, to make a brave show in the world and have his feet planted on a solid financial basis.   A poor peer then was a miserable object.   *Ten Thousand a Year* was the title of a best seller about the middle of the century, being published in book form in 1841, in which an estate of that value was taken as the maximum to which a gentleman could aspire.   Since direct taxation was infinitesimal according to our notions, such an income to spend would now stamp its owner as wellnigh a Monte Cristo.   The authorship of the book *Ten Thousand a Year* was kept a sedulous secret, but my grandfather strongly suspected it to be by a friend of his.   So, taking Samuel Warren by the arm and drawing him into a corner away from other guests, he declared himself compelled by conscience to make a confession : *he* was, he said, the author of the book that set all London talking.   Warren was so startled that he blurted out his avowal of the true authorship.   Ten thousand a year was perhaps

13

more than the Lord Chief Baron enjoyed at the height of his fame ; in any case with his vast family he felt himself unable to " support " a peerage, and so refused a position to which in every other way he was thoroughly entitled. He took a baronetcy instead. He felt considerable pride in his progeny, and on the birth of a grandson in 1869 wrote that this made " my 81st descendant alive, viz., 20 children, 54 grand children, and 7 great-grandchildren. I think it not improbable that I have more descendants than any male persons in England. The number is not extraordinary for a woman, but very unusual for a man."

Other reasons besides the mere difficulty of keeping them decently weighed now against families of twenty children or so. The refinements of life were increasing. Baths were beginning to come into fashion in the 'fifties, and baths involved a more copious supply of water, hot and cold. There was opposition to them, of course : my Uncle George quoted an old colonel who complained : " These young men keep washing themselves till there's not a bit of natural smell about them." Slightly earlier, washing was thoroughly unpopular in fashionable society. It is recorded that the brilliant and noble lady from whom Balzac drew his exquisite Duchesse de Maufrigneuse was one day at the house of her friend the Duchesse de Hijar. Someone mentioned Saturday. " Oh, don't talk to me of Saturday ! " cried she. " I hate Saturday." " But why, *ma chère*," asked the Duchesse de Hijar, " why do you hate Saturday ? " " Because," came the to us slightly surprising answer, " Saturday is the day when I wash my feet ! " People also began to demand more air, more light, more room. Even servants' sleeping-quarters, terribly squeezed and unhygienic in earlier days, were being improved until in the 'eighties those in decently run houses were no longer open to exception on such ground. But more potent than either of these motives, the gradually improving position of women militated against marriage meaning for them a mere succession of child-births and of infants to tend. Upper- and middle-class wives were coming more and more to be companions to their husbands, to share the same tastes and pursuits, rather than to be relegated to exclusively domestic duties. The ideal so well expressed by the German " Küche, Kinder, Kirche " was rapidly nearing its end in England. My paternal grandmother, Juliet Pollock, was an

AUNT CHARLOTTE : AGED OVER 90

From a photograph

example of this change. She was the niece of a Secretary to the Treasury and granddaughter of that Colonel Charles Herries who virtually invented the organised Volunteer movement, as opposed to the previous Trained Bands and their like, when he raised and commanded the London and Westminster Light Horse Volunteers in view of the expected invasion of England by Napoleon. How the Light Horse Volunteers would have stood up to Kellermann's cuirassiers or to Murat's lancers may be a question, but they make a pretty show in Rowlandson's picture of them being reviewed on Wimbledon Common by George III. Colonel Herries's inspiration so struck royal and popular imagination that on his death he was accorded burial in Westminster Abbey ; his monument there is but a few yards away from that to Field-Marshal Sir George Pollock who was to be uncle by marriage to Colonel Herries's granddaughter. Juliet—her true baptismal name was Julia but she preferred Shakespeare to the sugary sound of that eighteenth-century favourite and resolutely changed it— married my grandfather William Frederick, who later dropped the William, in 1844. After his death, my grandmother's servants always referred to their late master as " good Sir Frederick ". In the letters that accompanied their courtship Juliet and W.F.P. discussed not Shakespeare, but Plato and the musical glasses. Juliet was a lovely young thing as her portraits by Boxall, George Richmond, and Henry Phillips testify. She was besides gifted with exceptional intellectual interests. Without being anything of a blue-stocking, she was a forerunner of days when young women could study anything they liked whether for business or for pleasure. In Juliet Pollock it was pure pleasure, but that does not make study the less meritorious. On the engagement being announced, my great-grandfather, then Attorney-General, exchanged letters with Juliet's uncle. Each was in his way a personage and underneath the formal compliment can be read a keen desire not to tread on each other's toes. When Disraeli first became Chancellor of the Exchequer in 1852, Herries had been spoken of as a possible rival for the post. It was Herries who had inaugurated and conducted on behalf of the British Government the negotiations with Nathan Rothschild thanks to which Wellington's army in the Peninsula was financed, and made possible the later operations on which the Rothschild eminence in London, Paris, and Vienna was based. The only mark of gratitude that Herries would appear to have received was a china dinner service—not indeed from any Rothschild but from Von Bülow, the Prussian Minister of Finance. Herries's niece, Juliet, plainly inherited original qualities. A prominent lawyer and mathematician might well feel some anxiety about his eldest son marrying this brilliant literary girl, so totally different from his own wife, or indeed any of the women with whom he had mixed. If so, her charm and accomplishments quickly effaced it. Cordial relations ensued and continued till the end. When my great-grandfather died in 1870, Juliet Pollock wrote in her private diary : " He was a most loving Father and a delightful companion. I already miss the storehouse which I so often ransacked and which always yielded treasures."

CHAPTER II

THREE GENERATIONS

THE Court of the Exchequer was among the oldest seats of
Justice in England. Its establishment dated from the
beginning of the twelfth century. The judges who sat in it were
called Barons, though in fact they were not peers of the realm,
and were knighted like other judges on being raised to the Bench ;
their chief was the Lord Chief Baron, whose office ranked below
those alone of the Lord Chancellor and the Lord Chief Justice of
England. In the Middle Ages the Court of the Exchequer had
dealt overwhelmingly with finance ; but by the nineteenth century its work had become undistinguishable from that of the
King's Bench, and the Barons, the Lord Chief among them, went
circuit like other judges, trying civil suits and criminal cases at
Assize. The whole system was recast by the Judicature Act of
1873, when the Courts of Exchequer and Common Pleas were
finally merged with that of the King's Bench and the Barons disappeared. One Baron still remained on the Bench down to 1897,
my great-uncle Charles, one of the younger sons of the Lord Chief
Baron's first marriage. He died aged seventy-five, not a great
age for one of his family. I heard him with two other judges try
the Jameson Raiders. He was, too, one of the judges before
whom Horatio Bottomley appeared, and told me that Bottomley
had the most beautiful and persuasive voice he had ever heard.
I was in court when Uncle Charles tried a big election petition
case. In this a witness refused with obstinate and shocked
modesty to repeat the words used to him by the election agent
alleged to have resorted to threats and bribery. He was forced
reluctantly to write them down and the paper was handed up to
the Bench. With a ghost of a smile my Uncle Charles read out :
" He said he'd hit me on my bloody nose." This was half a
generation before Bernard Shaw's *Pygmalion*, but Uncle Charles
had no use for senseless prudery. He was a charming person
and a respectable but not remarkable judge : his chief claim to

17

fame was the sobriquet that got attached to him from Bulwer Lytton's popular novel, *The Last of the Barons.*

My great-grandfather was one of four brothers that survived, five others dying young, a perfectly normal proportion in those days. Their father was David Pollock, ever since known in the family as " the Saddler " and the first of it to come away from Scotland. The Saddler's father, John, was a Burgess of Berwick-on-Tweed and, according to my Uncle George, a bookseller. Books of course were then exclusively bound in leather so that the trade connexion between father and son is clear. David was six years old in 1745 when his father lifted him shoulder high to see a young man cross the ford at Kelso : [1] it was Prince Charles Edward, the Young Pretender, on his way to the last warlike Scottish invasion of England. So David Pollock came to London, went into the saddlery business, prospered, and became Saddler by appointment to His Majesty King George III. He had a fine shop at Charing Cross that stood across the north end of White-hall, where now is the pavement in front of Landseer's lions round the Nelson column. The Saddler died solvent in 1815, after being very nearly ruined by Frederick Duke of York, the King's brother. This was an unkindly act, for the Duke of York had stood godfather—doubtless by proxy—to David Pollock's third son. Being Commander-in-Chief of the army, the Duke had the spending of £50,000 voted by Parliament to pay for military accoutrements ; and let not the real value of money at the time be forgotten. Instead, however, of putting this large sum to the purpose intended, the Duke of York seems to have muddled it away, some of it perhaps passing to the Duke's lady friend, Mrs. Clarke, and the proportion that David Pollock should have had evaporated into thin air.

In the year 1808 Major Samuel Pollock of Mountainstown in Ireland, being in London, boasted to David Pollock of his three promising sons. The Saddler replied that he too had three sons who would all become famous men. In the Saddler's case the boast was justified. The eldest, David, who being disfigured by smallpox was known as " the ugliest man in London ",

---

[1] Not as Lord Hanworth erroneously says in his Life of " Lord Chief Baron Pollock ", to see him cross the bridge. The bridge was not built till some thirty years later.

became Chief Justice of Bombay, the second, Jonathan Frederick —he dropped his first name—dubbed " the handsomest man at the Bar ", Lord Chief Baron, and the third Field-Marshal Sir George Pollock the conqueror of Afghanistan, who died Constable of the Tower of London. In a lesser degree George Pollock repeated Nelson's sublime impudence at the Battle of Copenhagen. He was about to march in 1842 with his army after forcing the Khaiber Pass to avenge the murder of a British mission and the massacre in the Khaiber of a retreating British force by the treacherous Akbar Khan, son of Dost Mohammed the deposed Amir of Afghanistan. At Jalalabad he received a despatch from Lord Ellenborough, recently appointed Governor-General. Ellenborough had advocated active operations but was shaken by the news of two other British reverses. Since he knew his superior to be vacillating and timorous, Pollock calmly put the despatch in his pocket and did not open it till he and his army had attained their goal by forcing the Jagdalak and Tezin passes, hardly less formidable than the dreaded Khaiber. Pollock's expectation was justified : the despatch contained an order to retire to Peshawar by the quickest route. Now, he said to himself, I am in the heart of Afghanistan. The quickest way back will be via Kabul. So on Kabul he marched, did the work he had come to do, and returned to India, having assured peace for long years with the Afghans by the means warlike men best comprehend, a hand of steel. There was yet a fourth brother, John, a solicitor and in the end registrar of the Bristol Court. John, who appears to have been considered something of a black sheep, might, had he lived a century later, have cut a bigger figure in the popular eye than any of his famous trio of brothers. For he was a noted athlete and billiards player. It is recorded of him that on one occasion, for a bet, he walked from London to Windsor, won a match at racquets there, and walked back on the same day. Who knows but that in the age of international competitions he might not have become a Davis Cup player and represented England on the track in the Olympic Games ?

It is not my object to relate the lives of these worthies, which have been sufficiently chronicled elsewhere, but to sketch the part played by them and their descendants on the stage of Victorian England. The Field-Marshal's grandson had his part of responsibility in the spread of the Trust system of hotels and public-houses that has had influence in leading the country from the era of " gin-palaces " to the sobriety now characterising it. I remember myself as a boy the horrid spectacle of men, and women too, reeling drunk about the streets in London and, much later, that, now almost unbelievable, of Glasgow on a Saturday evening. The brewers themselves have had a share in this beneficent change in Great Britain : it was always a tenet in the faith of Sir Sydney Nevile, director of Whitbread's, that England sober was worth more to " the Trade " than England drunk. But it was the Lord Chief Baron's progeny that was the most spreading (" and how ! " an American might say) and active. One of his sons and two of his grandsons were raised to the Bench. The husband of a daughter became a Lord of Appeal, a grand-daughter married one Lord Justice and a great-granddaughter another. Two other sons were in turn Queen's Remembrancer, a legal office less visible, yet of real consequence. A fourth, Sir Edward Pollock, became Official Referee and one of the best skaters at the old Toxophilite Club, then the home of the highly restrained, even stilted, style known as " English skating ", now killed stone dead by the freer, more elegant " Continental " style. A fifth deserves to have more said of him.

This was Major-General Sir Richard Pollock, K.C.S.I., who, following the example of his uncle, the Field-Marshal, entered the Indian Army. He was known to all his friends as " Trim " and to his nephews and great-nephews as Uncle Trim. The nickname was not, as many supposed, derived from the character in Sterne's *Tristram Shandy*, but was conferred upon him by Sir Dighton Probyn, afterwards Comptroller to Queen Alexandra's household. The two were companions in arms in the Indian Mutiny. A fight against the rebels was not going too well. " Look ! " cried an officer on the staff. " Our fellows are breaking ! " " No, they're not," retorted Probyn ; " there's Pollock as trim as if he were on parade." The word stuck, and " Trim " Richard Pollock remained to the end of his life. He was appointed the first Political Officer at Peshawar, quarrelled with Lord Lytton on account of that Viceroy's " forward " policy on the Northwest frontier, and came home to accept work in the City for which his tact and businesslike habits well suited him.

When I knew him he was the sweetest and best-looking old gentleman imaginable : had he not been too intelligent for the part, a veritable Colonel Newcome. He had, by common consent, three of the most beautiful children ever seen. Dighton, the eldest, named after that friend of Mutiny days, created a sensation when acting in the Greek Play at Cambridge, where he was a scholar of Kings. He looked indeed exactly like the god Apollo whom he was playing. Dighton went to the Bar, became Junior Counsel to the Treasury, a post better known by the name of " Attorney-General's devil " that has the promise of a judgeship attached to it, but died too soon to be raised to the Bench of the excessively hard work thrown on his shoulders.

The same fate befell a precedessor of his in that office, Austen Cartmell, who was my " father in the law ", an amazingly brilliant financial barrister. The Attorney-General's devil has, in sober truth, a killing job. Cartmell could keep the details of five cases in his head at a time : the maximum for the most capacious legal mind is said to be seven. When we think that Napoleon habitually dictated to nine secretaries at once on different subjects, we get a measure of that great brain's retentive power. Of Adrian, my Uncle Trim's second son, later warmly appreciated as City Chamberlain, his final appearance in his robes-of-office being when after the last war Mr. Churchill was given the Freedom of the City of London, it was said that when he went out on to the links near his home at Seaford you could hear the ladies' hearts cracking all round. He was six foot two, as straight as an arrow, and in youth had been an exquisite step dancer as well as performer in a ballroom. Till well over seventy years he was one of the handsomest of men. Oscar Wilde had cast eyes on him, much to Adrian's disgust, and revenged himself for the rebuff he sustained by going about and saying to everyone : " Do you know the secret of Adrian Pollock ? The secret of Adrian Pollock is that he has no secret ! " The third of this astonishing constellation was Dighton and Adrian's sister Mabel, unquestionably one of the great beauties of a time when there were still famous beauties in London both on and off the stage. She fell deeply in love with Johnston Forbes Robertson, comeliest and most accomplished of actors, besides being a painter of no mean merit, and an unique pair they would have made. But this was before the days when actors had come into their own socially. Mabel's mother, a daughter of Sir Harris Nicolas and an autocrat of unbending temper, intervened at her most peremptory and hustled Mabel into marriage with a Hussar officer understood to have great expectations. The marriage ended in a childless separation, a lesson to all wilful mammas. Mabel died only in 1948, beautiful to the last.

My grandfather, though a barrister and distinguished holder of legal office, did not have his heart in that profession. On someone remarking in my hearing that the L.C.B. had done well for his heir, my father answered tartly : " Yes, if you call it doing well for a man to get him a position he is perfectly competent to fill." Sir Frederick Pollock the second was of the same mind as his friend Sir Henry Taylor, the author of *Philip Van Artevelde*. Taylor was a civil servant, and was offered a post that meant much advancement but would have absorbed more of his time than he cared to give up to office work. He wished to refuse but thought it might be his duty to accept. While still hesitating he learned that conditions were attached to the post offered him of which he could not approve. On this he wrote a spirited letter to the Secretary of State expressing his delight at being able to refuse an office which would have prevented him from pursuing his real work, literature. To my grandfather the bar represented a livelihood but nothing more. Literature, art, the stage, social intercourse of the highest level : these were his real interests. He was the second of four consecutive generations in his family to win a scholarship at Trinity, Cambridge, but failed to get elected Fellow of the College like his father, his eldest son, and his grandson. The Lord Chief Baron's success at Trinity, where by the way he had spotted a hitherto unsuspected error made by Newton, and the connexion he always maintained with Cambridge made it natural that his descendants should follow him there and, sure enough, their names are scattered over the College books for three generations. Two other Pollocks were up with me, and the Dean of Corpus, afterwards President, and in his time sixth Wrangler was the Rev. Charles Pollock, yet another of the Saddler's breed. My grandfather, though a weaker link in the academic line, remained a devoted Trinity man. He had his arms put up in stained glass in the College Hall, and it was in the

Great Court of Trinity that he made a *bon mot* often quoted and often, like most of its kind, attributed to half a dozen men besides its true begetter. There was for many years in Trinity a College tortoise, that crawled about the grass in the court. One of a party of seniors idly watching it one day asked : " I wonder what a tortoise would feel if you scratched its shell ? " To which W.F.P. made reply : " About as much as the Dean and Chapter would feel if you were to scratch the dome of St. Paul's."

59 Montagu Square, where my grandparents lived, came to house what I suppose was nearer to a Paris *salon* than anything else in London. Both of them had a rare talent for friendship. Their drawing-room was a centre for much that was artistic and literary in town. Thackeray was a special friend, and Dickens too. Thackeray and W.F.P. exchanged portraits of them in coloured chalk by Samuel Lawrence, nephew of the scintillating Sir Thomas whose fame nevertheless perhaps masked a lack of the perfect taste and execution visible in the work of the younger and less known man. I have in my possession that portrait of Thackeray, more vivid than any other done of the greatest novelist produced by the two centuries since the writing of novels began. Also a note, folded and sealed according to the manner of the time, addressed to W. F. Pollock, Esq. Its contents run : " Dear Pollock, Who do you think is in town ? Answer, Titmarsh." Then underneath, a speaking likeness in ink of my grandfather, tall, thin, eager, slightly romantic looking, with the legend in Thackeray's hand : " Pollock takes his hat instantly and runs with all his might to the Garrick Club." In this sketch my grandfather carries under his arm a long cane that I remember well as his constant companion. It is a nice bit of bamboo coated in resplendent red lacquer, with a leafy ornamentation, probably Chinese. Doubtless it was one of the Oriental knicknacks brought back from India by the Field-Marshal and given by him to his elder brother, the L.C.B. One such addition to the latter's home was an Indian servant who never learned to speak proper English but lived so long in England that he is said to have forgotten his own language—whatever that may have been, for there is no record. All conversation with him was in a pidgin of his own devising. In view of the origin of the bamboo cane and of my grandfather's friendship with Thackeray, I cannot help

Dear Pollock.

Who do you think is in Town?

Answer Titmarsh!

Pollock takes his hat instantly and runs with all his might to the GARRICK CLUB.

THACKERAY TO W.F.P.

surmising—but it is a mere surmise—that the stick figuring in Thackeray's sketch of W.F.P. was the model for Colonel New-come's famous cane the company at " the Cave of Harmony, then kept by the celebrated Mr. Hoskins " felt to have fallen on all their shoulders after old Costigan's bawdy song.

Macready was another constant visitor at Montagu Square. So were Anthony Trollope, George Richmond and later his son,

Sir William to be, one of the finest of Victorian portrait painters, whose work in redecorating St. Paul's Cathedral earned him unmerited disfavour, Sir Henry Taylor, Spedding, Fitzgerald and a host of other literary and artistic men of two generations, Carlyle and Tennyson too were my grandparents' friends.

Sims Reeves was another intimate. I remember that as a very small boy I was taken to the house and placed in the hall that I might watch the great tenor as he left after lunch and so be able to say that I had set eyes on him. What still more indelibly fixed the fact in my memory was that in taking his hat and coat Sims Reeves tipped Romney, my grandfather's butler, a sovereign. Such largesse was still a custom of the time, though already almost extinct. It must always be difficult to appraise dead executive artists at their true value. How can those who have not heard a voice judge its quality? In Sims Reeves's case there does exist a valid criterion to be applied. The songs with his rendering of which he packed halls all over the country have gone clean out of fashion, but he is the only singer or, for the matter of that, musician of any kind I have ever heard tell of, who could pack a concert hall with a public having paid money they had been told beforehand by prominent announcement on the concert bills would not be returned if Mr. Sims Reeves were unable through indisposition to appear. This is a more cogent proof of the genius in Sims Reeves's vocal chords than yards of enthusiastic description. Sims Reeves suffered from a delicate throat, and the threat of non-appearance was no bluff. If he felt unable to sing, you were just unlucky. You did not get your money back. But the public paid in its thousands nonetheless. Sims Reeves was growing old when London, following Paris, was bewitched by a young tenor named Jean de Reszke. Sims Reeves wrinkled his nose. " Ah," he said, " the Polish baritone." Jean de Reszke, who had in fact begun as a baritone, heard of Sims Reeves's quip. " Ah," he retorted, "the English soprano."

My father remembered hearing Macready read at Montagu Square. My grandfather edited the tragedian's *Reminiscences* ; my grandmother wrote a little book about him. Her taste had veered from the classics to the moderns. Shakespeare was her god and she loved hearing him read aloud. Macready was dead long before my time, but the readings she delighted in were often carried on at St. Julian's, a pleasant house just south of Sevenoaks, by her first cousin, Edward Herries, a dramatic reader of a high order. To me the readings were memorable for Edward Herries's white beard, so long and wide that it wholly covered his dress shirt, and of as flashing a white as the shirt itself. In youth he had been in the diplomatic service in Switzerland and in Italy and, being instructed to write a minute on the economic basis of peasant life in northern Italy, was reputed to have sent in the following report : " The economic basis of life of the peasants in northern Italy consists of spaghetti and polenta." On which Edward Herries's diplomatic career abruptly ceased and he retired with the consolation of a C.B. to a more palatable life in Kent with Shakespeare as his main companion.

The Macready era had passed. One story from my grand-parents of that grand actor, a most cultivated man, as his pre-decessors Edmund Kean and George Cooke had not been, may not have found its way into print. One night Macready was playing Macbeth and a bewildered super had floated into his way just as he was about to begin the great soliloquy. " Tomor-row "—went Macready's tremendous voice like the tones of a church bell ; then sotto voce an incisive—" Fool ! "—" and tomorrow " still deeper, followed by a still more cutting whisper —" Idiot ! "—then the splendid climax, " and tomorrow——" topped up with a breathless " Damn you, get off the stage ! ", which the wretched super did at a run, leaving Macready to continue to enthral an audience totally unaware of the by-play. A new young actor had come forward to pick up the torch. He was a Cornishman named Brodribb and after an exacting appren-ticeship in the provinces had come to town to join the Bateman company under the name of Henry Irving. Juliet Pollock was quick to spy his genius. She was an intimate friend of the Baroness Burdett-Coutts, and induced her to lend Irving £10,000 with which to start his own management at the Lyceum. His unparalleled success in the venture enabled him to repay the loan in record time. Another and almost more transcendent service was rendered by my grandmother to Irving. He was looking about for a leading lady, when Juliet Pollock recommended Ellen Terry to his notice. He had never seen her act, but had such confidence in my grandmother's judgment that he engaged Ellen

Terry on the spot, thus founding one of the most famous and extensive partnerships in the history of the English stage. Small wonder that there was always a box at the Lyceum for Juliet Pollock and her family, or that Irving visited more at Montagu Square than probably anywhere outside the circle of the theatre that was his world. My sister and I virtually had the run of the Lyceum, always welcomed by genial, bluff Bram Stoker, courtly even to small children, Irving's personal manager and famous afterwards as the author of *Dracula*, and kissed—heavenly thought! —by Ellen Terry. My sister has a treasured postcard written to her aged thirteen by Irving after the first night of *The Dead Heart* : " Alice ! My heart is dead, but not to you." I witnessed part of Henry VIII and of *King Lear* and once the often-repeated *Merchant of Venice* from the seat on the O.P. side of the stage, where Irving sometimes put far more important visitors, like Gladstone, who did not want to be seen in the audience. Since I hope some day to write more substantially about Irving, I will set no more on record here but that he was beyond question the greatest actor, save one, there has been in my lifetime. He and that one other were indeed the only actors to whom the epithet " great " can be applied without hesitation.

The actor thus to share Irving's pinnacle was a Frenchman, Mounet Sully, and he too was a friend of my grandmother's. Mounet Sully, whose superb career did not end till his death in 1916 at the age of seventy-five, differed so much from Irving that a fruitful comparison between the two would need much space. What the two had in common was, first, a power unequalled by any others of getting inside the skins of the characters they were portraying, and, second, the power to excite noble emotions in their audience to a pitch I have never seen or experienced elsewhere. Both my grandparents were devout lovers of France. He had travelled extensively in the country, a thing less common and easy than in the day of bikes and motorcars, and according to my mother had a singularly precise knowledge of French domestic arrangements from the kitchen upwards : this may explain the fact that in his own home he relieved his wife of all the household accounts. He had a story that remarkably illustrates the meticulous efficiency and exasperating rigidity of French official methods which French authors, Courteline the deadliest

27

of all, have made the butt of their wit without obtaining a change in them by one iota. My grandfather was watching a man watering the street. It was raining. He said to the man : " Mon ami, pourquoi arrosez-vous la rue pendant qu'il pleut ? " To which the man in charge of the watering cart replied with a withering look : " Sachez, monsieur, que la pluie est un phenomène naturel, et que l'arrosage est un phenomène administratif." He was employed officially to water the street, and watered the street should be, no matter how much rain fell from heaven the while. My grandmother's French interests lay in Paris. They knew a host of people there, including Taine, the de Franquevilles, the Turgenev circle, and especially that of the Comédie Française, where, besides Mounet Sully, Got, the *doyen* of that famous company, and Delaunay, exquisite actor of de Musset, became close friends. I suspect that it was from my grandmother that Irving got the idea of staging *The Bells*, one of his most lasting triumphs. Under the title of *Le Juif Polonais*, this play by Erckmann-Chatrian was a favourite at the Théatre Français and the part of Mathias a fine vehicle for Got's talent, although he played it quite differently from Irving. It was she too who in 1871 suggested that the Français should make a visit to London during the disturbed period of and following the Commune in Paris. From her admiration for Turgenev came mild Russian leanings : she kept a poodle in London by the name of " Moscow " and had her grandchildren call her " Toushka ", short for *matoushka*, the Russian for " little mother ".

A similar tribute to their joint admiration for Alexandre Dumas was that on his accession to the title my grandfather always addressed Juliet Pollock as " Milady ", a somewhat curious compliment when the character of that dæmonic vamp in *The Three Musketeers* is remembered. Sir W.F.P. was remembered in Paris longer than, outside his immediate friends and family, he was in London. When I had a play produced in Paris just before the second World War, I was delighted to be hailed by the critic of the Figaro as the grandson of the translator into English of Dante's *Divine Comedy*. Dante was done for the first time into English verse by my grandfather. The idea was not perhaps wholly happy : prose is really a better vehicle for the purpose. Yet the work, long forgotten in England, was still remembered in Paris.

Juliet Pollock's friendship with the Baroness Burdett-Coutts was for a while clouded at the time of the Baroness's marriage to her young secretary, by name Ashmead-Bartlett. He told his employer one day that he was engaged to be married, on which she, determined not to lose a perfect secretary, spoke words to this effect : " Oh, no, you're not ! I mean to keep you close to me and, to see that you stay, *I* shall marry you." So it came about that this gay, capable woman, attractive even in middle life, the richest in England to boot, who had refused the hand of Louis Napoleon and of the Duke of Wellington, married a clever commoner with his way to make in the world. It must be unique in the history of matrimony for one and the same woman to receive a proposal from the victor of the most terrible war in a whole era and from the nephew of the vanquished in it, the one a Prince and Duke in three countries and the other about to become an Emperor in his own. Had she accepted the latter, the heiress of Thomas Coutts's millions would have sat on the throne of France and all history might have been changed. The girl whom Ashmead-Bartlett jilted to make his way was well known in London society, and my grandmother was among those who thought he had behaved shockingly. But the Baroness had her way. She married Ashmead-Bartlett, forced him to change his name to her own, lived happily with him, and won her friends back by her imperturbable good humour.

The Lyceum by no means exhausted my grandparents' appetite for the theatre. This was the heyday of amateur theatricals, not as now run by regular clubs, but got up at home, in the drawing-room, the pieces put on for the entertainment of friends invited often being written by the performers. The celebrated charade in *Vanity Fair* was an affair of this kind. Such evenings were frequent in Montagu Square, where the combined talent of family and friends was fully equal to the task. Walter Herries Pollock, my father's second brother, one of the most brilliant writers and editor of the *Saturday Review*, in a day when weekly reviews counted, had great success on the stage with his play *The Ballad Monger*, adapted from Théodore de Banville's *Gringoire*, and his lyric *The Devout Lover* was an immense favourite. It was he who gave Irving the correct title for *The Lyons Mail*, which had been literally and wrongly translated as *The Courier of Lyons*. He was himself an amateur actor of much repute, though I thought him eclipsed by his wife who, I am convinced, had she gone on the stage, would have made a niche for herself to fit in between Lady Bancroft and Yvonne Arnaud, the most entrancing comediennes of their two generations. The third brother, Maurice, was a painter of the Barbizon school, not without talent. He completely lost his health at an early age. Mounet Sully, who had by natural sequence formed a real friendship with both the brothers, in speaking to me years afterwards of Maurice, said with much emotion : " Quelle belle lumière éteinte ! " Both were gifted with outstanding personal charm ; men like Robert Ross, the dramatic and art critic, who had worked under my Uncle Walter, retained a vivid affection for him long after he had passed from the scene. He was too one of the small band, notable also being Captain Hutton and Egerton Castle the novelist, who developed a taste for swordsmanship in England where since the age of duelling it had fallen into sad neglect. My Uncle Walter, an accomplished fencer, was indefatigable in getting up not only exhibitions of modern fencing but also bouts with rapier and dagger, rapier and cloak and like historic reconstructions. A caricature of him by Spy in *Vanity Fair*, shows him standing, tall, slender, somewhat stooping, with a thoughtful look and an elegant auburn beard.

My grandfather's town life, literary outlook, and continental tastes to some extent cut him off from the more traditional if not less individual ways of his younger brother George in his family and multitudinously mechanical home at Hanworth. Not that my grandfather lost touch with scientific developments : attendance at lectures given at the British Institution was then a regular part of the life of persons aspiring to a cultivated mind, just as was practical acquaintance with the arts. Thus my mother was an excellent pianist, her mother a good performer on the harp ; Juliet Pollock sketched admirably in water colours. How men and women of that generation found time to undertake all they did is something of a mystery. They wrote long letters, they kept full diaries, mere dressing demanded much more of their time than does ours and a lady's long hair might take very nearly an hour a day for the brushing of it alone ; yet they never seemed to be hurried and always appeared to have time for extensive social, literary, artistic, or scientific occupations.   One part solution of the mystery is doubtless that they had far more service at their command than have their descendants, so that there was a corresponding division of labour.   Another may very likely be that modern time-saving inventions like the telephone and the motor-car in reality absorb so much time and effort in their manipulation as more than to offset the rapidity of their performance.   The wireless has killed amateur music, the telephone and easy telegraph letter writing ; but the net result appears to be greater hurry all round with very little, if anything, more to be shown in the way of accomplishment.

Meanwhile my Uncle George was producing a family in its way not much less notable than that of his father.   Like the Lord Chief Baron he was a man of distinctly liberal mind.   When the matrimonial fight between Mrs. Norton, Sheridan's grand-daughter, immortalised by George Meredith in *Diana of the Crossways*, and her husband was at its height, the L.C.B. put his drawing-room at her disposal so that she might see her children, and Uncle George, his sister Mary with him sometimes, played chaperon reading the *Encyclopædia Britannica* in a corner.   Dr. Lushington, a well-known lawyer engaged in the Norton case, told my grandfather the following curious story.   George Norton's accusation was that Mrs. Norton was Lord Melbourne's mistress.   Proceedings had been started, when a former footman at Mrs. Norton's came to her husband's attorney to say that one day when Lord Melbourne was calling he had looked through the keyhole and seen Mrs. Norton lying on the floor and Lord Melbourne bending over her.   The attorney decided that such a bit of evidence was impossible to produce.   No one would believe that, if adultery had taken place, it could have been in such circumstances.   If told in court the tale would have seemed concocted.   Later Dr. Lushington summoned up courage to mention this to Mrs. Norton.   " Oh yes," she cried with a laugh.   " I remember perfectly.   I told Lord Melbourne that I could put one leg round my neck, and he bet me I couldn't.   So I lay down on the floor and did it straight away."

My great-grandfather had bought and enlarged a house at Hatton, close to Feltham, in quite the ugliest part of Middlesex, apparently for no better reason than that he could drive the fourteen perfectly flat miles from Hatton to the Law Courts and back every day, an hour each way behind a pair of fast horses. Later the Southwestern Railway Company arranged trains specially for his convenience. My uncle George, who lived in the same district as his father, had three sons, each eminent in his own walk of life. Rivers, the eldest, became one of the most expert gynæcologists in London ; Bertram, the youngest of the three, Headmaster of Wellington, where his reforms are still vigorously applauded, and later Bishop of Norwich ; while Ernest as Lord Hanworth rose to be Master of the Rolls. This high judicial office, it should hardly be necessary to say, has nothing to do with a bakery. Yet it is the fact that on my cousin Ernest's appointment to it being published he received a pathetic request from a poor woman to bestow on her a supply of rolls, she had not tasted any for so long. There were not wanting those to say that Ernest should have gone to the Church and Bertram to the Bar. The latter, a running blue at Cambridge and a precise scholar, had a first-rate brain. He excelled as an administrator. He had the confidence of Queen Victoria and of Edward VII and it was freely said that, had the latter lived, Bertram would have become Archbishop of Canterbury. He was a most lovable man, an incisive speaker, no respecter of persons, a champion of the Prayer Book against interested " reforms " and, without being exactly handsome, a man of truly magnificent presence. The Archbishop of Canterbury of that time had thought to dispose of so stubborn a churchman by bestowing on him a secondary bishopric. King Edward, learning of this, sent for Bertram and said : " Don't accept, I'm keeping something better for you." The something better was Norwich and a seat in the House of Lords. Had the two brothers changed professions, Ernest would have made a popular and effective archbishop, Bertram a first-rate Lord Chancellor. Ernest owed his success to his intelligent common sense and to his personal qualities. These brought him to the office of Attorney-General at the end of the 1914 war ; at the Peace Conference he won all hearts by the amusing imitations he gave of the bigwigs there. When Stanley Baldwin overthrew the Lloyd George coalition he privately offered the Woolsack to Sir

Ernest Pollock who, out of loyalty to his former chief, refused but later accepted the Rolls and a viscounty as compensation. Had two men other than Stanley Baldwin and Ernest Pollock been concerned, this would have been called a job ; for the latter, however successful he was in Common Law practice, had small title to become the chief of the Bench on the Chancery side, where a very different style of law is applied. Ernest was charmingly modest about it and said to me : " The others pull me through." In an unobtrusive manner he was devoutly religious. My own belief is that in the modern world where devotion, to meet with success, must be tinged with common-sensible comprehension of changing conditions, he would have been better suited on the Episcopal Bench. He had not really the stuff of lawyers like Lord Wright and Lord Greene, his successors at the Rolls.

The Lord Chief Baron, who had thus produced in the two generations succeeding his own so many lawyers, churchmen, soldiers, and doctors, for there were many others besides those mentioned in the last two categories, one grandson winning the V.C., and a great-grandson holding the rank of Major-General in the recent war, had an individuality far stronger than those would give him credit for who only read the mention of him in Disraeli's diary. At the time of Ernest, his grandson, becoming Attorney-General the *Daily Telegraph* printed a two-column leader on my great-grandfather and his descendants. Dizzy had called him " a weak man ". This may have been a strictly party judgment. But there was no love lost between the two. Dizzy was once in his vain, prosy way describing how when he became Chancellor of the Exchequer the robes of office, handed down from one Chancellor to another, were worn out and how he at his own expense had " nobly " had new ones made. But " I thought," said he, " that I should like to keep the old robes as a matter of curiosity," and so he carried those illustrious rags away with him. " Now," turning to the Lord Chief Baron, " should you call that petty larceny or not ? " " No," said my great-grandfather. " Oh, no ! I should simply call it an interesting survival of hereditary instinct."[1] The then common cry

---

[1] This story has been told, but erroneously, of my Uncle Charles, " the last of the Barons ".

of " Old Clothes ! ", no longer heard in London streets, lasted into my youth, and never came from one not of the seed of Israel. It is in any case hard to believe that the epithet " weak " in the ordinary sense of the word could be justly applied to one whose judgments bulk so large in the Common Law of England as those of the Lord Chief Baron. Among other things he was finally responsible (in R. *v.* Kohl, 1865) for laying down the law as to the duty of a jury in considering evidence offered in a murder trial : a jury, he said " ought to have the highest degree of certainty which the practical business of life admits of. Demonstration is not required ; absolute certainty is not required, for it is really unattainable in any case whatever " ; and there followed a conclusive analysis of the nature of circumstantial evidence.

In 1840, Sir Frederick Pollock had much increased his already great reputation at the Bar by his defence of John Frost and others on a high treason charge at the time of the Chartists riots. He had against him Campbell, the Attorney-General, afterwards Lord Campbell and Lord Chancellor. A feud existed between the two. Campbell envied Pollock's success, especially since the latter had once taken the lead from Brougham on the Northern Circuit, to which they all belonged : Pollock judged Campbell unscrupulous and shallow. A generation later my father more than supported this view : he thought Campbell a bad, inaccurate lawyer and that the Woolsack with him on it touched a regrettably low level only to be challenged by Lord Halsbury's tenure of office. There was no question, in the trial mentioned, about Frost's guilt. He had planned an armed rising and attacked Newport in Monmouthshire with a force of 5,000 men. He and his fellow-leaders were condemned to death, but legal objections were so successfully drawn by Pollock that the sentences were commuted. This was the last trial for high treason in England till that of Sir Roger Casement in the first World War. It was emphatically not my great-grandfather who produced a sweet incident in court. A woman was being closely cross-examined about the movements of her husband, who had returned home very late and come up straight to bed. " As he was getting into bed," she said, " his words were——" Here she was sharply interrupted by Counsel : " You must not tell us what he *said*,

THE LORD CHIEF BARON

because that is not evidence : you can only tell us what he *did* ! " [1]

In the first half of the nineteenth century, few ways were open to professional men of taking exercise. Lawn tennis had not yet been invented, golf not come out of Scotland, rowing after men had left the university was unorganised : riding was virtually the only thing, and few men rode who were not more or less country gentlemen or hunting men, which lawyers hardly had the time to be. My great-grandfather invented an original form of exercise for himself. He did indulge sometimes in dancing, but his standby for keeping fit and working off surplus energy was to jump over tables and chairs placed round the room as in a miniature circus. He was seen at the age of nearly seventy-five to do this in a hotel at Norwich where he was on Assize, having just received a pair of white gloves, the traditional sign that there were no criminal cases for the Judge to try.

My father has told in *For My Grandson* how the Lord Chief Baron said to an emissary of the Heralds' College, come to announce what the L.C.B. thought an excessive fee : " You may go back to Garter King of Arms and tell him with my compliments that he may go to the Devil sable in flames gules with a pitch-fork ardent sticking in his backside proper." This little passage however did not disturb good relations with Garter King of Arms who was a personal friend. The Victorians were anything but mealy mouthed. When one of the L.C.B.'s sons announced his intention of marrying again, having already a large family, an indignation meeting of younger relatives met to discuss the question whether the marriage could not be prevented. " If he must have a woman," said one of them, " why can't he take up with some perfectly respectable female ? " This plain-spoken advocate of concubinage was Sam Martin, the son-in-law of the L.C.B., known to the world as Sir Samuel Martin, Baron of the Exchequer and a Privy Councillor, and father-in-law of Lord Macnaghten, one of the three greatest judges of the nineteenth century.[2] So

---

[1] I owe to my late cousin E. S. P. Haynes, like myself a great-grandson of Lord Chief Baron Pollock, and author of the well-known series *A Lawyer's Notebook*, both this story and various points about our ancestor.

[2] There is some doubt as to the occasion of this remark, but none as to the spokesman and his words, which were related by Lord Macnaghten to his son, and by my father to me.

long as relations of the kind were kept quiet, scandal avoided, and the female in question discreetly visited in her little house in Fulham or St. John's Wood, everyone was happy. Thus indeed did manage a celebrated leader of the bar a generation later, a pillar of nonconformity blessed with a singularly dull wife.

The Lord Chief Baron Pollock, like most Victorians, acquired a wide mind. He had lived under four Sovereigns and seen social England, and even physical England, change out of all knowledge. He had presided at his own table when men wore stocks so tight that they could not turn their heads without turning the whole body too, an awkward manœuvre when sitting at dinner. My great-aunt Mary remembered seeing him, probably being then Attorney-General, look straight down the table before him. "James," he would call to the butler without turning at all. "Yes, Sir Frederick." "James, ask Lady So-and-so if she will take wine with me." Now Lady So-and-so was sitting immediately on her host's right hand, but unless he swivelled round in his chair he could not see her. A hasty colloquy between James and Lady So-and-so. James returns to his master's left ear. "Lady So-and-so will be highly pleased to take wine with you, Sir Frederick." "James, is Lady So-and-so's glass charged?" Another visit to Lady So-and-so's side. James returns. "Lady So-and-so's glass is charged, Sir Frederick." Then the climax : "Lady So-and-so, I have the honour to drink wine with you." And the glasses would be lifted and drunk without a single glance between the honoured guest and the distinguished host. It is barely credible that protagonists in the social comedy, at all events its hero in this case, did not see the humour of the situation. That my great-grandfather did have both a keen sense of humour and a broad mind is testified by a story passed down from my grandfather to my father and from him to me. The L.C.B., no longer indeed holder of that office for the past four years, lay dying. It was August 1870 and he was a month from his eighty-seventh birthday. His family, and how large it was we have seen, were gathered round him. The old man signalled to his eldest son to approach. My grandfather drew still nearer and bent down over the dying man to receive his last instructions. "My boy,"

came the words almost without breath, " my boy, always
remember that Joseph was no gentleman."

* * * * *

Such were the sons of David Pollock, " the Saddler ", and
their sons and the third generation of them, all save one, of whom
I must speak apart. The Saddler as aforesaid was son to a
Burgess of Berwick-on-Tweed, and it was the Saddler who first
brought the Scottish blood of Pollock out of Scotland and into
England. What manner of men were then the Pollocks ?
Whence came they, and what had been their story ?

CHAPTER III

FONS ET ORIGO

THE original Pollock, the Ur-Pollock, as scientists of a bygone generation might have called him, was of course not born with that name. This may be truly said of the seed from which all families shoot up and out. The first of the royal house of Stuart was a retainer. Stuart is French for Stewart and Stewart is Steward with the final " d " pronounced hard by a Scottish tongue. The *New English Dictionary* tells us that there is " no ground " for saying that a steward was the man who kept the sties, the habitat of swine, but that he was in charge of part of the house. There is however a sturdy tradition in East Anglia, where in pre-Norman times swine formed a noteworthy portion of domestic and even national economy, that the part of the house under the steward's charge was precisely that which lodged the swine. The steward of an Anglo-Saxon chief was certainly not personally a swineherd, but the trusted manager of a whole branch of his master's wealth, just as a mediæval butler, from whose calling all the Dukes and Marquesses of Ormonde and both Samuel Butlers, celebrated in prose and verse, took their name, was not one who, like the modern though now vanishing Victorian factotum, opened the front door and decanted the wine, but held sway over the internal economy of a powerful man's household, it might be that of the King himself. A great number of family names come from trades or callings. Such are the two foregoing examples. Such is the name of Fletcher, a reminder of the importance of archery to mediæval England ; such also the eminent name of Smith, and there is no joke in the epithet when we think of Adam, and of Sidney, and of Sir Harry and his Lady. Others, like those of the Highland clans and of innumerable Joneses and Williamses from Wales and Johnsons from England, tell that their holders are descended from one who was the son of Donald or Gregor or William or John. Your real name is your baptismal name or, outside the Christian pale, that given you by your parents or tribe. Your family name is, as our English word has it, a sur-name, that is, a name tacked on. But with the growth of population, as it became increasingly difficult to distinguish between one John and one Richard and another, the surname or, as the French call it, *nom de famille*, and the Russians more briefly *familiya*, grew more and more prominent until to bear one became a legal necessity. In many parts of the world this was a more modern development than is often supposed. Thus in France it was an edict of François Ier, who was contemporary with our own Henry VIII, that fixed on his subjects the obligation to answer to a surname. Indeed the Jews in France did not fall under this law imposing surnames until after the French Revolution. In Germany the sons of Abraham had long before that time been forced to take them. Since they had no trades and were cut off from the other chief source of surnames, they took refuge in fanciful names culled from nature, such as Mond, Hirsch, Rosenthal, Blumenfeld, Baumgarten and their infinite varieties, or sometimes had less pleasing names, such as Hoden, pinned on to them in derision. Even in our own day in a European country, or at least in one district of it, the Christian name remains the only thing. You may look for Luigi Bertuccio from dawn to dusk and not find him. The village knows a dozen Luigis but, to spot the one you want, you must know not his surname, but his nickname—as " the lame ", " the thief", " the blond ", " the bastard "—given him by his community to distinguish him from all other Luigis. So it is, or was until recently, in southern Italy, as we learn from Mr. Norman Douglas's *Old Calabria*, one of the most amusing as well as instructive books to be written in our time. Traces of the same custom, existing till near the end of the nineteenth century, can be found in southern France.

The other main source from which families take their names is the place whence they come. The reason why the Jews were cut off from this is that in the Middle Ages they were forced to live together in ghettoes and had no other place of origin. Some place-names have obvious significance. For instance, the French Dupont and our Bridge, Deschamps, and Field ; an extremely pretty as well as clear place name is Troutbeck, which was that of a well-known Coroner of Westminster fifty years ago. These come down from men who dwelt by bridges and in fields and,

like John Peel, by a stream full of trout. But it is not often
that the first holder of a place name can be positively identified,
which is the case with the first Pollock. Now Pollock is the name
of a place in the County of Renfrewshire between Glasgow and
Paisley, which lies seven miles west of Glasgow. In the Gaelic
tongue it would seem to mean " the lake with the dark pool ".

To the lake with the dark pool then, about the year 1100,
came a Frenchman. There must have been about his coming
some colour of romance or urgent personal reason ; for what
Frenchman would have left the comparative comfort and more
civilised contacts of his native land for the wilds of then almost
completely savage Scotland, unless compelled by high imagination or imperious necessity ? It would be pleasant to think that
this Frenchman had a premonition of the close connexion later
to be found between the country he left and that to which he
came. Did he dream across the centuries of " the auld alliance "
that was to bind French and Scottish hearts together and still
quickens intelligence between them ? From the thirteenth to
the eighteenth centuries French and Scots fought, conspired, and
enjoyed life together. A French princess became Queen of
Scotland and a Scottish King of England found refuge in France.
It was only by virtue of the Franco-Scottish blood in them that the
Hanoverian line came to our throne. There can be no question
but that the more generous flow of Scots blood now in our royal
family serves to make them popular in France and that the visit of
Princess Elizabeth to Paris was touched with flaming triumph
in part because she is the daughter of a Scotswoman. These things
are less actively known than unconsciously felt. When I married
a Frenchwoman of Béarnais stock, my father said : " C'est l'union
de l'Écosse et de la Gascogne." It was one of the few occasions
on which the sense of his Scots descent came out strongly.

Fulbert was the Frenchman's name who thus appeared in
Scotland at the end of the eleventh century and fixed himself
by the lake with the dark pool, and became Fulbert de Pollok,
or, according to later and more general spelling, Pollock. What
manner of man was this Fulbert, we can only conjecture. One
thing that seems certain about him is that he had great wealth.
Within a short time he and his sons and grandsons—Peter de
Pollok and John de Pollok and David de Pollok and Robert de

Pollok, names, all except Peter, that recur among Fulbert's descendants to this day—were making rich endowments to the important Cluniac Abbey of Paisley, or Pasly, as it was then written, founded in 1163, and before the end of the twelfth century there were endowments too to the Kirks of Bute and to the Abbey of Kinloss in Moray. Mediæval wealth, as all know, was largely employed *ad majorem gloriam Dei* in building churches, endowing and aggrandising ecclesiastical establishments. The motives for such expenditure were various ; some good, some bad. Good or bad, they all required a substantial amount of temporal possessions to give them effect. Whence then did Fulbert de Pollok and Peter his son acquire the wealth demanded by this munificence ? One answer alone seems admissible : Fulbert must have brought it with him, in gold and precious stones that, besides land, constituted the main form of wealth in that unsophisticated age. It is totally incredible that within the space of one or even two generations a foreign family should have obtained the broad lands from which to endow monasteries and build churches, had they arrived as needy refugees. Fulbert may have been a " displaced person ", but he clearly succeeded in shipping the family treasure chest with him.

Unless the Sieur Fulbert, now become Fulbert de Pollok, had an overpowering urge for adventure that bade him set forth across the tumbled waters of the Irish sea or perhaps even rounding Ireland in the open Atlantic to seek a new destiny in the misty north, one other motive and one alone can have driven him from his home in France. This was if he had been not indeed a willing pilgrim on uncharted seas like the Vikings who crossed the waste ocean and found " Wineland " where even now the vine grows in North America, but a fugitive from the justice or the vengeance of some greater lord whom, staying in France, he would have been powerless to resist. There exists one faint indication, or rather one most dim presumption, that this may have been the case. According to a tradition handed down in the family, the origin and even the course of which cannot be traced, Fulbert claimed descent from Childebert, the third son of Clovis, King of the Franks, that tremendous warrior and statesman who converted his people to Christianity, was the first to weld them and the Romanised Gauls into a nation, and may be considered, more than any one man, the founder of France. Clovis left his mark on France in many ways. To this day the common woodman's axe throughout France has the shape of the formidable Frankish battle axe known as the Francisque, whose reputation was besmirched for awhile by the spurious Vichy Government taking it as an emblem. Clovis it was too who gave the three lilies to the royal arms of France. While yet a pagan conqueror he bore on his shield the sign of three toads ; but at the moment of his baptism by the good Bishop Rémy Clovis's ugly toads were miraculously changed into the three fair lilies that for fourteen hundred years remained the ornament on the banner of France. So tells us the monkish chronicle that is our authority for that proud event which made France a Christian land. And before nine of those centuries had passed, the right to wear on his escutcheon the lilies of France was granted by a King of France to a Scottish soldier who had served him well ; and from that Scot they passed into the arms of the Pollock family and are part of their blason to this day.

The tradition of Fulbert's descent from Childebert and thus from Clovis is no modern invention, for it is extant in at least one of the branches of the Pollocks who emigrated to America in the seventeenth century. One suggestion may be made in support of the tradition, though of so slender a texture that it can be offered as barely more than issuing from the domain of fantasy. Among the Franks the contract of marriage was held almost more sacred than the wedding itself, a view that prevailed in mitigated form until quite modern days in France where the *contrat de mariage* or, more popularly, *les fiançailles* was a ceremony of the utmost consequence and nearly as binding as the subsequent marriage. On the night of the marriage contract it was the Frankish custom that the bride and bridegroom should spend together the hours of darkness in absolute chastity, hoping for a dream to pierce the unknown future with a ray of light. So Queen Basine, who had abandoned the King of Thuringia for love of Childeric, King of the Franks but dethroned and in exile, slept with yet apart from her new husband to be, and dreamed. And she dreamed of a great beast, the beast on which the goddess of the Franks, identified by monkish scribes as Diana of the Romans, was wont to ride when she went hunting, and in her dreams the beast was the son that she should bear to Childeric. And she did bear a son, and that son was Clovis. Now the beast on which this Diana of the Franks rode was a wild boar, and the crest of the Pollocks found on a seal as early as the beginning of the thirteenth century, those Pollocks who sprang from Fulbert who claimed descent from Clovis, is a wild boar, and the motto that accompanies the crest is " Audacter et Strenue ", from which the description of the beast in the dream sent to Clovis's mother, " ferox et strenuus ", is not far removed. To that very slight extent therefore a presumption may be said to exist of a link between the offspring of Fulbert de Pollok who came to Scotland in or about the year 1100 and Clovis King of the Franks who died Anno Domini 511. That there is a striking similarity between the Pollock crest and the Clovis chronicle cannot be denied. It would not be reasonable to imagine that, in an age when that chronicle was locked up at Tours and unknown to all but a few monks, Fulbert had taken a crest in order to bolster up a claim to royal descent by an allusion to a dream of which, unless he received knowledge of it from his ancestors, he could never have heard. Either the wild boar crest with its motto is a pure coincidence or it had truly had its origin in the dream of Clovis's mother and had been handed down to Fulbert and by him to the new family he founded in far-off Scotland.

There is yet a further consideration. In the eleventh century nothing whatever could be gained from a claim to Merovingian descent. After his death Clovis's kingdom went to pieces that were only picked up and cemented together again by Charlemagne and, later, the Capetian monarchs. On the contrary anyone making such a claim must have been exposed to instant and pressing enmity from the reigning King of France and from the more powerful among his feudal lords. His position was much like that of " the White Rose ", that Marquis of Exeter descended from Edward IV, whose head Henry VIII caused to be chopped off. Even a far less serious pretender to royal or princely rights might be an intolerable threat. The Dukes of Normandy, still more to be dreaded since William's conquest of England, and the Dukes of Brittany must look with an evil and a menacing eye on anyone presumptuous enough to claim descent from the son to whom the redoubtable Clovis had left precisely that share in the kingdom of France that abutted on and even involved their fiefs. The vital importance—vital in sober truth—of the conjuncture to anyone merely suspect of wishing to set up as a pretender can best be appreciated when it is remembered that Henry Plantagenet, Count of Anjou through his father and having for mother the Empress Matilda, inherited also Touraine and Maine, and was invested Duke of Aquitaine and Duke of Normandy. Besides the lower reaches of the Garonne in the south, he controlled those of the Loire and the Seine. He was the greatest baron in France. He was violent, martial, indefatigable, and politic ; and in 1154 he became King of England. From potentates such as these, a claimant, even in his cups, to descent from Clovis must be in mortal danger. If indeed Fulbert was rash enough to talk in public of such an ancestry and his boast came to the ears of so high a man, then he had the strongest motive to decamp from a native land sure to provide him with long imprisonment if not a speedy tomb, and to put as many leagues of land and sea as he could between himself and the wrath to come. Scotland was an ideal sanctuary.

The view is sometimes held, and now more often than formerly, that family history is of no consequence. This on the inverse of the principle expressed by Napoleon when implored to consider posterity. " What has posterity done for me ? " came the answer like a cannon shot. That pregnant saying by one of the greatest exponents of expediency is worth reflexion in an age when everyone plans for the future and justifies the complication and expense of his plans by pointing to the good that will accrue to generations after us. Napoleon's abrupt retort has clearly a wider application than a refusal to be put off from a practical course by merely speculative motives, as all motives based on the future must be. It implies observation of the fact that all serious advance in the organisation of society is based on enlightened self-interest : enlightenment residing in the recognition of the further fact that no one can advance himself seriously without advancing others also and that consequently one neglecting the interests of others will end by injuring his own. This was conclusively pointed out nearly two hundred years ago by Adam Smith, an author now disastrously ignored. The classic proof is afforded by the history of the slave trade to

America and its results. Because the traders in " black ivory "
and the planters who ran estates on slave labour ignored the
interests of their slaves or rather denied that they had any right
whatever to personal interests, the United States is faced a century
or more after those causal events with a problem the gravity of
which none can yet fully measure. Seventy years ago Lord
Acton, on being asked to define a serious-minded man, answered :
" A man who has spent more than two sleepless nights thinking
of the negro problem in America." At that date most people
must have thought the dictum absurdly exaggerated. Now, like
so many other judgments of that very prescient teacher, its under-
lying truth is becoming apparent. More harm is done in this
world by idealists, save only those of genius, than by realists.
Realists are accused of having too low a standard of morality.
But an idealist is capable of ignoring standards of morality
altogether, in obedience to his fixed idea. The slave trade was
justified by plenty of idealists anxious like Torquemada to save
men's souls by sacrifice of their bodies. Whoever thinks a priori
to do good is likely to do ill, and, since building for the future
is bound to be a priori, nobly meant structures thus erected often
turn out to be costly, and sometimes harmful, towers of Babel.
Work for yourself and you work for others. Neglect of this
precept is at the bottom of much disappointment and much
mischief today. It is a neglect largely practised by those people
to whom history is a mere concatenation of boring facts or a
collection of backstairs scandal. Not that the backstairs scandal
is to be despised. On the contrary, it forms part of what that
admirable historian, G. Lenotre, called " la petite histoire " and
made peculiarly his own. Sometimes it even becomes part of
history proper, as when we learn by word of mouth, since I am
not sure whether any writer has thought it decent to put on
paper, how Barrère discovered from Robespierre that his name
was on the Incorruptible's list of arrests for the morrow and
therefore to save his own neck sprang the Tenth of Thermidor
on a world sickened of ideological murder. To anyone capable
of reasoning it must be obvious that history is as vital to man
as its roots are to a tree. All that we are, all that we have,
comes out of the past. Only fools imagine that they can build
afresh from the beginning. If we ignore the teaching of the past,

we are like lunatics living in an ephemeral world of their own sick fantasy. Outside the realm of religion, the achievements and the errors of our forefathers are our chief guide in life. It was well said by a French eighteenth-century writer that a nation is an entity made up of innumerable entities which are families. Even today in England, where the family tie has been weakened in the course of the past century, this truth still holds good, particularly among our better working classes who celebrate family events with the same gusto that obtained in past generations and go on family jaunts and holidays with completely co-operative affection. If we wish to know ourselves or to measure our capacities, we are bound to preserve and to study the records handed down to us, among which family records are to be prized, especially as showing how the ramifications of family are intertwined with and impinge upon regional and national history, becoming part of it and so affecting its course. Mr. Robert McCormick, the violently anti-British proprietor of the *Chicago Tribune*, has accused us of " preferring ancestry to accomplishment ", which preference, he went on to emphasise with a certain want of consistency, explained the fact that Great Britain was able to impose her foreign policy on the United States and thus to " rule the world ". Many Britons, painfully aware of our humiliation in Palestine, Egypt, China, and India, would be glad to know where to look for this British world rule. Mr. McCormick appeared unconscious that, if our love of ancestry enables us so to force our will on the rich and powerful United States of America, there must be something to be said for it. Without pursuing further the complex that seems to inspire this Chicagoan worthy, we really must admit the past, ancestry included, to have something to do with achievement in the present. And therefore the study of families as well as of nations in the past must be thought worth while, always, as aforesaid, by people capable of reasoning. It is true that Descartes' " Cogito, ergo sum " attributes the power of reasoning to the entire human genus. Perhaps it might be prudently modified by a corollary to the effect that since so many men appear barely capable of reasoning, they must be held hardly human.[1]

---

[1] The reader interested in pursuing the fortunes of the Pollock family from the twelfth to the nineteenth century is referred to Appendix A.

CHAPTER IV

MAINLY MY FATHER

PAUL FORT, whom the younger men of his generation dubbed " le Prince des Poètes ", gave to the finest of his historical plays the title *Louis XI—Curieux Homme*. In the same sense of the word my father was a curious man. This is not to suggest a comparison between the enigmatic and dreaded monarch who in France closed the book of the Middle Ages and a modern scholar whom one authority called " the English Nestor ", and another " the most learned man since Bacon ". But, as with Louis XI, my father's qualities were to be found only behind a screen that cut him off from many of his fellow-men. It was not that his behaviour was eccentric in the ordinary way. He did not, like his friend Professor A. V. Dicey, produce at first sight the impression of being drunk. " Totally intoxicated, Sir," reported to his Tutor an Oxford freshman who had fled in horror from Dicey's first lecture of the term. My father dressed well and tidily, suffered from no physical strangeness or tic, had simple and commendable tastes, and though a very dissident member, indeed ex-member, of the Church of England in which he had been brought up, was at least a stout Erastian, " as my father was before me," I remember his saying. He did not then offend by militant agnosticism. But he had something about him that made the average person find him odd. Sometimes that average person thought him rude, or crabbed, or boorish, according to fancy ; but average opinion was probably best summed up by a secretary at the British Embassy at Washington who said to an American : " We think him rather peculiar." A minor diplomat was surely the last person to get behind the screen. The subject of that remark would have been astonished to learn that after his death various Americans in writing of him made free use of those other less complimentary epithets and attributed to him hoary chestnuts of bad manners told, when he was still a boy, of Ranke and others celebrated for forgetfulness of this world's decorum. F.P.—for so he signed all intimate letters and liked to be called—had a great liking for Americans as a whole, derived from warm friendships with O. W. Holmes, Professor Goodwin of the celebrated Greek Grammar, Richard W. Hale a well-known Boston lawyer, Mrs. Charles Thursby the sister of Arthur Brisbane, and others. In the simplicity of his heart he thought all Americans must have the same liking for him. F.P.'s unworldly manners formed an aspect of him that annoyed many average Americans, among whom I think none was to earn even passing fame, for the simple reason that on his numerous visits to America my father was expected by the average person to act like a showman of himself and to delight the crowd. When he did not, the crowd felt annoyance and naturally thought its annoyance must spring from a fault in him. That a screen did surround his qualities is undeniable. The explanation is twofold, but not difficult. In the first place he had suffered in boyhood from defective eyesight and, as in the case of Rudyard Kipling, this was corrected only very late : in the 1860's and 'seventies oculists' work and the need for it in childhood was far less well understood than nowadays. My father remained throughout life extremely short-sighted. With proper distance and reading glasses he saw perfectly ; but he had the disadvantage that he could only see what he looked at directly. It thus often happened that in the street or a crowded room he passed by one known to him without being aware of it. Then that person, if he did not realise the reason for his being overlooked, was offended. Early bad sight, moreover, had made my father, as it is wont to do, very shy, and this shyness became an ingrained habit, causing him to with-draw into a shell whence he had to be tempted out. Secondly, and this was far more important than any physical cause of aloofness, he could not abide the commonplace. Even this does not put the matter rightly. An active dislike of anything involves having paid it attention. To my father the commonplace simply did not exist. To commonplace things and commonplace people he presented a perfectly blank and unresponsive surface. Consequently the many commonplace people against whom from time to time he came up railed at what they considered his intolerably ill manners. They naturally did not get a chance

of discovering the very fine sense of humour, among other
qualities, on which Lord Wright after my father's death commented with happy appreciation. Sometimes after the interview
it would be exercised at their expense. It must further be
admitted that when F.P. met new people he was inclined to
class them as commonplace until the contrary was proved. Ways
of overcoming the barrier thus erected were devised by two much
younger lawyers. One counselled a man who was to meet this
reputed ogre to start talking about himself, his experiences, and
his hopes, and to go on till he struck a spark. The receipt
worked well. After a minute my father's interest was awakened
and he began to talk with the fluency that all his friends knew.
The other, a well-known judge, was approached by a friend
invited as guest to a legal dinner and placed next F.P. " I'm
absolutely petrified," he said ; " I know I shall spend a dreadful
evening." " Not a bit," said the first ; " just tell him a couple
of ' blue ' stories, and you'll find he'll thaw out at once." Which,
according to the judge in question, was what happened. My
father, a most sober man in all respects, had a sound sense of
the ludicrous possibilities of impropriety. He had been a member
of the Rabelais Club which, though it existed for the study of
the works of the Curé of Meudon, also inculcated a proper use
of the humour called *rabelaisien*. In an early notebook he jotted
down a toast he heard given at a French dinner (presumably of
scholars, lawyers, or philosophers, for I hardly see him in other
company, and obviously from the context a Franco-American
dinner) : " Je lève mon verre," said the speaker, " au beau sexe
des deux mondes—ou plutôt, aux deux mondes du beau sexe."
The word *monde* is here equivalent to *mappemonde* or " globe "
and to those unacquainted with the nicety of this *double entente*
the shape of the globe may suggest the true interpretation. He
had a pleasing story told him by Guy Le Strange of an Italian
peasant girl's prayer : " Madonna, you who could conceive
without sin, I supplicate you to arrange things so that I may sin
without conceiving ! "

Fred Pollock, as he was also known to his many friends—
and the warmth of his friendships is in itself a complete answer
to the allegation of crabbedness—may be regarded as the last
of the Victorians. He was not of course the last in point of time,

for others younger by fifteen or twenty years still survive him. Many men born in the sixties and early seventies of the last century, when Queen Victoria had yet thirty years to reign, still flourish ; my contemporaries at Eton and myself saw Victoria's first Jubilee and took an active part in her Diamond Jubilee, waving torches and singing a Latin hymn of triumph at her in the great court at Windsor Castle. But my father was the last of that band of great intellects that came to fruition some time from 1860 to 1880, whose work gave its stamp to the second half of the nineteenth century, and went on working till death took them, some sooner like Clifford and Maitland, some in old age like Gladstone, Tennyson, and Pollock, some in the ripeness of life like Swinburne, Huxley, Tyndall, Meredith, Lister, W. S. Gilbert, and Acton. That the epithet " Victorian " became attached to their age was a mere accident and one not really appropriate. The Queen who reigned so long as to impose her name on a period of sixty years had singularly little in common with what made it notable. Out of touch for long even with politics, a science by its nature changeless, she came by the sheer act of her survival to incorporate ideals that she never understood or even much approved. With the bubbling mental forces around her, challenging everything, accepting nothing at its face value, destroying to build anew, violently obnoxious to castellated prejudice and ignorance, she was wholly out of sympathy and, for the greater part, did not so much as recognise their existence. Her competent, dominant, commonplace personality fitted in admirably with the expansion of England, to use Seeley's phrase, on its geographic and material sides ; and, while her autocratic capacity did great service to the nation in ways a modern democracy could not understand, that democracy which in turn she did not understand raised Victoria's fame to the level of legend.

My father once remarked that, except as regards politics, the Prince Consort died too soon, saying : " He had educated the Queen up to appreciate Mendelssohn : there she stopped." He conceived it as possible that Prince Albert, a highly cultivated and serious man, and probably for that reason as well as others repellent to the English aristocracy, would himself have gone forward with the development of his age and drawn the Queen with him. We might then have had the curious spectacle of a sovereign patronising the Metaphysical Society, attending Irving's first nights, and reading George Meredith : such leanings as have not been displayed in England since Charles II. Left to herself, immersed in a posthumous cult of " the Great and Good ", the authoress of *My Highland Diary* was plainly refractory to intellectual progress. Imagination was not her strong point. It needed the genius of a Disraeli and a Kipling to place Victoria on her ultimate pedestal. She had curiosity, as witness her interview with Carlyle, but was incapable of meeting men on their own plane of thought : she thought they ought to come to hers. A Catherine of Russia, even a George III, the George of his youth, was better fitted to apprehend the force of intellectual currents round them. Victoria was wholly out of touch with the men who gave its bent to the nineteenth century in the arts and sciences, on whose discoveries, reasoning, inventions, and imaginations we now live, and who were united, if by nothing else, by the bond of an inner resolve not to cease from mental strife till they had shown the truth that was in them.

" Edward VII had a strong German accent," said my father. " What is odder, he had a German-Jewish accent. I wonder—" this added with sly reflexion—" where he got it ? Perhaps from his creditors." As became a historian and a lawyer, F.P. was interested in the practice as well as the theory of kingship. He maintained that the Sovereign's influence on affairs of State, circumscribed though it be by constitutional restrictions, was far more important than most people supposed. Recognition of this importance clearly prompted Edward VII, as was told my father by one of the doctors present, on being informed by them that Queen Victoria had ceased to breathe, to utter the fervent words : " Mein Gott, es ist zu spät ! " That Edward, at last come to the position he felt he could well fill, was wrong, since it was not in fact too late for him to do much excellent work as King, does not blunt the point. Recognition of this again, at the very close of my father's life, so sharpened his interest in the impending abdication of Edward VIII, as to make him spontaneously write the letter to Lord Simon, of which mention was made in the press on his death, setting forth the principles on which an Act of Abdication should be based and enclosing a short draft

51

of a Bill : the Act of Abdication as passed was found to follow very closely the lines laid down therein. Monarchy had his approval, wherein he differed from his great friend F. W. Maitland who was wont to say : " I have no use for modern kings." But modern royalty tends, F.P. thought, to be confined behind a transparent wall of glamour, opaque to the light radiated from common life. To illustrate this he quoted a story told by Charles Booth, the author of *Life and Labour of the People of London.*

One morning Charles Booth was awakened very early at his home in Great Cumberland Place, where both he and my father lived, by a messenger from Marlborough House. The messenger himself had been hauled from bed and despatched, if possible, to bring Mr. Booth on the instant to the Prince and Princess of Wales (later George V and Queen Mary). Booth made haste and arrived about six o'clock at Marlborough House, where he found the Prince and Princess in a state of much agitation. The Prince excused their importunity and said that he and the Princess the evening before had been reading a book in which mention was made of a man having died of starvation in London. They thought it could not possibly be true but were so much upset by the idea that they had passed a totally sleepless night. At dawn they had roused their people and demanded who could tell them the truth. Someone had known the name of Mr. Charles Booth as that of the highest authority on the London poor, so they had sent to beg him to come at once and enlighten them. Booth could only answer that to his great regret it was perfectly possible for people to die of hunger in London.

This story, which reflects nothing but credit upon the Prince and Princess of Wales, showed too, said my father, what cloistered lives they led, so that they could be ignorant of a fact notorious to all the world. Frank avowal of ignorance is far better, he maintained, than the pretence of expert knowledge often assumed by exalted personages at their own dictatorial promptings or those more well meaning but not always more instructed of masters of ceremony. He illustrated this by three stories. Frank Tarver the French master at Eton was entertaining Queen Victoria at tea and met her at the door. " That is a very fine old staircase, Mr. Tarver," said the Queen, entering. " Yes,

ma'am," answered Tarver, who had in fact just spent a great
deal of money on having it built. " I'm delighted your Majesty
should admire my staircase ; but it is not precisely old——"
The Queen interrupted : " I said, it is a very fine *old* staircase,
Mr. Tarver." Royalty must not be contradicted. George V,
on coming to the throne, was made to entertain a gathering of
leading men, among them W. L. Courtney, the learned and
brilliant editor of the *Fortnightly Review* who had been Professor
of Poetry at Oxford. Courtney was led up to converse with the
King who set the ball rolling with : " Now, Mr. Courtney, don't
you think that Shakespeare was a very overrated man ? "
Courtney, who related this with gusto, was so much surprised
that he could only ejaculate : " Well, Sir, no, I do not think
so." Edward VII, remarked my father, dealt more diplomatic-
ally with the priming he had received before a similar interview
with Sidney Lee. " Ah," said the King, " you write about
Shakespeare, Mr. Lee ? " Lee gracefully acknowledged that
this was so. " Ah ! " rejoined Edward, by now at the end of
his literary tether. " Then go on writing about Shakespeare,
Mr. Lee ! " Very good advice too, said F.P.

These anecdotes have now a further point than they had in
F.P.'s mind. They show what a distance has been covered in
half a century in the relations between the Sovereign and
individual subjects. Not one of these three stories could be true
of today. It took Edward VII some time after he came to the
throne to live down the not very savoury reputation he had won
for himself as Prince of Wales. Among the complaints made in
good society was the King's alleged excessively meticulous
attention to the niceties of military uniform. A good deal of
latitude, even some slovenliness had crept in under Victoria :
Edward insisted on perfect correction. My father always
defended Edward against this charge. " There is no excuse,"
he would say, " of having a grand show, if you are not going
to get the little things right." At a later date he added :
" Edward VII was a great master of buttons."

Fred Pollock, as already noted, came of a long-lived family.
His father was cut off by disease at over seventy years, but his
grandfather and many of the almost excessive number of his
uncles and aunts lived to be over eighty and at least two to be

ninety-three and ninety-four. He died himself at ninety-one after a series of accidents in old age that might have killed many a younger man. When seventy-eight he was knocked violently down from behind by a cyclist in Hyde Park and fractured his skull. St. George's learned to its surprise that the unconscious man brought in was a governor of the hospital. The surgeons predicted a fatal issue. Within a month Pollock was about again. Not long after he slipped on a wet stone and ruptured the muscles of the thigh just above his left knee. Complete rigidity of the leg seemed certain. A few months and Pollock, having almost kicked out the medical valet imposed on him, was once more at the London Fencing Club. Some years later a lightning operation was required to relieve a strangulated hernia, the surgeon—the late Sir Percy Sargent—accomplishing in twenty minutes what usually takes over an hour. Death from shock or subsequent pneumonia was feared ; but the patient made a swift recovery. Such experiences must obviously shorten life ; it is curious to speculate by how much in this case.

The toughness that overrode these mishaps with cheerful ease came doubtless not only from a hereditary tendency to cling to life but from a happy physical constitution. Under 5 feet 10 inches in height, F.P. weighed barely more than ten stone ; he had no superfluous flesh against which to fight. His habits were normal. He was never for a moment interested in food fads, nor fell a prey to faith in quack medicines. Every day of his life, save when he was ill, he ate meat twice or, if not meat, fish ; every day he drank wine at least once and often twice ; every day he smoked at least three pipes. It was an inspiriting sight at the dinner given to celebrate the fiftieth anniversary of the *Law Quarterly Review*, at which he, as first and retiring editor, was the guest of honour, to see him surrounded by the flower of the Bench and Bar ; at the age of eighty-nine he made the best speech of the evening, then sat down to the enjoyment of a large cigar and a glass of old brandy.

Without claiming profound knowledge of wine Fred Pollock liked it good. In the spacious days of the wine trade before Dora, Prohibition, and puritanical import duties in England on one of Nature's noblest gifts to man, he had been on a visit with the Franco-Scottish Society to Bordeaux, where he was entertained by Nathaniel Johnston, head of the firm of wine merchants of that name, and a renowned mayor of that queen-city of the vine. He loved to recount the answer given him by the fine old merchant prince, when asked wherein lay the difference between burgundy and claret : " Monsieur, le vin de Bourgogne est une cocotte, le vin de Bordeaux est une grande dame."

As F.P. never had any doubt on the subject, the question raging about the beginning of this century as to whether alcohol had a food value left him cold ; but he expressed pleasure on hearing Emile Duclaux, Pasteur's first successor at the Institut Pasteur, answer it with an emphatic affirmative. Certain it is that brandy administered at the right time and without stint saved both his and my mother's life more than once. When he had a cold as was not infrequent, having inherited a weakness that way from his father, he drank rather more than usual. " But," he would say, " I never ventured on Aldis Wright's prescription for exorcising a cold." Aldis Wright was a cele-brated Vice-Master of Trinity, Cambridge and the editor of the classical Cambridge Shakespeare. " What was that ? "—" Why, when Aldis Wright caught a cold, he went to bed and then drank off a whole bottle of Audit ale. In the morning, Wright said, you must be either cured or dead." Although my father did not cure colds with Trinity Audit ale, reputed the strongest and certainly the most delectable beer brewed, he always kept some in his country cellar. One day a bottle, without label, was opened by mistake for cider and a glass offered to Lady Claud Hamilton, Professor Tyndall's mother-in-law. Lady Claud was elderly, and very melancholy. That day she almost danced a mile uphill to Tyndall's house.

Fred Pollock, then, ate meat, he smoked, he drank. He also walked. In his remembrances *For My Grandson*, a storehouse for the future social historian of the nineteenth century, he speaks, belittling them somewhat, of his experiences as an Alpine climber ; he says little of his walking. Yet walking made up a great part of his life. Down to extreme old age, if he could not go for at least one good walk a day he became fractious : indeed, to be prevented from walking was about the only thing that could upset the balance of his almost invariably serene humour. He must have started walking for pleasure very early in life—I should guess, at Eton, where his uncorrected eyesight prevented his playing games well ; his last walk was taken within a fortnight of his death. During Term, that is, the Law Terms by which his movements were regulated for sixty-five years, it must have been rare for him, until the accident to his leg, not to walk in the morning from Marble Arch to Lincoln's Inn, in the afternoon from Lincoln's Inn to either the Athenæum or the London Fencing Club, opposite St. James's Palace, and thence often back to his house. Say, on an average, roundabout six miles. In the country during vacation, when he often worked most of the morning, from five to eight miles ; often more on Dartmoor where he was a frequent guest of William Collier, brother of the first Lord Monkswell and a famous wine merchant in the West country. Every Sunday, when in town, till of middle age, he walked something over twenty miles with the Sunday Tramps, that " fellowship " as he calls it, which he founded together with Leslie Stephen ; besides a host of other well-known names the roll of the Sunday Tramps comprised at various times those of George Meredith, John Morley, Haldane, James Bryce, F. W. Maitland, Theodore Davies, George and Robert Trevelyan, Douglas Freshfield the great mountaineer, Arthur Verrall the most brilliant Greek scholar of his generation, Grant Allen, Sir James and Harry Stephen, brothers of the lamented J.K.S., and McColl, editor of the excellent, now long defunct, weekly *The Athenæum*. When I came down from Cambridge, together with Thoby Stephen, Leslie Stephen's son, I revived the Sunday Tramps ; and they flourished throughout a whole second generation. F.P. never tired of walking ; walking never tired him. It seemed rather to release a hidden spring. As he walked, his mind became easier, his talk more flowing, and it is no wonder that those who walked with him remember with delight the natural warmth and quick wit that inspired his talk.

" Your father," wrote the then Chief Guide of the Sunday Tramps to me on his death, " is much more the G.O.M. of the present-day Tramps than Stephen who remains with them as a kind of historical figure, whereas there was always a feeling that F. Pollock was not far away and might turn up at Victoria any Sunday morning."

Together with Mr. Justice Bramwell, he invented a formula for the benefit of irate landowners on whose property the Tramps might trespass, never failing to point out that the common notice " Trespassers will be prosecuted " is a mere piece of mendacious bluff, since trespass is not a criminal offence. The formula ran as follows : " I give you to notice that I claim no right of way or other easement over this your land, and I hereby tender you the sum of sixpence by way of amends." Later this became embellished into a kind of anthem, which my father would execute by himself, enacting, and chanting, the parts of the priest as he intoned the first words, then to be taken up and repeated by the trebles, the tenors, and the basses in the choir, and so on until the whole swelled into a majestic unison on the word A-men (ds). He had a clever trick of, as it were, imitative recital, by which he could represent a whole scene in some such anecdote as the above, and cause his listeners to dissolve into laughter.

Besides walking, my father's only form of exercise was fencing. He had studied in youth under an instructor named Waite who himself had been a pupil of the elder Prévost. Camille Prévost, the latter's son, was the most famous of all nineteenth-century *maîtres d'armes*. Waite must have been a man of some originality for at this time fencing in England had sunk to a low level and nothing better was generally taught than rough sabre and elementary foil-play. Later my father worked under good French *maîtres d'armes*, besides making a thorough study of the literature and thus the science of fencing. He was one of the band mentioned before in which F.P.'s brother Walter, Egerton Castle, Captain Hutton, and Hugh Pollock a grandson of the Field-Marshal were conspicuous, to whom the scientific revival of interest in fencing was due in England. Hugh Pollock was a fine *sabreur* and for many years his feats in cutting ribbons in the air and severing at one blow a sheep's carcase were a feature of exhibitions at the School of Arms belonging to the Inns of Court Volunteers. F.P. practised the foil till he was well over eighty ; after the accident to his leg, fortunately the left one, he was immobile on his feet but still remarkably active and accurate with the foil in his hand. I never had a chance to fence with my Uncle Walter, a brilliant performer, but did on several occasions with Egerton Castle who had learned from some of the best French masters and enjoyed a great reputation, and am confident that F.P. was the stronger fencer. Indeed, he earned from the great Mimiague, his last master at the London Fencing Club, the high compliment of being called *difficile*. He never fenced with the sabre but had mastered and was fond of displaying the intricate sabre exercises of Cut, Thrust, Guard, and Counter taught in the Light Horse Volunteers of his ancestor Colonel Herries. After F.P.'s death Lord Maugham hastened into print with the statement that " he was not a good fencer ". This so much incensed three former British champions and internationals who used to meet F.P. constantly at the L.F.C. that I had some difficulty in restraining them from writing publicly to rebuke the author of it. What was even stranger than so ill grounded an opinion, was that none of these three, nor I myself, had ever heard of Lord Maugham as a fencer.

It would be absurd for me to attempt to assess my father's value in the domain of the law, to which he gave the greater part of his life. His mastery of all branches of it was notorious and probably unequalled in any age. Nor would this be the place to go into detail. But I may again quote Lord Wright, one of the outstanding judges of the succeeding generation, when he wrote of " Pollock's extraordinary freedom of mind, his penetrating insight undimmed by his wealth of learning, his faculty of hitting off a simple and convincing solution of a problem, however complicated it might seem." And again : " There are some men whose personalities transcend any particular things they have done. Some men are greater than their works or deeds, though these may have been great. There comes from such men an afflatus of impulse and inspiration. This is what we always felt with Pollock." Another superlative mind had written in no less superlative terms nearly half a century earlier. This was Professor F. W. Maitland who in one short work wholly destroyed a comfortable theory set up by that august body the Church of England and buttressed by assumptions sanctified through the passage of three centuries. Of Maitland that great American lawyer, Oliver Wendell Holmes, wrote that " he was acknowledged to be supreme ". That Maitland and my father were close friends does not make the

COLONEL HERRIES IN THE UNIFORM OF THE LONDON AND
WESTMINSTER LIGHT HORSE VOLUNTEERS

From a painting by W. R. Biggs, A.R.A.

testimony less significant : Maitland was incapable of not speaking as a witness of truth, even about a friend. Nor is it lessened by the charming tone of levity in which it is written. In 1883 Pollock was elected Corpus Professor of Jurisprudence at Oxford. Maitland wrote to him :

" To F. Pollock, Professor of All Laws in all Universes and Universities and reputed Universities.

May it please you Enormity to accept the congratulations of your sincere votary and humble brother [1] over the fact brought to his notice by the *Times* that you have become more vested than ever and having had the animus to profess the law in Oxford have now the Corpus also.

Ave verum Corpus Juris !

F. W. MAITLAND."

Pollock's judgment on his friend was simple and complete. " Maitland was a genius," he said.

Law was my father's life-work. He transfigured the conception and the teaching of law in England. " Our lady the Common Law," in his own pleasant conceit, was to him the embodiment of the historic growth of English ideas and especially of English justice,

" the Law of England ", as Lord Wright has said, " seen in all its amplitude in time and space, progressing down the ages and expanding beyond England over the nations of the British Commonwealth over India and over the United States ; indeed he thought of the Common Law as the law of free nations and as the bond of union between the English speaking peoples, on whichever side of the Atlantic or Pacific their homes were."

It would however be a mistake to suppose that my father's other manifold interests were pursued as mere dilettante distractions. His rapier-like mind was incapable of not fixing itself seriously on anything by which its attention was caught. His accuracy was impeccable. Painting, classical sculpture, architecture, music, literature, history, languages, philosophy, all came within his ken ; and his knowledge of most of them equalled that of professional exponents. He spoke with great sureness French, German, and classical Italian, though porters, waiters, and cabmen with foreign tongues were always stumbling-blocks to him ;

[1] i.e. in the Law.

59

read with ease Dutch and Spanish ; and had more than a nodding acquaintance with Persian and Russian. His classics were beyond criticism. He could discuss Greek poetry on equal terms with Swinburne and Verrall, Greek philosophy with Henry Jackson. Classical and mediæval Latin were to him as his mother tongue, and he could without the slightest trouble converse in Latin with the best Roman ecclesiastic ; I have heard him do it. After ten days spent in Greece he began to speak modern Greek. Lord Justice Kennedy, who was Senior Classic at Cambridge with my father as second Classic, told me that Pollock was unquestionably the better scholar, " the best in my time ", and that he forfeited his right to the Senior title only because he was after the Chancellor's Medal, which he won, and in those days to enter for it a man had besides being a first-class classic to have taken the mathematical Tripos : F.P. was senior optime. This aptitude for languages was not a heaven sent gift, as in the case of Lord Leighton and a few other lucky mortals. It came only with steady application, after the hard linguistic grounding that boys in the last century got at Eton, aided by an astonishingly retentive memory and tireless reading. My father's mathematical knowledge, whetted by the genius of W. K. Clifford, his alter ego at Cambridge, in whom some qualified to speak have since seen, had Clifford lived, an earlier Einstein, enabled him to follow with understanding modern developments in physics and astronomy. These fitted in very well with the philosophy F.P. had derived from his study of Spinoza. "A man drunk with God ", Novalis, the romantic poet, had called Spinoza. It would be hard to sustain a comparison between any other modern man and Spinoza, either for elevation of personal character or for devotion to things of the mind. Nor could any other rise to that height of absorption of self in the divine essence of all things. But it may safely be said that my father had drunk deep at the fount which Spinoza's genius caused to flow. Later this influence became strongly tinged with another Eastern strain— for it must not be forgotten that Spinoza was of Oriental extraction—when my father came under the charm of the Persian poets. He studied the language with Professor Cowell, with " Persian " Browne of Cambridge, and with Guy Le Strange. This remarkable man, in the judgment of experts one of the most profound Orientalists, was, I know not how, always an intimate family friend. The Le Stranges are one of those ancient East Anglian families proud never to have held any hereditary title of nobility down to the seventeenth century when one could not escape being made a baronet. Guy, who had lived largely in Italy and France as well as in the lands of Kinglake's *Eothen*, now called the Middle East, came back in the end to live and to die in Cambridge. He was one of the most fascinating of men. He was almost blind of one eye, in his last years completely so, saw very poorly with the other and was afflicted with a severe stammer that he mastered so cleverly as to make it an additional attraction to his lively conversation, using it consciously to give point to innumerable anecdotes stored in his observant mind of great scholars and travellers and of exalted personages and their sometimes unexpected bastards.

Guy Le Strange was not to my knowledge specially interested in the aspect of Persian poetry that mainly captivated my father, namely its mysticism, which became a dominating strain in his spiritual life. I shall have occasion to speak of a manifestation of this in a supreme moment. Another link with the East was my father's friendship with Cornelia Sorabji, the first Indian woman to become an English barrister. This unique young woman, of whom no one could say whether she was more beautiful than intellectual or intellectual than noble, came of a Christian Parsee family. Her career, as unique as herself, is recorded in her own works *India Calling* and *India Recalled*. On coming down from Oxford, where she was a pupil of Dicey and my father, she speedily became friends with some of the best brains in England, including Haldane, Sir Edward Grey, Asquith and his second wife, and later Mr. Justice Atkinson and Sir Stafford Cripps. She was a great favourite of Lord Roberts. The Baroness Burdett-Coutts formed a special attachment for her. Among those friends I think Sir Edward Grey perhaps took first place in her heart, but my father had an advantage over Grey in the equal love Cornelia Sorabji had for my mother as well as for him. Though she was not in the least given to mysticism, her immense knowledge of India, of which she spoke virtually all the current languages and her ability to look at her native country without the prejudices inherent in most native eyes, gave talk with her, apart from her competence in English law as well as in the customs of India, a peculiar value for my father, who had inherited an interest in what was then a jewel in the Imperial crown of Great Britain and had cultivated it by wide reading and by learning from men like Sir Henry Maine, Mackenzie Chalmers, Sir George Robertson, Sir Courtenay Ilbert, Sir Francis Younghusband, and Sir Alfred Lyall, who had had long personal acquaintance with the Asian sub-continent. It pleased him, when the untrustworthiness of Indian evidence came up in conversation, to quote Chalmers's opinion that in all his experience in India, where he had served as a judge, he had never heard so much perjury as in the County Court of Birmingham. There was too an affinity with Younghusband's religious leanings, and F.P. joined with the famous traveller in Thibet and the Pamirs to found a movement in 1914 that they named " Fight for Right " ; but it was too abstract to have success with the British public. My father's one visit to India, to give the Tagore lectures at the University of Calcutta, was prolonged by him for some months in order to see as much of the country and its peoples as he could. He had numerous other Indian friends, such as Sir Dimshah Mulla with whom he collaborated to write a classical work on the Indian Contract Act, and profited by his journey throughout India, staying as a guest among others with Sir Pertab Singh for whom he conceived a warm admiration, to begin the study of Sanskrit. The sincerity of his interest in India may be seen in that charming novel written in letter form by him and Mrs. Fuller Maitland, *The Etchingham Letters*. The composition of it occupied the greater part of one Long Vacation. F.P. took unrestricted pleasure in the work. Only the bare framework had been settled beforehand by the two collaborators and every letter from each of them contained some new development unexpected by its recipient.

A short time after my father's death I was surprised, indeed a little staggered, to hear an accomplished Oxford professor call him " the most learned man since Bacon ". At the first blush this praise seemed to me exaggerated. On consideration I believe it may be true. It is difficult to compare men of learning in different ages : the extent of knowledge has so grown in the last two centuries that the circle of it available to a man in the seventeenth century was minute if set against that open to one in our own. Doubtless Francis Bacon had all the knowledge available to his generation. That can hardly be said of anyone now. The last man who could aspire to universal knowledge was, in F.P.'s opinion, Whewell, the Master of Trinity, Cambridge, who died in 1866. Since Whewell's day there have been many famous men of learning, such as Mommsen, Harnack, and Lord Acton. But the vast knowledge of even the last named was circumscribed ; that of the two former more so. It is only by attempting to compare the learning of Acton, whose pupil I was, with that of my father that I am able to form any opinion as to the validity of the judgment quoted above. Acton's knowledge of modern history and political theory was unique in its breadth and thoroughness. His knowledge of ecclesiastical history and of the early Fathers was not less. That possessed by Pollock was certainly far less extensive and detailed. But he had read almost every important book on these subjects and, although he had not Acton's miraculous visual memory for books, he never forgot what he read and always had the facts ready in his mind. *His Introduction to Political Science* has remained what it was on publication, the best book on the subject. Though not a professed Shakespearean scholar, he had the bulk of Shakespeare's plays so incrusted in his memory that he hardly ever had need to refer to the text and was the originator of more than one illuminating emendation. His knowledge of mediæval and of classical history was complete : it was superior to Acton's in that to him they were always living subjects. Again F.P.'s strictly classical learning and of course his knowledge of the laws of many countries was definitely wider than Acton's, as also of Greek and in general profane philosophy, the East, poetry, music, sculpture, and painting. The arts did not greatly interest Acton. Church architecture was always F.P.'s delight : " it is as hard," said Mabel Robinson, a close friend of my parents, " to get F.P. past a church as to get a drunkard past a public house." His acquaintance with French and Italian cathedrals must almost have equalled that of Anatole France. On a balance, and saving alone modern history in its fullest sweep, I am driven to the conclusion that my father's learning was barely, if at all, less than that of so renowned a man as Acton and in some respects greater. If this is so, the judgment that started this strain of thought may be not unwarranted. The process that led to F.P.'s becoming, to put it at the lowest, one of the most learned men of his time was quickened by the ease with which he worked. He could turn from one subject to another without the loss of a minute and with undiminished avidity. I never knew his brain to be tired.

Dr. Johnson without James Boswell would have remained to the world noteworthy as an early lexicographer fond of incisive definitions. Without the Rev. Richard Millward, John Selden would be known as an erudite but difficult writer on obscure legal and constitutional subjects. Neither could have lived, as both do live, as representatives of the highest English good sense on an infinite variety of topics, as talkers whose style in speech surpassed that of many professed stylists on paper, and as a source of admiration and delight to generations that succeeded them. It is a matter for regret that my father had no Boswell, no Millward to chronicle his table talk. He would have been the first to repel a suggestion that it could be put on the same level as those two illustrious samples of what the best talk can be. But he was for ever saying things worth putting on record. By the time I began to realise this, I was no longer enough with him to take notes even intermittently, and too much occupied to have time to do so. His comments on people and things were often caustic but almost always just. Some of them have found their way into print, as that on Ramsay MacDonald. He used to meet Ramsay sometimes at the Athenæum and had a personal liking for the man. This did not prevent his saying, first, that the Socialist P.M. was a worm ; then, after some reflexion, that he must apologise to worms, for he had never heard of a worm that was frightened of its own tail. The formula clearly tickled him not a little, for he wrote it to Oliver Wendell Holmes. Then it was improved by the apology following in a second letter, the delay between the two giving an added savour for their recipient. Of F.P.'s friendship with Holmes I propose to say little here. Their unique correspondence extending over fifty years is in print,[1] and in my introduction to it I wrote of their relations at length.

[1] *The Pollock-Holmes Letters*, Cambridge University Press, 1942.

My father was an accomplished versifier and, one might almost say, an inveterate rhymester. His *Leading Cases* has caused joy to generations of lawyers and to more than lawyers, for the *Other Diversions* that complete the title contain verses not legal only. In a book of memoranda of 1880 he noted a translation by himself of his *Epigram on Beethoven's Symphonies*, published therein, and originally written in really magnificent German. To the best of my belief the English remained unpublished, so I give it here :

> Nine times he spake, the lord of mighty strains,
> And bound the world ninefold in magic chains,
> Master of soul and sense, of love's young breath,
> Men's noble deeds, labour and fate and death ;
> The end is light : he calls with voicëd spell
> Joy from her starry sphere, with man to dwell.

On another loose page, the year not noted, I find :

" Dec. 9. (Milton's birthday)—sent to the Rector of Lincoln after talk of epigrams his folk were making, and seeing in O.W.'s poems a cry of ' Where is Milton's austere pen ? '

> Sermonem, Miltone, tuum desiderat Attis,
> Casta prius solitum jura docere patres.
> Hoc agit eximie : certe exoriere sepulcro,
> Quem priscum laudat semivir ipse virum."

F.P.'s *Chanson de Rodilardus* (Rabelais' cat), written during the Russo-Japanese war, won praise from so good a judge as Robert M. Johnston, the Harvard professor, of whom I shall speak later. French was Johnston's second, or rather first, mother-tongue, for he had been born and brought up in Paris. He held, with Anatole France, though France's opinion was then not yet publicly known, Béranger to have been the last truly classical French poet, and he found in my father's verse an echo of that master of almost Horatian incisiveness. The last stanza pleased him specially :

> Sur la mer du Japon
> Depuis la mi carême,
> L'on joue du canon ;
> Moi, je lèche la crème :
> Ronron, ronron,
> Ce monde est bon.

To such verses as those I have quoted F.P. evidently devoted time and thought. But he was also fond of tossing off lines that came to him after a few minutes', or even seconds' cogitation. One he suddenly produced at a luncheon-party in the midst of a heated discussion on the Bacon-Shakespeare controversy. After a short, brooding silence, he sat up and said :

> " He that would Bacon place where Shakespeare sits,
> Must have unbaken brains or shaken wits."

Here I may interpose another remark on the same subject : " What makes it really impossible for anyone of literary taste to believe that Bacon wrote Shakespeare's plays is the quality not of Shakespeare's poetry, but of his prose. A man who thinks that the author of Bacon's prose could have written Shakespeare's prose deserves to be damned with authors of books without indexes who lie ten miles beyond hell, where the devil himself cannot go for the stinging nettles." And another of the little imitative improvisations I have mentioned consisted in imagining all the principal Elizabethan authors holding a meeting, perhaps at the Earl of Oxford's house, to discuss which of them should write the works of which. The discussion became more and more involved when of a sudden one of them cried out : " Happy thought ! Let each one of us write his own works ! " And so they all went home and did.

One of F.P.'s most remarkable improvisations was on its being told him, perhaps quite untruly, that Robert Trevelyan, whom I trust it is not insulting to call one of the best of our minor poets, had written a number of sonnets for which he could find no first lines. My father sat silent for a while and then produced the following :

> Robert, thou son of George our parodist,
> Why boggle at that line which should be first.
> Since it may not be worser than the worst,
> And neither first nor last will e'er be missed ?
> On many sonneteers the sun uprist,
> With that same gift of evil rhyming curst
> To set upon them still in rhymes immersed.
> Lean and desk thumping with a futile fist,
> Nor will it vex him if thou beest one more
> To vex the patient page with crabbed ink,
> And smoke too much, neglecting meat and drink
> And ask of fellow scribblers what they think :
> For these things make him neither glad nor sore.

I am unhappily conscious that a line—not the first—is missing, but I wrote down the sonnet only long afterwards and have never been able to recapture it completely.

Once being incensed by an entry in a bookseller's catalogue he wrote to my cousin E. S. P. Haynes :

" From bookseller's Catalogue : Blake—Illustrations of the Book of Job . . . 21 sublime etchings by Blake . . . This is the second time I have found this blunder—the first time (a good while ago) there was something about the artist's *needle*, and all at once there came into my head :

> Good fool, if you think I engraved with a needle
> You're fit to be whipt with Sir Joshua for beadle.

If I had been a medium by trade I might have passed this off as a message from W.B. Certainly he wrote many much better epigrams but, I think, also a few worse."

Blake was one of my father's lasting enthusiasms : the call of mystic to mystic. Another in lighter vein was rattled off on December 10, 1927 : this was the date of his birth :

> A most elderly man said, 'Tis clear
> I can't have a birthday, my dear,
> For now that Einstein has removed Space and Time
> There's no Day and No Month and no Year.

In *Outside the Law* F.P. printed a jingle on *The Wasp : a Moral Poem* telling of all the dreadful things that will happen if you try by various means to kill one. But one couplet was omitted from the printed version :

> And if you smite him with a sword,
> You'll buy Van Dycks from Humphry Ward.

Humphry Ward was *The Times* art critic and carried on discreet business on the side as intermediary between buyers and sellers of works of art. F.P. did not consider it in the least a comedown to turn to the limerick. He became a first-class hand at the job. An early one of his that earned widespread fame was :

> There was an old man of the Trent
> Who talked to himself as he went,
> But so loud and so much, and moreover in Dutch,
> That no one could make out what he meant.

I quote two more, in order to show their author's later style. The subject of the first was an American " socialite ", as U.S. papers would now call her, afterwards to marry a British peer, and reputed to have had an injection of petroleum wax on the bridge of her nose. This was the limerick :

> We have a young beauty named Deacon,
> Whose nose seemed her features to weaken.
> So she filled it with grease, and said ".Now I'm at peace,
> For my profile's a perfectly Greek 'un."

The second was the immediate response to a challenge to write a limerick on the name of Fletcher, the possessor of it in question, who was present, being Walter Morley Fletcher, M.D., a Fellow of Trinity, Cambridge, later Sir Walter and secretary of the Research Council. F.P. was on to it like lightning with :

> We have a young Fellow named Fletcher.
> Do you think he's a fiddler or etcher ?
> Can he act, sing, or paint ?
> None of these things he ain't.
> He's of medicines a carrier and fetcher.

At a tea-party where he was disappointed of muffins he suddenly got off :

> A scholar suff'ring crusts devoid of jam
> And other plagues—as you are and I am—
> Still like a prudent clerk minded his soul,
> And taught a soulless parrot to say " Damn ".

On being asked by a French lady present what were muffins, he replied : " Muffins are what bishops eat for tea at the Athenæum, and then they go away taking other members' umbrellas with them."

Although I cannot offer anything like a serious collection of my father's table-talk, I have a number of stray sayings of his jotted down that are worth recording. One subject that always tickled his curiosity was the Day of Judgment. " Just to think of the secret that the Archangel Gabriel has had up his sleeve all the time ! " he said. " It used to be objected as impossible that all the resurrected could be present in the Valley of Josaphat. But of course there is no difficulty at all : broadcasting has made it the simplest thing in the world. And no trudging to the Judgment Seat—all stations connected by television." Another view of the matter concerned Dr. Montagu Butler, the last of the three great Victorian Masters of Trinity, about whom F.P. wrote with affection and admiration in *For My Grandson*. Butler, it was well-known, had a weakness for singing the praises of Trinity College in season and out of season. So, said F.P., he was sure that on the Last Day Montagu Butler as Master of Trinity would at the end rise to propose a vote of thanks to the Chairman for his admirable conduct of the proceedings. " ' Some,' he would say in his beautiful, chanting voice, ' have done well, and others '—this with a tactful glance at the damned— ' have done less well, but whatever we may as individuals think about our Chairman, we must all agree in this—that he is, in the best and the widest sense of the word, a Trinity man.' "

F.P. had much less liking for Jowett, the Master of Balliol, and said of him : " Jowett had the supreme talent of putting a polish on a most ordinary man."

He was a considerable friend of Arthur Cohen, K.C., a lawyer of much fame, and thought most outbursts of anti-semitism in history had been caused by commercial jealousy or by the King's need for money. He said : " A great deal of nonsense is talked about semitism and anti-semitism. There is a lot of Jewish blood in the world. People should remember that we are all descended from Father Adam. Did you ever know the real reason why Adam and Eve took to wearing fig leaves ? No ? Why "— triumphantly—" so as to lay the foundations of the old clo' trade ! " He liked to tell the story of a friend of his father's who had remonstrated with a Jewish peddlar for crying out : " O' clo' ! O' clo' ! " The man stopped and regarding him gravely said : " Sir, I can say ' Old Clothes ' as well as you can. But if you had to call out ' Old Clothes ' twenty times a minute, you would say ' O' Clo' ' as I do."

Of Law reporting : " On the Day of Judgment one of my credit notes will be the amount of red tape I have *not* put into the Law Reports. Just imagine the red tape the official mind might have spun over sending a case back to a reporter for revision or a judgment to a judge ! When I became editor, one of the reporters used to write me whole screeds about points in the work. I answered on half sheets of notepaper twisted into a cocked hat. But finally I had to send him a letter telling him

that I would *not* be addressed as if I were a government department." And he invented a tremendous curse on a bad law
reporter, ending up : " But 'twill be a poor, pitiable damnation,
neither. Hast not enough soul in thy guts, I warrant, to light
a taper for Beelzebub to use a piss-pot."

Of titles : " The one serious advantage of being a baronet
is that you can't be Knighted."

On being offered some " British Champagne ", and tasting
it : " Suitable for wedding breakfasts—it might almost be
ambitious cider."

He related a trick a publisher had tried to play upon him,
ending up : " Well, he began as an Anglican, went on to be a
Positivist, and ended in the Church of Rome : so I suppose he
must have had a peculiar sense of veracity."

On going to the Spinoza tercentenary in 1932 at The Hague,
where he represented the Universities of both Oxford and
Cambridge, he said : " I must take care they don't put me in
a bottle at the Spinoza Museum as an antiquity with the label :
" Section Préhistorique. Age moyen. Spinoziste anglais en
bon état de conservation." Starting on the same journey he
remarked : " One should always have a Horace with one," and
produced from his pocket a Horace he had had at Eton, adding
on the spot a marginal note to those he had made in pupil-room
in 1862.

On the silliness of a discussion at the time of the Disarmament
Conference about offensive and defensive weapons : " The only
strictly defensive weapon I know is a thick mud wall."

He also said : " I know the solution of the disarmament
situation—but I shall not send it to Simon. At a given moment
all the powers will send him a wire : ' Delighted join in making
omelette.' Identic reservation : ' *My* eggs are not to be
broken.' "

On Paley's *Evidences* : " If you assume that the twelve apostles
really existed and that they were a jury of Guildhall merchants,
his position is unattackable." Then he quoted Fitzjames Stephen
as ridiculing miracles by narrating an Arabian Nights story as
if told according to the rules of evidence : " At this point,
gentlemen of the jury, the witness says that a black man came
out of the wall and said ' Fish, fish, are you in your duty ? ' "

Fitzjames Stephen, it will be remembered, was the author of the often quoted definition of metaphysics as a blind man in a dark room hunting for a black hat which isn't there.

Of religious dogmatism, arising out of Bishop Gore's *Belief in God* : " The ordinary apologist and the ordinary freethinker are mere dust and ashes—I don't know which is the more tiresome."

Someone spoke of important evangelicals. F.P. said : " Important evangelicals ? Ah yes, elderly gentlemen with the best intentions who sit round a table and talk, and know nothing about anything."

Longfellow's *Excelsior !* he called " The worst complete bad poem ever written by a good poet. But what we shall never know is what idiot gave the State of New York the word Excelsior for a motto."

Concerning wireless : " What wouldn't Moses have given for a good loudspeaker to broadcast the Ten Commandments ! "

On hearing Lord Tyrrell's bad dinners at the British embassy in Paris contrasted with Lord Crewe's good ones : " What is the good of being a Catholic if you don't learn how to dine ? Catholics have to study the art of eating—that is, those who observe Lent. Catholics and Quakers have always been reputed to dine well : the Puritans never had any objection to either eating or drinking—so long as they were not made amusing."

On surtax : " By charging supertax on the whole of income, without deducting the amount paid in income tax, the Treasury is guilty of precisely the same tricks that the State condemns in moneylenders for concealing their real rate of interest."

My father, as was well known, was no respecter of persons. Many successful public characters came under his keen eye.

" Lord Brentford," formerly Joynson-Hicks and, when Home Secretary, popularly known as " Jicks ", " is an example of how far a man can go with one or two poor ideas if he has obstinacy enough in applying them."

" Gilbert Murray is the sort of man who wouldn't mind having a pistol in the house if he was certain of its not being loaded."

" The fortune of the Harmsworths is one of the things that

tempt one almost to be a Socialist. Oh well, the original Harmsworth showed that, when an unscrupulous European chose, he could play the American game as well as an American. Besides, the fuss made about rich people amassing money is quite useless, because it gets dispersed somehow."

" I suppose the Lord created Beaverbrook to make Rothermere appear tolerable."

" Grey would have been a perfect Foreign Secretary in a world as honest as himself."

" Lansbury is the perfect specimen of the natural fool."

" Asquith thought of the British Empire as a formless thing that did not conform to the rules of the House of Commons and was very tiresome when you had to talk about it in public."

Asked if he had read E. M. Forster's *Life of Goldie Lowes Dickenson*, the author of *Letters of John Chinaman* and *The Meaning of Good*, F.P. answered : " Not yet. I'm not in a hurry to read one old woman on another. Lowes Dickenson never took joy in the world as a spectacle. He was always wanting to improve somebody or something."

In the 1930's Lady Houston, widow of Lord Byron, who married a shipowner and had the distinction of leaving intact to his relatives the seven millions her marriage with him brought her, was making a splash, first, by her patronage of aviation, which was of serious value to the nation, but secondly by her political views which were futile. F.P. drew the following diagram :

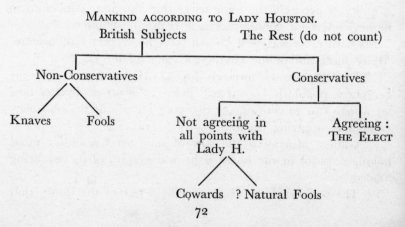

MANKIND ACCORDING TO LADY HOUSTON.

British Subjects   The Rest (do not count)

Non-Conservatives   Conservatives

Knaves   Fools   Not agreeing in all points with Lady H.   Agreeing : THE ELECT

Cowards   ? Natural Fools

When he was about forty, my father was invited by Rawlins, K.C., afterward M.P. for Cambridge, to meet Lady Frere, the widow of Sir George Bartle Frere, a prominent empire-builder of the generation then passing. (Sixty years later we have only empire-breakers.) Rawlins had the idea that F.P. would be a good man to write Bartle Frere's life. So my parents dined with Rawlins to meet Lady Frere and F.P. was put next her at table. The following dialogue ensued :

Lady Frere (*with interested condescension*) : Where do you go to church, Mr. Pollock ?
F.P. (*curtly*) : I do not go to church.
Lady Frere (*in aweful tones*) : And why do you not go to church, Mr. Pollock ?
F.P. (*thoroughly ruffled*) : I shall not tell you.

After this nothing more was said about the biography.

"It is an open secret to the few who know it," wrote F.P. in his biographical memoir of Clifford, "but a mystery and a stumbling-block to the many, that Science and Poetry are own sisters." This abiding sense of the one-ness of all things of the mind, which insensibly glides into that of the one-ness of all things, may have first come to my father from Spinoza, or it may have been only so strengthened and broadened. It was certainly at the root of F.P.'s spiritual development and was part of the rock on which his friendship for Clifford was built. What Clifford's place as a mathematician was or might have been had he lived I am incapable of estimating ; but that he would have become a philosopher of high rank appears certain. F.P.'s memoir of him had for its motto the phrase of Paul Louis Courier : " La verité est toute pour tous ", and the following passage from the memoir might have been written with equal appositeness of its author.

" Students of Spinoza will easily trace the connexion between his theory of mind and matter and the doctrine set forth in Clifford's Essays on ' Body and Mind ' and ' The Nature of Things-in-Themselves '. . . . Briefly put, the conception is that mind is the one ultimate reality ; not mind as we know it, in the complex forms of conscious feeling and thought, but the simpler elements out of which thought and feeling are built up.

The hypothetical ultimate element of mind, or atom of *mind-stuff*, precisely corresponds to the hypothetical atom of matter, being the ultimate fact of which the material atom is the phenomenon . . . To speak technically, it (this theory) is an idealist monism. Indeed it is a very subtle form of idealism, and by no means easy of apprehension at first sight."

It is clear that neither F.P. nor Clifford thought of reality as being conditioned by Euclidean geometry or Greenwich time : F.P. frequently had little digs at those who imagine eternity to be a mere extension of the latter, in which they will go on feeling and reasoning as they do in this world. He was fond of telling this parable : " The cheese-mites once held a meeting to decide what was the origin of the world. Some maintained that it was the plate. Others favoured the belief that it was the knife. But not even the most enlightened among them could in the wildest flights of their imagination even conceive of the existence of a cow." Yet this recognition of human ignorance led neither to agnosticism, nor to discouragement, but rather to a firm faith that by conscious improvement man can realise his place in the divine infinitude. As to immortality he said, " If I had to put into one sentence what I think about personal immortality, I should say that in eternity many things do not matter and, for aught we know, the individuality of which we think so much may be one of them."

The faith that direct communion can be achieved between the individual mind and the divine essence is a mystic faith. Many were the hours that F.P. spent in the last quarter of his life in talks with Evelyn Underhill, one of the foremost among latter-day exponents of mysticism. And in the final hour it was mystic faith that was uppermost in his mind. He had written for the Omar Khayyám Club perhaps the loveliest verses that ever came from his pen. They were entitled *The Queen Rose* and were on the theme of a line from another Persian mystic :

Of a surety the rose knoweth the secret of the nightingale.

The last words I heard him pronounce were in Persian and I feel convinced that they were his own translation into that language of the final stanza of *The Queen Rose* :

74

At last the Lapwing [1] piped to me : " My Son,
Thy fill of doing gets thee nothing done ;
We flit in this brief show from flower to flower
Of many roses, but the Rose is one."

So reciting, he fell into the sleep from which he never woke.
In that ultimate gleam of consciousness maybe he had found
the secret.

[1] Supposed to have been King Solomon's bird and to possess his wisdom.

CHAPTER V

ACCENT ON FRIENDS

MY father's oldest friend within my memory was Lucy Clifford, the widow of William Kingdon Clifford, who had meant so much to him at Cambridge and in the early years afterwards. In his memoir of Clifford he relates how Clifford was unable not to be polite to a man he disliked and despised. The same trait was visible in F.P. Yates Thompson, the proprietor of the *Pall Mall Gazette*, had printed something that my father thought reflected on Clifford's memory. F.P. was furious and made my mother promise to cut Mrs. Yates Thompson ; he would do the same on his side. True to her brief, my mother did cut that astonished lady dead ; being rich and influential she was not accustomed to such treatment, especially from the wife of a barrister by no means affluent though of good position. But my father unexpectedly ran into Yates Thompson, blissfully uncon- scious of having given offence, and being affably greeted was incapable of acting up to his intention. He responded stiffly but decently. On Yates Thompson learning that his wife had been cut by Mrs. Pollock, an uncomfortable coolness ensued. Yates Thompson was a noted collector of books and *objets d'art* and an important figure at the London Library, on the committee of which my father served for many years. Later I met Yates Thompson and found him pretentious and disagreeable ; clearly he was remembering this little incident in my disfavour. Another man to carry a feud into a second generation was Edmund Gosse. My father made no secret of his contempt for one he considered slovenly and unscholarly. When asked why the British Academy, unlike its more famous French prototype, was founded without a section of pure letters, F.P. answered : " Because that was the only way of keeping Edmund Gosse out." When I was elected to the Savile Club Gosse was plainly displeased and showed it. Puffery was one of my father's pet aversions and this was the art to which Gosse owed not a little of his rise in the world of letters.

Once at the Savile, long before I became a member, merriment was caused by a book about Edmund Gosse written by an American. Almost every other paragraph began with the words : " Then Edmund . . ." A number of the men in the club, then one of the hubs of literary London, agreed each to send a postcard to Gosse, with the words " Then Edmund " written on it. The anecdote shows the strength of Gosse's position while still a young man, for R. L. Stevenson, one of the party, wrote privately and without informing the others to apologise to Gosse : he was afraid of Gosse doing him a bad turn. This was related to me by C. F. Keary, another of the signatories, in whose mouth R. L. S.'s disloyalty left a nasty taste.

Other more amiable figures dimly crossed my childhood in London. There was the painter, L. R. O'Brien, P.R.A. of Canada, whither he carried off my parents on a thrilling visit to canoe on a tributary of the mighty St. Lawrence. O'Brien was tall, wiry, full of spirits, a draughtsman and water-colourist of rare imagination. He revelled in the scenery of Dartmoor and North Devon, where he joined us more than once. Then there was Maxim Kovalevsky, burly jovial Russian, exiled from his chair of law at Moscow for having replied to an order to lecture on the Russian constitution that there was no such thing to lecture about. He was the opposite of Vinogradoff, for whom my father, on resigning it in 1903, obtained the succession to his chair at Oxford, the stern, silent, dour type of Russian that has so much astonished Western diplomatists in the person of Molotov. Kovalevsky's laughter must have rung far down Great Cumberland Place ; I had never before heard so gay and explosive a sound. Though he already enjoyed a European reputation Kovalevsky was a young man, for when I met him more than thirty years later in Russia he was barely sixty. Another visitor was Oliver Wendell Holmes the elder, author of *The Autocrat at the Breakfast Table* and representative of all that was best in that Athens of the New World, Boston. He was a sweet, white-haired old gentleman, and so stout that he had trouble in keeping me on his knee where I suppose he felt bound to seat me out of his affection for my father. Sometimes I was taken to see Kinglake, the author of the gigantic history of the Crimean War and of the still wholly delightful *Eothen*. Kinglake, who was a friend of my grandparents, lived just west of the memorial chapel in the Bayswater Road, where afterwards was built Hyde Park Place. His little house was one of a row in the Regency style still to be seen at Brighton and in a few London backwaters. I was even younger then and am sorry to remember no more of Kinglake, one of the most brilliant of Victorian talkers as well as writers, beyond his making a pen-and-ink sketch of me, now a treasured possession, at his rose-embowered window with a balcony and the metal awning proper to its period. William Cory, who had been F.P.'s tutor at Eton and wrote for me the poem reprinted by Henley in his *Lyra Heroica*, beginning " When George the Third was reigning a hundred years ago," I barely remember at all. Cory exercised a great influence on his generation, by his combination of classical scholarship and humane interest in history and poetry, and maybe held one of the founders of the wider modern education now prevalent in our public schools. Among his other pupils was Lord Rosebery.

Here I may correct a mistake made in F.P.'s obituary notices that mentioned his having resigned his post as Professor of Jurisprudence at University College, London in 1883. It was an annual appointment, but considered a permanency. Though then only four, I have a vivid recollection of my father's anger and my mother's consternation when he came back one afternoon from Lincoln's Inn and told her that the post had been filched from him by a personal intrigue. The loss was soon made good by his appointment the same year to the more valuable chair of Corpus Professor at Oxford, now moved to University College and, while I write, held by that distinguished jurist, Sir Arthur Goodhart. The true universality of our universities is shewn by this important chair having been held after my father by the Russian Vinogradoff and by Goodhart, an American. But of all my parents' friends in that early period the most prominent for me was Mrs. Clifford. Until her death between the two World Wars I can never remember a time when she did not occupy a significant place in my mind. She was a woman as remarkable for character as for talent. Untimely bereaved, she was left with two infant girls and in straitened circumstances that could only be partially relieved by the efforts of Clifford's friends. So without any experience to guide her, she bravely set out to be a

" TOUSHKA ", LADY (JULIET) POLLOCK

From a painting by Sir William Boxall, R.A.
and George Richmond

writer. At that time there were few women novelists : Jane Austen, whose fame had as yet barely reached its height, the Brontës, George Eliot, Mrs. Gaskell, Miss Mitford, Charlotte M. Yonge, formed a short if distinguished list of predecessors. The standard of novels then was high. Of Mrs. Clifford's own genera-tion, were Mrs. Oliphant, Miss Braddon, Ouida, and Mrs. Humphry Ward by far the most important. The solemnity of Mrs. Ward's subjects and no less serious thoroughness of their treatment by her made a powerful appeal to late Victorian high-brows. Though her first publication was only just before that by Mrs. Clifford, Mrs. Ward's position was already secure. She was the niece of Matthew Arnold, acknowledged prince of English literary critics, and her husband, of whom mention has been made, was a clever man of business who devoted himself to her success. The Humphry Ward family was always on the horizon of my youth. We frequently met in London, and I was invited to a house-party at their country place at Tring. Mrs. Humphry Ward had a somewhat formidable reputation, but to me she was always kind, simple, and gracious. Arnold Ward, her son, became a brilliant scholar of Eton and Balliol, and was in the Eton XI. Mrs. Ward seemed to me superior to her books and she surely did not merit the vindictive caricature of herself and her husband perpetrated by Arnold Bennett in *The Honeymoon*. She so dominated the literary world of women that for another to pose as a serious novelist was an act of some temerity. Lucy Clifford's first book was not less serious in its subject, but she struck a new note by her passionate handling of feminine psycho-logy. *Mrs. Keith's Crime* was clearly inspired by the agonising end of her own married life. Its success was immediate. Mrs. Clifford followed it with others, equally successful, among which I best remember *Aunt Anne* and *A Woman Alone*, notable for their intimate and emotional treatment of feminine character. She had a play produced by Mrs. Kendal. Since novelists, except real best-sellers, can rarely live on the sales of their books, she turned to journalism and for many years was literary critic on the *Standard*, then a leading Conservative paper under the editor-ship of Mudford, a personality in Fleet Street hardly less strik-ing than had been Delane of *The Times*. Years later I did some work for the *Standard*, which expired in 1915, and met its society correspondent. He was an extremely jovial person, first rate at his job, and besides that enjoyed the position of press-agent to a big group of hotels : the sort of thing every journalist dreams of, for apart from a good salary it meant frequent free dinners and lunches and being put up as a guest at Brighton and other popular resorts where the group operated. John Lane was particularly kind to me, showed me the ropes and the pitfalls ; I was delighted. One day he said to me : " You know who I am, don't you ? " I answered, of course I did : he was a brilliant journalist, etc. etc. " No, no," he stopped me. " I don't mean that. I'm Lucy Clifford's brother." I then learned what I should never have known otherwise, that Mrs. Clifford had a brother whom she never mentioned, that she had violently quarrelled with him (about what I have no idea), and that they had worked on the same paper for over twenty years without ever meeting or exchanging a line. I thought it reflected well on the man that, instead of taking it out of a younger friend of the sister who had erased him from her life, he should on the contrary have gone to the trouble of being friendly.

To be cut out of Lucy Clifford's life meant something to a writer or a journalist. Not only was she a successful novelist and critic, but she was charming, witty, popular, and an extremely capable hostess. Her house in Westbourne Grove, later as success grew to be exchanged for one in Chilworth Street, was the centre of much that was alive in literary London. Her little drawing-room was a writer's microcosm. Henry James, a devoted friend, was often there on Sunday afternoons when in town. In early days too Rudyard Kipling. So were Ford Madox Hueffer, F. Anstey of *Vice Versa* fame, Elizabeth Robins beautiful actress and novelist, Violet Hunt, Somerset Maugham sometimes, McColl the influential editor of the weekly *Athenæum*, George Street, and many others : authors, literary agents, publishers—among them George and Frederick Macmillan and Gerald Duckworth—actors and editors.

I have a keen memory of the enigmatic impression made on me at Mrs. Clifford's by Courtenay Thorpe, the actor rarely seen on the stage but highly regarded by connoisseurs. Thorpe had an undoubted touch of genius. His Torvald in Ibsen's *Doll's House* was overwhelming as a scathing revelation of commonplace, self-satisfied egoism. But he had no need to act for a living, being the principal proprietor of an antique furniture shop in Ebury Street. His taste and knowledge in this department were profound, and he was accounted the best judge of Oriental lacquer in the country. His little house in Pimlico was a treasure of interior design and decoration. When I was introduced, he let out an ecstatic cry of " Are you *He* ? " As I was not conscious of being a new messiah or any identifiable " he " except a humble undergraduate, I doubtless showed some embarrassment, to be dissipated on realising that Courtenay Thorpe had mistaken me for another young fellow at Cambridge, *nomine* Pollitt, who was attracting attention by his astonishing female impersonations at the Footlights Club. On discovering his error, Thorpe I am afraid was distinctly disappointed. His last appearance on the stage was as the Ghost in John Barrymore's production of *Hamlet* at the Haymarket. Most of the parts in the play, like that of the Prince, are actor proof ; just as *Hamlet* itself, for we have learned this from Sir Laurence Olivier's film, is producer proof. No one has ever seen a really bad Ghost. But Courtenay Thorpe instilled into the part an eerie majesty that has not been touched in our time. He had a personality of uncommon power and, were the theatre in England better organised, would have achieved worldwide fame as one of the leading actors of our stage. Young men too, among them Hugh Walpole and Noel Coward, got a helping hand from Lucy Clifford in their upward climb. Not a few diplomats and M.P.s were to be met at her house. The hostess was a capital mixer and, if conversation ever flagged, she could always rely on Violet Hunt's vitriolic tongue to start a fresh hare. Violet Hunt is taken off as " Rose Waterford " in a vivid thumbnail sketch in Mr. Somerset Maugham's *The Moon and Sixpence*, where George Street too makes a dim bow under the unashamed homonymity of " George Road ". Lucy Clifford was a proud woman and proud of her success. Her courage, kindliness, and energy won and kept for her a host of interesting, valuable friends.

Aunt Lucy, as she inevitably became to my sister and me, and her two girls were regular guests of my parents at Hind Head. One acquainted with that sprawling mass of suburbia today would not know the place as it was in the 1880's. Hind Head was then a moor, a *lande* of heather and Scotch fir ; and even that hardy evergreen failed to make foothold on the upland leading to the Gibbet, a blasted heath if ever there was one. For human habitation, there was The Huts, the old coaching inn where before railways the London to Portsmouth traffic had changed horses after the pull up to the 700 foot summit ; beyond that for near two miles round nothing save sparse cottages in the combes jutting out from the sides of Hind Head, and these inhabited by rough, uncouth men, thought mainly to be descendants of fugitives from justice, who earned a livelihood by making and selling heather besoms.   One of these was said to have expressed annoyance that another could sell his besoms for twopence. " I steal my heather," he pondered, " and I steal my staves ; but I can't sell for less than sixpence." " Ah," answered No. 2, " but I steal my besoms ready made."   That there was still an awesome feeling about Hind Head is certain.   It was so lonely, so wild, so fey.   The murder of the sailor that had caused the gibbet to be put up whereon were hanged his three murderers seemed as it might have happened yesterday.   A fine engraving by Turner shows the gibbet still standing and, though it had been replaced by a Cornish granite cross with suitably uplifting inscriptions on its four sides, tales were still rife that on stormy nights the wind could be heard to whistle through the gallows chains and the murderers' skeletons to rattle.   Natives would whisper how when the luckless sailor, who, being paid off in Portsmouth and walking to London, had rashly shown his money in the bar parlour at The Huts, been followed and been stabbed to death at the top of the rise, his blood had flowed down into the great pocket of heather on the north side of the Portsmouth road and the devil had come and licked it up : thence, they would say, came the name of The Devil's Punch bowl.   It was hard to think that Hind Head and its wicked repute were but forty miles from London.

John Tyndall was the first man, not a native of the place, to go to Hind Head.   That famous professor of physics, who had startled the orthodox world by his Belfast address in 1874, had advantages denied to most iconoclasts.   He had married the granddaughter of a duke, so could not be dismissed in England as an outsider ; and he was a renowned mountaineer, so, although mountaineering as a sport was in its infancy, he could not be set down as an unathletic ninny. Read today his Belfast address seems a model of moderation. Tyndall wore an Abraham Lincoln beard for which since then, because Tyndall was one of the most welcoming hosts imaginable even to a small boy, I have an affection now without an object. The last man I remember to have seen with such a beard was the butler in my tutor's house at Eton : now it is as extinct as the dodo.

Tyndall had been introduced to Hind Head by an older scientist, Professor Williamson, owner of a farm some two miles off, on the way to the neighbouring village of Shottermill. Williamson may have been a prominent chemist in his day, but he was an exceedingly dreary old gentleman with an invalid wife and an equally dreary son. My father would say that his only merit was to have known Berthelot, the famous French chemist. Tyndall, F.P.'s senior by twenty-six years, in turn induced him to buy a cottage a mile or so down the Portsmouth road and a couple of acres of land. Gradually the cottage, named Hind Head Copse, was improved and enlarged into a simple but agreeable country home and about eight more acres of ground, mostly rough, picturesque woodland, were acquired. There for many years we spent our holidays in great content amid a society of youngish people whose parents were led by my father's example to buy land, then cheap, in the surrounding district and to build. Tyndall, the discoverer of Hind Head, was aghast and furious. Not indeed at my father's friends who mostly built pleasant, inconspicuous houses on the slopes of the hill, but at strangers who, following Tyndall's own lead, settled and built on the edge of the topmost common. Tyndall's health was delicate. I do not know where the weakness lay (the *D.N.B.* says insomnia and indigestion), but he required very pure, fresh air, yet hardly ever left his house or took any exercise, he who had been one of the pioneers of the great Swiss mountains. The air of Hind Head he found precisely the thing. So enraptured was he of it that, having built a large, ugly red brick house in the most conspicuous possible place, with the widest possible views, he could not restrain himself in the frequent letters he wrote to the press from chanting the beauties of the spot and in particular the marvellous health-giving qualities of Hind Head air, fully equal in his opinion to that of his beloved Switzerland. The inevitable followed. Houses were run up close to his. They obtruded on the view from his windows. He retaliated by erecting monstrous screens of wattled heather, shaped to look like mountain tops, so as to block out the sight. But the screens themselves acted as an advertisement, so curious were they. Not many years had gone by before the land round The Huts, which blossomed forth into a real hotel, became studded with villas. To use the horrid land agents' term, Hind Head was being developed as a residential neighbourhood. Tyndall died there and his widow continued till her death to live in the great ugly house behind the now bedraggled and crumbling wattled screens, amid his magnificent collection of Alpine photographs, then much rarer than today, busied with the Sisyphean task she never accomplished of writing a monumental Life of the eminent Victorian. I heard the brother-in-law of her mother, Lady Claud Hamilton, tell the following curious story. He had been in youth an attaché at the British embassy in Paris. One day at a dinner-party he sat next an old, still pretty, lady who turned to him and said : " Comme mon mari a dit à Louis XIV . . ." Naturally enough, he took the old dear for a harmless lunatic, only to learn after dinner that by her first marriage she had been the wife of Duc de Liancourt-Rochefoucauld who, born in 1700, had in Louis's old age been a page of honour to the Roi-Soleil and in 1787 had married a girl of sweet seventeen, still enjoying life in the middle of the nineteenth century. So that I have spoken to a man who knew the widow of a courtier to a king born in the year 1638.

From the very sandy soil of Hind Head my mother made a beautiful garden. She had what gardeners call " a green thumb " and was paid the compliment by Evans, the head gardener at the Stewart Hodgsons' place at Haslemere, of having a rose of his invention called after her. My father was more keen on trees and once transplanted with success a thirty-year old yew-tree, no inconsiderable feat. I do not know if the " Lady Pollock " rose is extant in England, but since the last war I have found it in a rosegrower's catalogue at Bordeaux. Evans was one of the leading men in his calling. His fruit and his flowers took constant prizes at shows and were the joy of hospitals to which the Stewart Hodgsons sent their surplus. He was a tall, bearded, dignified Scot of immaculate manners, always that I remember dressed in perfectly fitting tweeds and always with a high billycock hat such as Mr. Winston Churchill is one of the last notable men to sport. Evans produced a great effect. But everything about the Stewart Hodgsons was great. She was a tall woman of aristocratic grace and by no means stupid ; he was a partner in Baring's and a very grand gentleman, bearded too. I have been told that he was opposed to the Argentine policy that nearly brought disaster on the firm. Whether or no, he was of course involved in it and died not long after, it was rumoured, of a broken heart. The family, including an adorable daughter Ruth,[1] retired from their palatial place above Haslemere and twenty or thirty thousand a year to the luckily transient penury of ten times less and a charming dower-house belonging to the estate. In the days of their grandeur the Stewart Hodgsons formed the ideal of a great English country household. For all his wealth, they were neither standoffish nor patronising. They had splendid furniture, fine pictures, a frieze by I forget what Pre-Raphælite painter, almost royal gardens, the most noble horses. Without precisely keeping open house they were hospitality personified, and were much admired and respected throughout west Surrey and Hampshire, though respect and admiration do not necessarily follow on wealth and a lavish board. Any of us could probably tell of cases where the contrary effect was produced. I don't think the Stewart Hodgsons were sporting people to any great extent. They were intelligent, patrons in a reasonable degree of the arts, used their position with a virtuous discretion, gave generously to local efforts, and the carthorses bred by Mr. Stewart Hodgson were famous throughout England.

One glorious luncheon given by the Stewart Hodgsons was when Haslemere, greatly daring, challenged Surrey at cricket. This, mark you, was in the country's prime, before Tom Richardson came to the height of his powers, but when Lockwood and Lohmann were bowling and W. W. Read and tiny Abel, nicknamed " the Guv'nor ", were high in the averages. Haslemere could put up some good batting in the persons of Lawrence, K.C., a brilliant stylist, afterwards raised to the Bench, Max and Guy Mort who were nearly of county rank, and the three Harrison brothers, sons of Frederic Harrison the philosophic man of letters

[1] Mrs. Oliver Hawkshaw.

and high priest in this country of Auguste Comte's religion, that I have been given to understand was Christianity without Christ or, as Huxley said, Catholicism without Christianity. All three had their public school colours. Haslemere's best bowler was Basil Watson, later a well-known London magistrate ; Max Mort was fast but erratic. On minor occasions I had played for Haslemere, which must have often been hard put to it to find an eleven, but now was among the spectators, shivering with excitement. The match was of course understood to be of the " friendly " variety and none of Surrey's stars came down from the Oval ; but Beaumont and Bowley, two of the lesser county bowlers led their eleven, backed up by a number of colts and second-class amateurs. It would be pleasing to imagine that Tom Hayward, afterwards the leading English bat, save only W. G., and master of Jack Hobbs, was among the colts ; but I think not. It was a thrilling one-day game, naturally won by Surrey but not by too crushing a victory. Luncheon was served on immense trestle tables sent down by the Stewart Hodgsons and afterwards there was a vast spread of tea, fruit, and various cups. It may seem curious to those accustomed to the vagaries of modern English summers that such reliance could be placed on the weather as to make these arrangements possible when no indoor alternative existed, for the rustic pavilion of the Haslemere C.C. could not have accommodated a quarter of those invited to the feast. But it is a certain fact that summers were summers when I was a boy, and winters winters. One hardy annual at Hind Head Copse was a visit on August bank holiday by thirty or forty London women, some with small children too, under the wing of Miss Octavia Hill, that pioneer of housing reform, of whom my father was a fast friend. Octavia Hill was against tenements or what would now be called Council flats, and all for small houses ; but the growth of London's population has been such that flats have won hands down. She had strong views on the giving of indiscriminate charity. One day on a visit to the House of Lords to promote her housing scheme, a fervent peer said to her : " Miss Hill, do you mean to tell me that, if a starving man came up to you and asked for help, you would not give him sixpence ? " Octavia Hill answered : " Do you mean to tell me, Lord So-and-so, that if a starving man came up to you and asked for help, you would *only* give him sixpence ? " Miss Hill's party to Hind Head were fetched in the morning from Haslemere Station in a convoy of brakes furnished by The Huts, wandered about in the grounds, had a copious meal on trestle tables in the open, washed down by dozens of ginger beer and lemonade, were sent for a ten-mile drive in the afternoon, followed by tea again in the open, and finally drove off cheering loudly and singing to catch an evening train back to town ; the interval of the afternoon drive being just long enough for family, friends, and servants to clear away midday dinner and prepare for tea. A big marquee was set up in case it rained. But I remember few occasions when it was needed. You really could count on the weather.

It was the same in winter. Until the advent of the safety bicycle in the 'nineties, all our movement was either on foot or in pony-traps, of which my father had two plus a stable cart. But at Christmas Hind Head was snowbound. Then the dogcart and governess car were replaced by a sledge. That the regularity of heavy snow does not exist in my imagination but was maintained over a number of years is proved by the fact that one sledge was worn out by constant use and was replaced by a second. Both were the work of a local artisan. They had room for three people sitting in front and three with a squeeze, standing on a ledge at the back also used for luggage. Going uphill those on the ledge jumped off and pushed. It was cold at Hind Head in winter. Central heating was unknown in those days. The Copse or the Cottage, as the house was indifferently known by its frequenters, was kept warm by generous log fires in the rooms, fed by our own wood, and by an ugly but efficient coke stove in the hall that could be made almost red hot. Hard frost lasted as a rule from two to three weeks over Christmas and the New Year. Parties of friends would tramp a mile and half through the snow to Waggoner's Wells, a trinity of ponds in the combe near Grayshott, which, afterwards large village, when I first knew it was nothing but one minute general shop for the supply of the combe's people. A stream ran through them and the first pond never froze ; but the other two set hard and, strangely, were never covered with snow, perhaps owing to the protection of tall pine woods. In summer one could bathe there, but it was very cold. There I learned to skate fast and play hockey on the ice.

Our two star performers were Evan Whiteway and Hum Lloyd. Evan was the son of a retired Indian Civil Servant. He was eight or nine years older than me and at this time an undergraduate at Trinity, Cambridge, where he was a Rugby blue. He was one of the handsomest creatures I ever saw and excelled at all games. Save for his disarming laziness I have no doubt he might have been a double or even a triple blue. Some time later I saw him give a beating at lawn tennis to " Willie " or " Bill " Marshall, the distinguished architect, who had built himself a house between Hind Head and Shottermill. Marshall had been, before Alfred Lyttelton, the leading English exponent of real tennis, and having taken up lawn tennis late in life played it in the same way, putting a terrific cut on every ball and capable, it seemed, of placing the ball on a sixpence anywhere in the court, equally sure fore- and back-hand. Coming from six foot three, his service was deceptively severe. To beat Marshall at the younger game, a man had to be good. Whiteway hit the ball with a perfectly flat racquet, crushing force, and could volley from every point in the court. But, like most other things, the game did not interest him.

Hum Lloyd, Evan's great friend at Cambridge and at home, was a far more interesting person. His laziness surpassed Whiteway's, in whom he certainly helped to develop this trait. But he was astonishingly gifted. He was a nephew of Dr. Lloyd, Provost of Trinity College, Dublin, before the better-known Dr. Salmon ; after her husband's death Mrs. Lloyd, with three nieces and her nephew, settled at Hind Head. Marshall, who had married the eldest Miss Lloyd, built them a house on a plot bought from my father. They were the nicest, cleverest sort of Irish. The eldest of the three, Alice, of whom more hereafter, married Albert Dew-Smith of Cambridge, and Ethel, the youngest, a real charmer, Sir John Sykes, K.C.B., one of the most effective men in the control of the liquor trade. Hum was the bad boy of the family. He could play every musical instrument. He could read and play any music at sight. He could dance. He could act. He had a humorous, even witty turn of mind. He had a sweet light baritone voice and could sing anything from Schubert to the latest music hall ditty. Had he wished, he could certainly have become first violin in any orchestra in Great Britain. But he just would not work. Instead he preferred to pass his time lounging and doing puzzles. Now the moral of this tale is not what might be expected. In course of time Hum Lloyd married an extremely pretty young woman possessed of no greater ambition than his own, and went to live at Bosham, at the time an obscure place on the south coast. A decade passed, and more. Then came 1914 and war. Like flint and steel, music and puzzles produced a flash in Lloyd's mind. He conceived the idea that musical notation might be used for sending cyphered messages. More than one " talky " has made play with the notion in later times. But till then it was unheard of. Lloyd wrote of his idea to someone in Whitehall. Contrary to the treatment often accorded to such messages, it was greeted with enthusiasm. Attention had been drawn to an unusual supply of musical scores, arriving in England from Holland, but musicians to whom they were discreetly shown could see nothing uncommon about them. It required a combination of musical genius with a puzzle mind to ferret out from such deep cover the hidden instructions to German agents in this country. Lloyd left Bosham and was soon the head of a special anti-espionage department. One of those working under him was Sydney Waterlow who had been with me at Eton and Cambridge and for some years was my brother-in-law. Waterlow, between the two World Wars British minister, first in Sofia, then in Athens, had a knowledge of German rare in an Englishman. Yet it would seem not to have bettered Hum Lloyd's. Where and how that idle apprentice managed to gain mastery of so difficult a tongue, I know not. Perhaps in the same way as Midshipman Easy's of Spanish, which came to him at the Zaffarine Islands. On an astonished Spaniard ejaculating to Easy that the islands were uninhabited, Jack retorted : " Plenty of ground sharks." The fish off Bosham may have been equally accommodating. As will have been noted, the moral is that idleness can pay a handsome dividend.

In 1919 Hum Lloyd who had proved too valuable to our country to be easily let go was retained in his hush-hush service and went to Berlin as undercover British agent. He quickly penetrated the bluff of German disarmament, which was indeed no secret to any observant person in Berlin and later obtained precise information on the methods used by Hitler and his gangsters to fix themselves in power. If published or even privately acted on by the British Government, such reports might have averted war. But in common with information sent by journalists with their eyes open they were sacrificed to the blind gods inspiring the Peace Ballot and its insane devotees. All this is such ancient history that there can be no indiscretion in reporting it now.

Hind Head Copse, I have said, was a place of work as well as of play. It was there that my father received instructions from the Government in the once famous Venezuela case, and there that within forty-eight hours he produced the report which settled the trouble. E. S. P. Haynes, who has earned a niche in letters by his series of *The Lawyer's Notebook*, was stopping at the Cottage, and relates the matter as follows :

" At the beginning of the weekend an official messenger arrived in a vehicle overflowing with formidable documents. These related to a dispute which had arisen between the President of the United States and Great Britain in regard to a boundary question in Venezuela. The question was in itself sufficiently complicated ; but President Cleveland had issued a message in regard to it which created a possibility of war. Sir Frederick Pollock shut himself up with the papers and did not get much sleep that night ; but after intense concentration he managed to grasp the issues sufficiently to send the messenger back with a report on Sunday before lunch. After lunch we had a magnificent walk through the surrounding country and I have seldom heard him discourse with more brilliance on questions of public and private international law."

F.P.'s report had the result of the dispute being referred to arbitration, and all danger of war was averted. Forty years after he wrote to Haynes, who had reminded him of their walk that day :

" When the Arbitration Tribunal did make the award nobody minded what it was, the gold in the territory in dispute having turned out to be a vain thing imagined by company promoters. I wrote a study of the origins of the Monroe Doctrine based on the original correspondence between the Americans and our F.O., which the U.S.A. Senate ordered to be printed as an official paper. I believe it is still found useful by specialists. Such are the byways of diplomatic history that accident may bring back to memory. The big historian brushes them aside in a lordly way—or did—but at his peril."

Of afternoon and evening there was always sure to be stimulating talk. In early years at Hind Head George Meredith was an occasional visitor and for some long forgotten reason nicknamed me " the bad raspberry " ; later he became fixed at Box Hill and had to be visited there. Kipling too came to Hind Head. I was first taken by my father to see him in his lodging in Villiers Street, by Charing Cross. This was at the beginning of his fame and he rented a bedroom so exiguous that there were in the place only two chairs on which F.P. and I were put ; Kipling, as the two men talked, sat on the bed. They had much in common and should have enjoyed lifelong friendship. But it was interrupted in an unhappy way. Kipling and my father came to know each other through Mrs. Clifford ; I suppose she had made acquaintance with him by her reviewing his early books. He saw her constantly and was on affectionate terms with her. One day at a tea-party somewhere they were standing together when he said : " Good gracious, isn't that the plainest woman you ever saw ? " Mrs. Clifford laughingly assented. The lady then coming into the room not very long afterwards became Mrs. Rudyard Kipling. It was an unkind stroke of fate. Kipling could not forget that he had made this frivolous, quite unjustified, remark to Mrs. Clifford and ceased to frequent her. There may too have been some jealousy of Kipling's former friends on the part of Mrs. Kipling, for he wholly stopped seeing my father and my Uncle Walter with whom too he had been very friendly. Not until after the first World War did I see Kipling again. It was in Paris. My wife and I were at the Comédie Française and ran into him in the foyer during an interval. I went up and said : " You can't remember me, Mr. Kipling. I'm Jack Pollock." His face lit up at once. " What, are you Fred Pollock's son ? " My wife and I spent some time with him. He was exactly as I remembered him, keen, boyish, affectionate, immensely interested in everything round him. The play was Henry Becque's *Les Corbeaux.* Kipling was thrilled by it. " Oh, she can't be going to marry that horrid old man ? " he said. But she did. Kipling was really grieved by Becque's inexorable realism. The last time I saw him was again in Paris. His devotion to France where his son, killed in action, lay buried was well known. He was one of the first three Englishmen ever to receive the Doctorate, *honoris causâ*, of the Sorbonne : the other two, honoured at the same time, were my father and a chemist whose work on poison gas had been of capital importance in the Allied cause. Now Kipling was guest of honour at a great banquet at the Cercle Interallié. It was the heyday of French, and English too, faith in a German change of heart and trust that by saying " Peace, peace " that desirable state might be perpetuated : a faith and a trust which led to the disastrous treaty of Locarno and sacrificed the last vestige of control by its dupes over German rearmament. Therefore it came as a shock to the assembled company when Kipling made a grave, resolute speech warning the French in courteous terms of the danger they were running. How right he was, 1939 was to prove.

The best of the three ponies at Hind Head Copse was of the Dartmoor breed, an absolute little thoroughbred. Toby had been carefully chosen for F.P. by Charlie Collier, the eldest son of William Collier, the famous wine merchant who had a virtual monopoly of supplying the Fleet at Plymouth. To the youngest, George, still alive and still riding at the age of eighty-nine, I owe a great deal. He taught me to ride and to shoot and helped to teach me to think clearly. The Colliers were among the finest sporting families in South Devon. Both Charlie and George, now the head of the wine business, that then included its own cider, the best I ever tasted, and the confection of a divine sloe gin, were noted horsemen ; their cousin Imogen no less, and the horses she bred for years took prizes at Olympia besides at shows in the west. All the navy was at her feet for she was as fascinating as she was a daring rider. But she married a man from the Midlands. William Collier, to me " Uncle Willy ", was a marvellous raconteur of West of England stories, and kept a pack of dachshunds for drawing the badger. At Wood Town, his attractive place six miles from Tavistock and on the edge of Dartmoor, there was regular otter hunting too, a form of sport delightful to me because I think I never saw an otter caught and killed. Foxhunting on Dartmoor, except to the truly expert, resolved itself into your letting your horse, far wiser at the job than any visitor, choose his path and set the pace. Even this sport, which seems to me thoroughly legitimate since the fox is a cunning, untamable animal and vastly enjoys life while it lasts, has for me a nasty moment in the kill. As for shooting birds, I gave that up when I was eighteen and shot a wild duck that fell into reeds, and was lost. It then came over me that killing harmless, beautiful creatures unless for the necessary demands of the pot is a revolting practice.

This last mishap took place at Clovelly. Readers of *Westward Ho!* and all travellers on what were once the Great Western Railway and the South-western Railway know of Clovelly, that village flung up by the sea, so it looks, on to a steep Devon cliff opposite Lundy. Not Lundy Island, please note : the " y " by itself stands for " island ", and to say " Lundy Island " is like saying " Chiswick Eyot Island ". Which, likely enough, other people equally ignorant of their own language do say. No more exclusively Devonian bit of Devon can ever have existed before motoring let in the outer world. Even sixty-five years ago trippers were brought to Clovelly by steamer from Ilfracombe. But they could stay only an hour or so, and when they had gone Clovelly was once more its unique beautiful self in which nothing essential had changed since the sixteenth century—or perhaps since the birth of Devon. The only other way to Clovelly was a twelve-mile drive from Bideford with a formidable hill to surmount : no joke for horses. In Clovelly is one and one only street ; and but two ways to go—" up-along " and " down-along ". The street is steep and cobbled, divided into stretches of a few yards traversed at the bottom by a cross-row of cobbles, lest a parcel falling should roll over and over from the very top of Clovelly down-along into the harbour. Save cat and dog, nothing goes down-along and up-along but that two-legged featherless creature man and surer-footed donkeys to carry up from the harbour baskets of coal and other heavy supplies. Wherefore near the harbour was a black-smith's, the donkey's shoes wearing out quick on the cobbles. So it was at least when I first knew Clovelly and played in the shop of old John Mill who had built boats for Clovelly for fifty years, and was taken out in fishing boats by my father and O'Brien the Canadian artist and by " young Mr. Fane ", the squire to whom all Clovelly belonged and whom all Clovelly loved. Even an almost infant heart was torn by the lamentation when Fane was drowned at sea. Clovelly and Clovelly Court, the squire's seat at the top of the cliff, had belonged for centuries to Fanes and Hamlyns and to branches of those families. This fatality left the estate to a sister, Christine. Never did anyone better shoulder responsibility. Christine Fane became the autocrat of Clovelly. She married one of the well-known Gosling family, making him change his name to Hamlyn, that the estate might not lapse from tradition. No one was allowed to build in Clovelly without leave and leave to build was never granted. In return Christine Hamlyn saw that the whole village was kept in perfect repair and dowered with all modern improvements possible within the framework of Clovelly's topography. Thanks to her imperiously benevolent rule Clovelly was saved from ruinous " development " and remains what it was, stylised perhaps, with the frosted look of an exquisite artificial flower, but still unique, still beautiful.

Sometimes we stayed at the New Inn (I wonder when it was new), sometimes at the Court. It was there, as I have said, that I took a distaste for shooting. It was there too, but some years before, that a dreadful thing befell me. I was thirteen and just going to Eton. My father and I were invited to stay at Clovelly Court ; my mother was to join us later. For the first time in my life I went down to dinner in a country house, a house too where everything was " just so ". Now the coast of North Devon is famed for its lobsters and, sure enough, resplendent lobsters were served. I had never before seen one outside a fishmonger's shop. I took the portion offered me and, all unsuspecting, ate. Ah, horror ! Hardly had two minutes elapsed when a poor little boy in Etons reeled from his chair and vomited upon the carpet of Christine Hamlyn's grand dining-room. Hosts and guests alike were marvellously kind to the unwilling offender. My father, who was sitting some places further up the table, craned his neck and with an air of detached interest remarked : " Ah ! Just like his grandfather. He could never touch lobster." It had not occurred to him to warn the wretched grandson beforehand of possible catastrophe. Since then I have eschewed crustaceans.

Among my parents' town friends were some who never or rarely came to Hind Head Copse. Sidney Colvin and Mrs. Sitwell, for instance. No doubt the reason was that when they stayed in the country they had, for propriety's sake, to be given separate rooms ; and the Copse contained a strictly limited supply of rooms. The Colvin-Sitwell liaison was accepted without question by the London of letters and scholarship. He was a man of real intellect and Keeper of Prints at the British Museum. She was understood to be separated from a drunken clerical husband in East Anglia which, for some obscure reason, specialised in inebriated parsons. She was born Macpherson—a further Scots link with my family—and one of her nieces married my Uncle Maurice, the painter. Another, herself a painter, married Sir Charles Holroyd, Director of the National Gallery. Mrs. Sitwell and Sidney Colvin could not marry, even when the drunken parson conveniently died, because Colvin was a Fellow of Trinity under the old dispensation and on marriage must give up his fellowship ; and the two had not enough money between them to abandon this source of income. Ultimately one or other inherited money and Mrs. Sitwell became Lady Colvin, Sidney by this time having been knighted. My father met Thomas Hardy and asked if he was going to the wedding. " No," said Hardy in his deliberate, ironic way, " no, I'm not going to the wedding. I haven't got a good enough coat to go in. But I'm glad she's making an honest man of Sidney after all these years."

It was Arthur Strong who procured Charles Holroyd's nomination to the National Gallery. This astonishing man, a brilliant and very learned scholar, whose appearance suggested a fair-haired, benign spider, was said to be descended on the wrong side of the blanket from Chateaubriand. His brother became a saintly Bishop of Oxford. Even to a youth the penetrating quality of Arthur Strong's brain and the ascendancy he exerted over men of acknowledged attainments and position in the world were striking. He was successively Librarian to the Duke of Devonshire and House of Lords, and married Eugenie Sellars, one of the most beautiful women of her time and already a famous archæologist, after her husband's untimely death Assistant Director of the British School (that is, of archæology) at Rome. The Strongs often came to Hind Head. So did Donald Tovey, with whose father, a minor historian of much originality, mine was well acquainted, and his tutelary musical inspiration, Miss Weisse, whose school for girls was not too far off. So sometimes did the great Joseph Joachim, though he never brought his violin ; his nephew Harold, afterwards professor of philosophy at Oxford, had a small house at Haslemere. Other fairly frequent visitors were Arthur and Sylvia Davies : he, the eldest son of Canon Llewellyn Davies, F.P.'s Cambridge friend, was deprived of success at the Bar only by an intolerably quick temper ; she, George du Maurier's lovely daughter whose face is reflected in so many of her father's drawings, was adored by all the world but most of all by J. M. Barrie, who by now had his little house a few miles off at Churt. Both the Davieses were cut off comparatively young. Gertrude Bell, Persian and Arabian scholar, during the 1914 war to become a personage in those climes only less important than Lawrence himself, was often at the Copse : another of F.P.'s links with the East.

But of all the figures in those Hind Head days the most striking was Mrs. Rogerson, known to a circle of admiring young people as Aunt Chrissie. Born Christina Stewart, Mrs. Rogerson was a personality such as a man could meet but once in his lifetime, if that. Henry James said of her : " If she had been beautiful and sane, she would have been one of the world's great wicked women." Aunt Chrissie was certainly not beautiful and she knew it. To compensate for her lack of looks, she cultivated an appearance peculiar to herself, especially peculiar in the 1880's and early 1890's. Her thick dark hair was cut short, and she invariably dressed in a dark tweed skirt stopping short at her ankles, a white shirt of the finest linen with stiff cuffs and links, a stiff " heaven and hell " collar, a black sailor's knot tie, and Highland shoes with large silver buckles. She combined a waywardly extravagant imagination with fierce, practical competence. It was as though a dæmon of energy inhabited her strong, wellformed body and finely chiselled head. She was the finest hostess and carver at table I have ever seen, a first-class whip, an amazing hand with animals of all sorts—even cattle seemed to like her, a croquet player of nearly championship rank, an inimitable teller of Scotch stories that she reeled off in every accent, Highland or Lowland, and popular with every man, woman, and child who ever saw her. Once she delighted a Christmas dinner-party of twenty or more given at her house, " The Log House ", which she had designed herself and was indeed made of rough logs with the bark left on, yet a beautifully comfortable place, by calling out to her butler, an episcopal looking old man with the strange name of Goby : " Bring in more turkeys ! " And more turkeys were brought in and dissected by her unerring hand. She was normally a woman of distinguished manners but, when she wished, could rail and swear like a fishwife. It was as good as a play to see her at a horse or cattle market, bantering the auctioneer and giving dealers a bit more than she got from those imagining that they were on a soft thing with a woman. She both bought and sold, buying not to keep but to get fun out of the hurly-burly of small country fairs, and no doubt made a good profit on the turnover. Among breeders she had warm friends in Lady Dorothea and Lady Estella Hope, daughters of Lord Hopetoun who had a stud farm a goodish drive from Hind Head. Aunt Chrissie took me over there more than once to stay, and there at the age of fourteen I smoked my first cigarette and found it delicious. The Hope sisters were so much alike that they might have been twins, though there were two years between them, tall, slim, athletic young goddesses of twenty-four and -six or so, who knew all there is to know about horses. But their delight was breeding and training donkeys. These animals, carefully selected, were bred till a truly aristocratic appearance was produced, differing as much from the coster donkey as does a racing Bedouin camel from that melancholy beast of burden. Then they were broken with just the same care as good ponies. The result was a docile, well-mannered animal, a fast trotter, indefatigable, responsive : in fact, the ideal beast for the then popular and useful governess car, killed like so many other things by the development of motoring. The Hopes sold their donkeys, I believe, for roundabout £12 apiece, a very good price for those days. Both these charming women were still alive till the late war.

Aunt Chrissie at a market was as good as a play. Yes, and almost anywhere else. She was always dramatising herself and her surroundings. It was this itch for theatricality that formed a kink in her brain and earned her Henry James's harsh judgment. Before she settled at Hind Head, she had run a large soup kitchen in Marylebone for down-and-outs, with immense success too, till she suddenly became bored with the idea and dropped it without notice to anybody. The same fate befell an orphanage for over

thirty children she started at Hind Head and managed admirably.
But her chief notoriety came from the Dilke divorce case in which
she was seriously compromised. Yet she made a number of the
most respectable people, including my grandmother Deffell,
believe her a deeply injured and innocent woman. Mr. Justice
Hannen had made some very sharp remarks about her in court.
Instead of allowing these to be forgotten, Aunt Chrissie used them
(but only when she had guests staying in the house) to stage a
fearsome nightmare, in which she would with a loud voice shriek :
" Not guilty, my lord ! Not guilty ! "

The Log House was almost always full of people staying
and the scene of constant dances, charades, and romps, led with
incredible zest by this tireless hostess. Among frequent visitors
were Charlie (C. F.) Keary, H. B. Smith afterwards principal
secretary to the Viceroy of India and his *alter ego*, J. D. Duff of
Cambridge, a brilliant Latinist, both highly popular with the
ladies, and about those two Hum Lloyd composed the following
classic :

> How I luff
> Mr. Duff,
> Want to kith
> H. B. Smith.

Keary was nearly a contemporary of my father's, though he
always seemed much younger, and his valued friend. A scholar
with special knowledge of early coins and Viking history, he had
given up a good position at the British Museum to write fiction,
and to work at art and philosophy. Save for summer visits to
England he lived mainly in Paris, that suited the asthma from
which he suffered better than London, on scanty means. In the
end London killed him, when he came back to live there during
the 1914 war. George Gissing, he said to me, once told him it
was possible to live in London too on £150 a year, though less
comfortably. In Paris you could take a room by the month in a
small, clean hotel for 40 or 50 francs, the franc being then 25 to
the pound, and could dine decently for 1 franc 50 cents. Keary's
principal novels *Bloomsbury*, *High Policy*, and *A Marriage of Convenience*, have real merit, and his *Pursuit of Reason*, highly thought
of by some professionals of thinking, resulted in his writing philosophical leaders in *The Times Literary Supplement*. Keary's

Posthumous Poems were published in 1923 with an introduction by John Bailey. He had a deep vein of quiet, delightful humour and invented the most delicate description I know of the state where a man and a woman live together without being married : Keary called it *tout comme* . . . " just as if ". He and Mrs. Rogerson, with whom he was great friends, while professing to be in mortal terror lest in a freak mood she should marry him (in that event she would probably have turned him into a successful and popular novelist), had a wonderful game that they played of an evening for friends' amusement. There had come to live at Hind Head an adept of Annie Besant the theosophist. No one knew the lady and much fun was made on the theme of meeting her astral body in the lanes. Keary and Aunt Chrissie then pretended they could release *his* astral body and send it wandering. They would go out together in the night and presently the form of Charlie Keary would glide into the house, the eyes unwinking, the face completely expressionless, pass through the rooms and out again. Spectators were allowed to laugh, tease, annoy, say what they liked, do anything except touch this seeming wraith. Never did it, even literally, bat an eyelid. Then Aunt Chrissie and Keary in the flesh, talking and smiling, would reappear and she would swear, with such appearance of sincerity that anyone almost must believe her, that all the time she had been holding his corporeal hand by the garden gate. I never saw anyone else with such a perfect poker face.

Another visitor at The Log House was Marriott Watson, one of the lesser literary stars in the constellation the great light whereof was *The Yellow Book,* that a wit took off as " a book that bounders are bound to buy and binders will buy to bind ". Marriott Watson had composed, but whether ever published I know not, a tremendous heroic doggerel poem that he recited with brilliant effect. The protagonist in it was a man who had lost his arm and told with a realistic thrill in turn how it had been amputated after a sea fight, shot off in a land battle, wrenched off in an accident, bitten off by a shark, burnt to a cinder in a fire ; finally, Marriott Watson would deliver the last two lines with a sort of graceful indolence :

> 'Ow did I lose me arm, sir ?
> Why, I never 'ad but one !

Hind Head, down to 1900 and a bit later perhaps, with its inhabitants, friends, or neighbours, must, I think, have been a unique spot. Certainly The Log House was a unique house and its owner a unique woman. Before her surprising existence drew to a close, Aunt Chrissie had, at the age of over sixty, married one of the most brilliant journalists of his or any other time, married him when just down from Oxford and perhaps driven him to his grave : Keary, who saw George Steevens on the eve of departure for the Boer war, told me that he thought Steevens meant never to return, so disillusioned was he. Nor did he return, but died in Ladysmith, during the siege. Even then Christina Stewart-Rogerson-Steevens's career did not cease, for nearly ten years later she captured the imagination of the most rising of living English novelists and playwrights, and convinced him that she had, as he said, " a heart of gold ". The ghosts of Sir Charles Dilke, of her two husbands, the first of whom she almost boasted, whether truly or not, of having poisoned, and of those many who, having placed all their faith in her, found they had been cozened and sometimes defrauded could have told him better.

Towards the end of the Hind Head era, many of my own friends frequented the Copse ; Hendrik van Loon, later to win fame in America by fantasies on the history of the world, Sturge Moore, the least minor of minor poets, Lawrence Haward, afterwards director of the Manchester art gallery and as fine a connoisseur of music as of painting, Walter Fletcher and Sydney Waterlow, of whom I have written above, Sydney's brother Jack who went down with the battleship he captained at Jutland : young people were just as welcome to Fred and Georgie Pollock as those nearer their own age.

Hind Head is now virtually Hampstead . . . 'Ind 'Ead.

Où sont les neiges d'antan ?

Beyond all these friends were two friends of my parents who bulked so large in their lives that I must speak of them separately. They were George Meredith and Mary Duclaux.

CHAPTER VI

AND TWO GREAT FRIENDS

MY first meeting with George Meredith that I remember distinctly was when I was ten or twelve years old. He came occasionally as I have said to Hind Head and saw my father, to whom he dedicated *Diana of the Crossways*, almost as often as anyone save John Morley, of whom Meredith was an even closer friend, and I remember him vaguely at the Copse. I have a postcard from Meredith to F.P. dated October 25, 1882, with the following verses never before, I believe, published. They are written in G. M.'s lovely hand with his "d's" all formed like the Greek delta :

> Vowed, by Time upon his dial !
> Or, by magic draught & phial !
> Or, if you will, by lute & viol,
> Is it !—or by your boar with shaft in
> Flanks !—I will return your Lyall,
> When you shall next thread this valley,
> Mounting, & have stormed the chalet
> Which full many a Tramp has laughed in.
>
> G. M.

Plainly F.P. had lent the poet a book by his friend, Sir Alfred Lyall. The "boar with shaft in flanks" is the Pollock crest. "Tramp" of course means one of the Sunday Tramps, of which fellowship Meredith was an enthusiastic member. That first clear remembrance was when my father took me with him to Meredith's house at Box Hill. In those days, and indeed until motoring became universal, Box Hill, though close to Dorking, and not so far after all from London, was a remote and still wild spot, a haunt it seemed of the Great God Pan himself, and a fitting spot for a poet and Olympian writer to dwell. Meredith was nothing if not Olympian. On the visit I speak of my father and Meredith settled down for a long talk, and Meredith, thinking I should be bored, tossed a book to me. I never knew what the book was, nor read a word in it, so enthralling was the sound of Meredith's voice as my elders talked, and so entrancing his appearance. He was, I suppose, one of the most striking figures a man or boy could ever see in the course of his life. Of medium height, well-knit but slight, quick and active in his movements, he had a head that might have been that of Zeus himself, and did in fact somewhat resemble that of Mr. Walt Disney's Zeus in *Fantasia*. He wore a classical Greek beard, much set off by the red silk tie without which he was never seen. He always wore, that I remember, a suit of fine, grey home-spun tweed. If not precisely a dandy, he was certainly a trifle proud of his appearance. We can see him thus today in reproductions of Watts's portrait, the hair thick and a fine silver grey, the profile one of regular beauty. But Watts, and all photographers to whom Meredith sat, missed the animation of the face, the depth and luminosity of the large eyes. George Meredith's voice was music itself and his laugh, as J. M. Barrie truly said, quoting Meredith's own lines on Shakespeare, was " broad as ten thousand beeves at pasture ". The hours that he spent over solitary work in the famous chalet, whence came the greater part of his poems and novels, on the side of Box Hill above his house, were compensated by the ceaseless talk that flowed from his lips when unlocked in company. Then his listeners, were they young or old, mere students or men already renowned in various spheres of life, listened in never-failing delight to the most effortless and varied monologue that can be imagined. Until old age impaired his physical faculties, Meredith loved going for long walks, and talked as he walked ; but his talk did not need, as is the case with some men, the stimulus of movement to set it going—he talked as naturally as he breathed.

Meredith's tongue was not always kind. Rather he had a ready fund of sarcasm that made him harder, doubtless, to live with than to enjoy on occasion. No doubt too his fierceness must often have done him disservice. Once I asked him if he had known Tennyson. He then narrated the following curious incident. Meredith had, when young, an ardent and most natural desire to know Tennyson, twenty years his senior and already acknowledged one of the greatest of our lyrical poets. He got himself invited to a house where Tennyson was staying, and having arrived too late in the evening to meet him, got up early and went out for a walk. In a meadow by a stream he found Tennyson wrapped apparently in poetic ecstasy. Meredith waited in silent expectation. Then Tennyson said, in his rumbling bass that Meredith imitated in telling the story : "Macflecknoe should not have said that I am not a great poet." Much taken aback, Meredith recalled that Macflecknoe was an extremely minor critic of the epoch who had attacked Tennyson (Macflecknoe was not the actual name, by the way). "What possible importance," cried Meredith, "can have what such a worm writes about you ? Nobody will so much as notice his impertinence ! "—with more to the same effect. Tennyson stood darkly pondering. Then he opened his mouth and spoke these words : "But he should not have said that I am not a great poet." That was all. Then Meredith, tossing back his head in a characteristic gesture and letting that noble laugh ring out, concluded : "And after that I never wanted to see him again ! " Self-conceit and pretentiousness were two constant butts for Meredith's "Comic spirit".

At his apogee, that is between, say, 1880 and 1895, George Meredith's position in English letters was almost unique. He had obviously not a success with the large public comparable with that of Dickens and Thackeray, but critical readers recognised in him a quality not only new but of transcendent value. Dickens had used fiction to attack social abuses. Thackeray, following Fielding, had deployed his brilliant powers of satire, wielded with the perfection of English style, to dislodge hoary prejudice. But George Meredith was the first novelist to make his characters speak for themselves in the cause of moral progress, and the psychological action of his novels serve as illustration of it. The cultivation of talent for noble ends, the true place of women in the world, were his ever-recurring themes. The latter was the more noteworthy, because the newer in our literature ; here Meredith was a breaker of almost virgin soil. He was woman's champion and the precursor of women's rights. Contemporary with Ibsen, Meredith gave the world an astonishing gallery of women's portraits that changed our whole attitude towards sex problems and he directly paved the way towards the modern conception of the moral equality of the sexes. On his side Ibsen pursued similar aims. But there is this difference between the two writers. Powerful as he was, Ibsen could only create dowdy, tiresome, suburban females in dreary surroundings. Meredith's heroines are all beautiful, fascinating, vivid, almost all exquisitely dressed, and delightfully witty. All the advantage is with the English novelist. Meredith loved beauty. He adored his daughter, to whom his own looks had descended—enchanting vision to the eye that she was, the perfect embodiment of every man's imagination of the perfect Dresden China shepherdess—while he teasingly nicknamed his serious son " the old gentleman ".

Not that Meredith's men lack interest. Old Mel, Roy Richmond, Adrian, most of all Sir Willoughby, are memorable figures. Indeed, I am not so sure that *The Egoist*, with its intense cleverness, is not the easiest approach to Meredith's work for the present generation. It would be hard too not to appreciate *Evan Harrington*, the *Ordeal of Richard Feverel*, and *Beauchamp's Career*. Even in those novels less instantly sympathetic, like *Vittoria*, there is a dashing eagerness and a swing in the storytelling that is irresistible. Often Meredith is not easy reading ; in the later books, and in not a little of his poetry, where he fell into a habit of mystic writing—something like " mystic bidding " at bridge—very difficult indeed. There is the beginning of *Phoebus with Admetus*, admittedly one of Meredith's finest poems—

> God ! of whom music
> and song and blood are pure.

John Morley and my father put their heads together in an effort to construe these lines. Having arrived, as they thought, at the truth, they put the point to Meredith, only to discover that they were wrong. Years later two of Meredith's younger admirers, failing to understand a line in that rushing poem *The Woods of Westermain*—" One whose eyes are out "—put the question to Meredith. The poet opened his great eyes very wide and said in still voice, that told his opinion of the questioners : " Death." The answer was simple to Meredith because he knew it : to anyone else the phrase was pure mysticism. Yet mystic or not, no one mindful of Meredith's magnificent lines—like that already quoted, on Shakespeare, that on Gordon—" The Man of England circled by the sands," and those to Nelson—

> He leads ! We hear our seaman's call
> In the roll of battles won.
> For he is Britain's admiral
> Till setting of her sun.

or the fierce panting rhythm of *The Nuptials of Attila*, or of the deep music of *The Day of the Daughter of Hades*, will deny to Meredith's poetry the title " great ".

But there is one work by George Meredith that seems to be more likely than any other to appeal a generation after his death to a wide public and perhaps more greatly merits lasting life. This is *The Shaving of Shagpat*, an allegory of life, gorgeously apparelled in Eastern dress, of life as George Meredith conceived it : a tremendous, strenuous, exciting, beautiful adventure, in which woman, clear-sighted, self-sacrificing, purposeful, lovely, and loved, acts as guide and stimulus to weak, vacillating, sensual man. How, by the aid of Noorna bin Noorka, Shibli Bagarag became Master of the Event and shaved that humbug of humbugs, Shagpat, is there told with a wealth of thrills and of laughter such as no Arabian Nights entertainment can boast. But more than this. The Eastern form in which Meredith concealed his allegory—for, as he said himself, " the English do not like allegory "—freed his hand to paint such colours as, I submit, can be rivalled nowhere else in literature. *The Shaving of Shagpat* is a phatasmagoria of beauty, a Walpurgisnacht of pure images, chasing one another over the firmament of Meredith's unbounded imagination. There is indeed nothing like it in the world for breathless loveliness but some parts of Mr. Walt Disney's *Fantasia*. Mr. Walt Disney may be no Meredithian, but something of the spirit of *Shagpat* touched him when he conceived those scenes. It was *The Shaving of Shagpat* that William Cory, my father's tutor at Eton, read aloud when it first came out to his pupils, among them F.P., thereby implanting in him an enduring love for its author.

Once, with the audacity of youth, I staggered and indeed somewhat shocked a distinguished gathering at All Souls, by asserting that Meredith had pushed the art of psychological fiction to a higher plane than any other writer. On the whole I still think I was right. And to show that I was not alone in my judgment, I will quote the last bit of the loving fantasy that J. M. Barrie—no mean master of the pen—wrote after George Meredith's death. The funeral procession had driven away from Box Hill to the cemetery at Dorking, and then—so Barrie imagined—the figure of Meredith, sitting in his familiar study, began to come to life. "Old age was falling from him," wrote Barrie. "This is what is meant by Death to such as he." So Meredith, restored to youth, strode forth from the house and was welcomed by "his splendid progeny", the women he had created in his books.

"Box Hill"—I quote again—"was no longer deserted. When a great man dies—and this was one of the greatest since Shakespeare—the immortals await him at the top of the nearest hill. He looked up and saw his peers. They were all young, like himself. He waved his staff in greeting. One, a mere stripling, 'slight unspeakably', R. L. S., detached himself from the others, crying gloriously, 'Here's the fellow I have been telling you about,' and ran down the Hill to be the first to take his Master's hand. In the meanwhile an empty coach was rolling on to Dorking."

*   *   *   *   *

"Mary James Darmesteter has no longer a right to exist. As regards the English public Madame Duclaux has given no proof of her existence ; she has, she hopes, before her a modest future of French prose, and leaves her English verses to Mary Robinson." So wrote Mme Duclaux in the preface to her *Collected Poems*, published in 1902 under the name of Mary Robinson and, in brackets, "Madame Duclaux". Mary Robinson was her maiden name. She was born in 1856. In 1888 she married James Darmesteter, a French orientalist of genius, whose work on the Afghan language and literature is admitted by competent scholars to be unrivalled. He died in 1894, and seven years later Mary Darmesteter married Emile Duclaux, another Frenchman of almost equal eminence, for Duclaux was the associate of Pasteur and his immediate successor as head of the Institut Pasteur. Mme Duclaux died early in 1944 at Aurillac, where she had been living with her sister since the Germans took Paris.

In the midst of war's alarms and the mounting tide of Allied success it was natural that Mary Duclaux's death should pass without much notice. What was a shade surprising was to find so little that was personal about this very remarkable English-woman of letters even in the few articles that showed acquaint-ance with her works. I knew Mme Duclaux from my boyhood onwards and during many years saw her frequently. This long friendship was the legacy from one even longer between Mme Duclaux and my parents. A very, very long time ago there existed a habit among English people to spend a few summer weeks or months abroad—in order to save money. This hardly appears credible even to those who travelled in the early part of this century, but in the last it was undoubtedly possible : an allusion to it may be found in Pinero's *The Notorious Mrs. Ebbsmith*. On one such journey of holiday economy my mother and hers, a widow in none too affluent circumstances, met, travelling also, Mrs. Robinson and Mary, who was six years younger than my mother. The two young women formed an immediate mutual attachment that became only the stronger on their respective marriages and lasted till my mother's death some sixty years later. Mary's first marriage in 1888 took her to live in Paris, and except during the war of 1914 I suppose no year passed after that without visits of the one to Paris or the other to London, or both, while close contact was kept betweenwhiles by correspondence between both my parents and Mary and her sister Mabel Robinson.

It would be impossible to think of Mary Duclaux without thinking in the same instant of Mabel Robinson. Mabel— whom Henry James, also a lifelong friend, would always call " Mabelle " with a heavy stress on the last syllable—had an ever-present critical acumen and a subtle sense of humour that formed a necessary complement to her elder sister's brilliance. Those who knew them sometimes wondered that Mary, who dwelt in the realm of intellect and imagination, should have married twice while Mabel, gifted with a delightfully human and affectionate touch as well as brains beyond the common, should have remained single. " Tante Mabelle ", as she became to her sister's stepchildren and step-grandchildren, received an almost filial adoration from them. Yet it was certainly not a case of Martha and Mary. Practical though she was to her finger-tips, Mabel never sacrificed her mind to the household round. Probably she was the stronger character of the two and felt an antipathy to the idea of giving up any of her personal independence.

The Robinson sisters were the children of George T. Robinson, an architect of Irish descent practising in London, who wrote a great deal of art criticism in the *Manchester Courier* and as war correspondent in 1870 had been shut up in besieged Metz. The sympathy with France inborn in his daughters showed itself in deed, not only by Mary's marriages, but by Mabel's devoted work during and after the 1914 war in nursing the wounded at the Invalides in Paris. For, as many visitors to Napoleon's tomb never learned, the Invalides, besides being a military headquarters and the Emperor's final resting-place, bore out its name as an asylum for the war crippled. Mabel, who at the moment of my writing is still living, inherited from her Irish father more than a love of France. She espoused the cause of the Irish leaders, among whom John Dillon was a close friend, and in the days of the troubles went to and from Ireland carrying, sewn into her clothes, messages between men held as rebels and their agents. There can be no indiscretion after so great a lapse of time in revealing this piquant fact, for which my mother was my witness.

" The quality of Mary Robinson's work, its conciseness and purity of expression, were only gradually recognised," states an article on her in the eleventh edition of the *Encylopædia Britannica* published in 1910. That she should, when barely more than fifty years old, have qualified for inclusion in the *Encyclopædia* testifies to the importance of Mary Robinson's work. Yet the impression conveyed by the sentence quoted does not tally with that passed on by eye-witnesses of her early period. On the contrary, they maintained that her rare talent struck the world of letters like a lightning flash from the moment when her volume of poems, *A Handful of Honeysuckle*, was published in 1879. Not only was a poetess then born, of whom a good judge wrote later :
" Her verse has to me more of the real singing quality in it than

can be found in almost any of our living poets junior to Mr. Swinburne," but that poetess was a young woman of astonishing personal sparkle and wit. Down to the very eve of the late war Mme Duclaux conserved these qualities to the full. In youth she was something to rave about. Tiny and light as a fairy she was beautifully formed. Her face was a perfect oval, her mouth the legendary cupid's bow. Under a broad forehead, surmounted by a mass of dark hair, eyes nearly as large as saucers were pools of deep, limpid, flashing light, set off by strong, straight eyebrows. Born half a century later she would have knocked Hollywood's beauties endwise, and did indeed somewhat resemble the Mary Pickford of her prime, but with a vivacity, an intelligence, and a brimming delight in things of the mind that no screen heroine could touch. She was painted by Watts, by Millais, by Louise Jopling ; but no portrait of her I have seen catches the combination of her enchanting prettiness and the ethereal scintillation of her presence. She illuminated the whole room. Small wonder that the Robinsons' house in Gower Street became a centre of art and letters, where William Sharp, Randolph Caldecote, Edwin Long, then a flaming star of the Academy, George Moore in the first flush of his vogue, W. B. Yeats, Justin McCarthy, and many others congregated round this young magician, who in the next seven years produced four more volumes of poems, to be followed quickly by studies on *The End of the Middle Ages* and on *Emily Brontë.*

James Darmesteter fell in love with Mary Robinson's poems before he fell in love with her. He had received a copy while at Peshawar, and it was his translation of some of them into French that led to their meeting. Mary used to relate with gusto one of his experiences in India. Darmesteter was present at a banquet given at Lahore to Lockwood Kipling, curator of the Museum there, when a high functionary of the Indian Government in proposing Lockwood Kipling's health expressed the condescending hope that the young man far down the table would some day follow in his father's distinguished footsteps. Darmesteter and more than one other guest held their breath and choked laughter down : Rudyard Kipling had already published *Plain Tales from the Hills* and *Soldiers Three*, and to the blissful ignorance of officialdom was already famous the world over.

Darmesteter was not the only man to feel Mary Robinson's spell from afar ; Gabriele D'Annunzio himself wrote to Swinburne to beg for an introduction to this new priestess of his shrine. Her third volume of poems had for title *An Italian Garden*, and she was a frequent visitor to Violet Paget's house at Florence, which was a magnet to Italian, French, and English men and women of letters. But with her marriage to Darmesteter Paris became her home. It remained so to the end of her life, and gave her the opportunity as no other place could have done to develop what was in a way her most peculiar gift, that of inspirer, critic, and literary guide to wellnigh a whole generation. James Darmesteter was a man of genius not only by his works but by his personal charm too. His appearance was far from prepossessing ; he was hunchbacked from infancy and, like the painter Toulouse Lautrec, so undersized that, said one who knew and admired him, when you came into a room where he was you thought you were alone in it. It can now cause no hurt to repeat what Mrs. Robinson once told my mother. The good lady was aghast at the news of this engagement of her exquisite daughter who might have made a brilliant match.

"Mary," she cried, "how can you ? How can you love him ? He's a Jew ! He's almost a dwarf ! "

Mary opened her enormous eyes wide. "When I look at him," she said, "I don't see it." Not long after the marriage Mrs. Robinson changed her opinion. It needed less than a minute, said my father, even for someone not in love with him to forget his physical strangeness, so delightful and noble was his personality. His death six years later was a grievous blow.

When in 1901 Mary Darmesteter married Emile Duclaux, who unhappily died three years later, she settled in a sunny flat close to the Invalides and overlooking the stately garden and historical building that became the Musée Rodin. Mabel Robinson had the flat opposite on the same landing. They were spending the summer of 1914 at Sucy-en-Brie when the war broke out, and moved for safety to Melun. Mary has related how on September 2nd the streets were filled with women rushing for their houses and crying, " Les Allemands ! Ce sont les Allemands ! " " I felt no fear," she said, " only an immense strained curiosity ; but I must have been at heart far more afraid than they, for I could not have moved or cried. And then, by the old church, round the corner came our bonny Highlanders ! I stood still on the pavement and sang ' Scots wha hae ' at the top of my cracked old voice, and they (appreciating the welcome and excusing the minstrelsy) waved their hands to me as they passed." Three days later she asked an English soldier in the street : " Are we getting the best of it ? Is there much danger ? " Tommy answered her : " Well, miss, it's like this : the place is full up of generals, and I don't know how it is, but I've always noticed that where there's so many generals, there's not much danger." Twenty-four hours went by ; it was Sunday, September 6th. The tremendous cannonade thundering miles away died down towards noon. Mary went out and met " a demure, douce young Highlander taking his afternoon walk, as quietly as if it had been in Glasgow. ' How are things going ? ' I said. ' Do you think the Germans are coming ? ' The Highlander answered : ' I haf been hearing, Matam, that the Chermans will have been hafing a bit of a setback.' " So Mary Duclaux learned of the victory of the Marne.

The Rue de Varenne then was the home of the two sisters for nearly forty years till they were driven once more from Paris to seek refuge from the same invaders. At Aurillac in Auvergne they found safety and kindness ; when neighbours learned their nationality they would bring up wood and coal to " ces dame, anglaises ", however Vichy might curse the name of England. In the Rue de Varenne Mary wrote the main part of what she had described as her " modest future of French prose ". There had already been a *Froissart*, and *La Vie de Renan*, her most popular book and the best account of Renan extant. In English she there wrote *A Book of France* and *A Short History of France*, preceded by her *Marguerite of Anjou, Queen of Navarre*. In French there was a *Pascal* and a *Fénelon*, a *Madame de Sévigné*, and a *Victor Hugo*. If her output was not large in quantity, the quality was uniformly high. She wrote an exquisite French style and had an incomparable mastery of the language, though in speaking she never lost traces of an English accent. But more important than her written work was her personal touch. Her flat, with her sister's as an indispensable adjunct, became " le dernier salon où l'on cause ". The sisters were at home one day in the week,

Sunday for many years, then Wednesday. Now there is about the word *salon* a suggestion sometimes of planned reception. Mary Duclaux's gained a special charm from its spontaneity, and besides persons of note there were always sure to be more intimate friends and young people to help, with the delicious cakes and the bubbling urn on the table. After talk round the tea-table in the dining-room there was a general move into the drawing-room, where the talk continued.

" Sir," said Doctor Johnson, being asked what he had done on a certain occasion, " we had good talk." If ever there was good talk in our time it was at Mme Duclaux's. The talk was by no means all literary, though literature perhaps predominated, for Mary Duclaux was an influential member of the " Femina— Vie Heureuse " Committee which yearly allotted one of the prizes most desired by French authors after *le Grand Prix du Roman* offered by the French Academy. To the Rue de Varenne came many authors, among them in later years François Mauriac, his lined features reflecting the force of the tormenting moral and religious stress within, André Maurois seeking support for his candidature at the Academy, Raymond Escholier, Elie Halévy the historian and his brother Daniel, whose grace and wit had a breath of their famous father Ludovic, the creator of *Madame Cardinal* and Offenbach's librettist. Philosophy was often represented by Professor Desjardins, who had revived the Platonic Symposium in his *decades* at the Abbey of Pontivy, where illustrious men and novices at their feet met for ten days at a time each summer to discuss all things in heaven and earth, by M. Jacques Maritain, the brilliant and liberal Catholic writer later appointed French ambassador to the Vatican, and by M. d'Eichtal, of the Académie des Sciences Morales et Politiques, noted for his prodigious age and a funereal appearance that got him the nickname " Ni fleurs, ni couronnes " (No flowers by request) ; which, however, did not in the least prevent his being a delightful conversationalist. Science, too, was faithful to Emile Duclaux's widow. The great Metchnikoff and Dr. Roux, successively heads of the Institut Pasteur, were constantly to be met ; Metchnikoff, burly, cheerful, with a truly Russian jollity, Roux thin, austere, yet benevolent for all his sometimes shattering pronouncements. Once when I commented to him on the dangers of an amnesty which included even common criminals, he retorted : " The only surprising thing is that all the honest folk are not locked up." Jacques Duclaux, Emile's son, who might have followed his father at the Institut Pasteur after Dr. Roux's death, but preferred the quieter situation of professor at the Collège de France, specialist in the primordial subjects of colloids, and his children growing to brilliance in a third generation, brought with them a freshness that vivified the galaxy of elder stars. On my father once being asked what, if he were not what he was, he would choose to be, he answered without hesitation : " Professor at the Collège de France," that unique foundation endowed by Francis I, where there are no examinations, no syllabus, and no degrees given, where the professors choose their own subjects, and where lectures are open to the whole world and attendance by students is purely voluntary. It was Professor Jacques Duclaux who invented safety glass for motor-car windows, and did some of the most vital work on artificial silk. Professor Pasteur Vallery-Radot, grandson of Louis Pasteur and during the late war one of the French Resistance leaders, was another visitor. Sometimes there was Mme Noémi Renan, the daughter of the great Ernest, and her children, and almost always Mme Arsène Darmesteter, painter of much talent, ready to talk about everything except her painting. And whenever they were in Paris, Mme Arsène's brother, Sir Philip Hartog, and Violet Paget, or, to use her pen-name, Vernon Lee, and George Moore, and Miles Dillon, son of the celebrated John, and my parents. George Moore, who took himself very seriously but none the less talked well, would have been horrified could he have known that Mary and Mabel used him, however lightly and affectionately, as something of a butt and had secretly laughed at him even in the days of Gower Street.

In the varied talk that the clash of so many fine minds produced Mary Duclaux took the lead with an adroitness that concealed its skill, ever ready to fling a fresh subject into the arena and watchful that no one should be left out in the cold. She always had a special welcome for young married couples and loved drawing them out. Herself, she talked insatiably, the whole time it seemed, with extreme volubility, and in a somewhat high-pitched voice that surely indicated a mighty hurry to express the thoughts crowding in her mind ; but crowd they never so much, they melted into words with unsurpassed lucidity and never without a point of wit. No one could ever wish her to be silent. Images fell from her lips in a ceaseless cascade, yet she was far too good a hostess to monopolise the conversation and was eager to elicit talk from others. As a talker she by far outclassed any other woman I have met, and all but two or perhaps three men ; but it was her gift of listening too that made her so successful a hostess. Criticism with her, whether of the living or the dead, was not an edged tool but rather a perfumed pointer : truth was always the object, but it was to be sought with grace and put into forms of kindness. I once sat by her at a performance of *Hernani* at the Comédie Française. To most twentieth-century critics the turgidly romantic drama would have been an easy mark for their shafts : one need refer only to Anatole France's gibes at Victor Hugo. At the end Mme Duclaux turned to me and whispered : " C'est ridé, mais comme c'est joli ! " Truth and charity could not have been better mixed.

The name of Anatole France is a reminder that down to shortly before the war of 1914 there was one Parisian *salon* that rivalled that of Mme Duclaux. This was the *salon* of Mme Arman de Caillavet, which has been described in a book under that title by her daughter-in-law Mme Pouquet. Mme Arman's liaison with Anatole France was consecrated by long acceptance ; when they travelled abroad they went as M. and Mme France, and Mme Arman, whose husband was alive, sat on the right hand of the French Ambassador at Constantinople when he entertained Anatole France. Mme Arman was clever and pertinacious in the extreme. She worked up subjects for her illustrious *protégé*, made his worldly success, even wrote unaided, as Mme Pouquet tells us, a substantial number of pages signed Anatole France. " He owes me everything," Mme Arman said herself in a moment of tragic abandonment. " It was I who brought him out of his shell and got him into the Academy. Who knew him, pray, before I taught him to put on his tie properly and to kiss ladies' hands and to peel fruit the right way ? He was a miserable little anarchist, a bookseller's son who lived with his nose in dusty papers. He would be still if I had not extracted him from them." This description of Anatole France was born of distress and spite, for even before Mme Arman took him up he was known as a witty and brilliant journalist. Mme Arman was not popular with everyone. Once on a visit to Renan she showered the old man with heavy compliments. "Ah, vous me comblez, Madame!" cried the great writer. "Ah, Madame, personne ne m'a jamais dit tant de choses gracieuses!" And the moment she was out of the door Renan turned to a young friend and fairly riddled her with the irony of which he was the unparalleled master. One who knew them both has given me Renan's view of Mme de Caillavet: "A vain peacock, with a peacock's showiness and bright colours, but not his beauty."

Mme Arman's *salon* differed from that of Mme Duclaux in that it was run exclusively as a chapel for Anatole France. It was to exalt him and for that alone that she collected celebrities in her grand house in the Avenue Hoche, where Anatole France was brought in as an exhibit and made to perform like a juggler on a tightrope of talk. Mme Duclaux's method, I have tried to show, was not like that, but designed rather to provoke general talk of a high intellectual order. Did the two ever meet? I do not know, although they almost must have done so at the Renans'; there is no record. I never heard Mme Duclaux mention Mme Arman. But they were well aware of each other's existence. In the days when Anatole France was a student at the École des Chartes, where he got his pyrotechnic skill in handling historical subjects, he had as fellow-student Arsène Darmesteter, author of a *Dictionnaire de la Langue Française*, and as brilliant a philologist as his brother James was an orientalist. Arsène Darmesteter and his wife had a *pavillon* or bungalow at Vaugirard, then much frequented by artists and writers, where they were at home on Saturday evenings, after a small dinner of chosen guests, to any friends who cared to drop in. James and Mary were often there; so was Anatole France. The creator of *Crainquebille* and *M. Jérôme Coignard*, highly susceptible to feminine charm as he was, could not fail to be struck. How soon Mme Arman became aware of a potential rival to her power, no one can now say. But it is clear that she did become aware. She reacted with vigour. Anatole France was whisked away from the dangerous neighbourhood of Mary Darmesteter. To the best of my belief they never met again. Not that Mme Arman had anything personal to fear, for no woman ever lived less flirtatious than Mary. It was her literary possession, the grand show-piece of Mme Arman's *salon* that was threatened.

Anatole France had received a deep impression. How deep was seen on the publication of *Le Lys Rouge*, which contains a full-length portrait of Mary Robinson in the person of Miss Bell, the second but by far the most striking of the feminine characters in the novel. There are in the portrait touches too of Vernon Lee, as in the description of Miss Bell : " ugly and seductive, a trifle ridiculous and altogether exquisite, she lived at Florence, æsthete and philosopher ". But the main traits in Miss Bell are undoubtedly taken from Mary Robinson : the " seductive " and " altogether exquisite " in the phrase quoted belong to her, not to Violet Paget. Although Anatole France was careful to bring in the names of both real English writers— " Like Vernon Lee and Mary Robinson, she had fallen in love with Tuscan life and art "—it was impossible for anyone not to recognise Mary in the words " England celebrated her as her most beloved poetess ". There is in Anatole France's portrait of Mary Robinson more than an edge of malice. Malicious his pen always was, but here it is hard not to see intention in the malice. Was he piqued at Mary's indifference to him ? Was he taking this way to make a burnt offering to Mme Arman ? Perhaps both. Yet even in his malice he could not help making Miss Bell, who talking French addresses every-body with the English word " Darling " and surrounds herself, as symbols, with bells of every sort and size, a fascinating figure. Whatever his intention, there is in Miss Bell a bubbling well of mental activity, an effulgent appreciation of beauty, a spend-thrift richness of spirit that could belong only to Mary Robinson. One scrap of dialogue reads as if it had been taken straight from her lips :

Miss Bell descendait les degrés du perron, en mettant ses gants.

" Oh, darling, la ville et les montagnes et le ciel veulent

être pleurés de vous. Ils se font beaux aujourdhui pour vous donner le regret de les quitter et l'envie de les revoir."

When this episode is considered, it becomes clear what high value became attached to Mme Duclaux's *salon*, for André Maurois, who had married Mme Arman's granddaughter, to pay his academic court there, as he did. Mme Arman was long dead, but so determined had she been to sever all connexion between Anatole France and Mary Duclaux that even twenty years after Mme Arman de Caillavet and her *salon* had ceased to exist, the trail left by this anxious enmity could still be seen and all who had been in the orbit of the Arman clan still held aloof from the *salon* in the Rue de Varenne, save when led to it by a motive potent indeed. To the hope of gaining Mme Duclaux's good opinion André Maurois was ready to sacrifice Mme Arman's vendetta, and did so.

A woman of rare distinction alone could have wielded the power that Mary Duclaux had over so many men of note, painters, poets, scholars, writers, and scientists, for more than a generation. Its secret lay, perhaps, even more than in dazzling accomplishments, in her utter sincerity, and for all the spangled jet of her talk in a sort of radiant humbleness that is the portion of truly great souls. Of her own she wrote :

> For in my Soul a temple have I made,
> Set on a height, divine, and steep and far ;
> Nor often may I hope those floors to tread,
> Or reach the gates that glimmer like a star.

What better epitaph could be hers ?

CHAPTER VII

ETON

ETON has for long been the lodestar of English public schools. The time has happily gone by when a silly, parrot cry was raised against " the Old School tie ". Our public schools remain, as they have been from their foundation, one of the most solid stones on which our public as well as private life is built. Quite recently we have had the edifying spectacle of the most class-conscious, revolutionary, and tyrannical government in our modern parliamentary history led by an old public school boy, and of a mission from it that set forth to pillory the misdeeds of the great public schools issuing from that crusade with cheers for what they had been meant to damn. The precise date when Eton took the lead among public schools seems not entirely clear. The author of *Midshipman Easy*, for a typical example of the public-school spirit, named Westminster. The Rugby of *Tom Brown's Schooldays* was famous. Nor could anyone fail at any time to see the manifold excellences of Westminster, Winchester, Wellington, and a dozen others. But it may be said without injustice to them that Eton has become *prima inter pares*. Her ascendancy perhaps began before the middle of the nineteenth century ; much of it was certainly due to the admirable organisation achieved by Dr. Edmond Warre who was still headmaster when I went to the school. Others who followed him continued and perfected his work. During the past century too there has been visible a growing consciousness of the advantage possessed by Eton in the beauty of her buildings and surroundings, and in her unique site upon England's noblest river. Some reasons that used commonly to be given for the pre-eminence of Eton are certainly false. One was that Eton was a school for the rich. The expense of education in England, as contrasted for instance with that in France, may be a regrettable trait in our social life ; but it has to be remembered that with us education combines what the French know as *instruction*, that is, training

THE SADDLER AND HIS WIFE

From contemporary miniatures

of the mind, which is well, many Frenchmen think over well, supplied by the French system, with *éducation*, that is, as interpreted by them, training in manners and in the civic virtues of leadership, political balance, and moral standards, which the French school system does not and does not attempt to inculcate at all. So far no one has discovered how to supply the latter at school without the expense of good housing, good food, adequate playing fields, and equipment for games, and above all masters who attain to a very high degree of mental and moral accomplishment. If Eton is more expensive, though not so much more as is often imagined, than other schools it is because these desiderata receive greater attention there and have, for at least three generations of men, been judged by a higher standard than elsewhere. The proof of this pudding is plain enough : e.g. in a post-war regiment in a technical branch of the army, with a high standard for admission to it, twenty-two of the junior officers were found to be old Etonians. It must moreover not be forgotten that nearly nine per cent of the boys at Eton are scholars wholly supported by the Founder's endowment and that their parents may be as poor as church mice. The existence of these Collegers or King's Scholars has a profound, though often unconscious, effect upon the rest of the school known as Oppidans, many of whom are spurred on by a spirit of emulation in their work, however well they know that successful rivalry is beyond them. Another fallacious idea about Eton was, and among the ignorant may still be, that she owes her attraction to a supposed aristocratic bent among the boys there. This, to use the language of a boy, is mere tommy rot. In the eighteenth century it was perhaps true that Eton was a school mainly for sprigs of the nobility. George III's affection for Eton doubtless fostered this, although indeed there was very little snobbery in the Farmer King's character or manners. William Brummell, Lord North's private secretary, certainly sent his son George to the school with the object of George's acquiring the rudiments of *bon ton* ; and certainly George did so acquire them, for as Beau Brummell he became the dictator of European taste and left his name to be a legend more enduring than bronze. But for at least a hundred years no school can conceivably have boasted of a more democratic atmosphere than Eton, and that before the poor word " democracy " had become so overworked as it is today. Eton boys never took the slightest notice of a newcomer's parentage or the surroundings he came from. Neither did masters. The only things to matter are character, decency of manners, and cleanliness. Woe betide whoever offends against the standards exacted by the boys in these. One of the least popular boys at the school with me was a duke, now defunct ; he was among the few I remember really to be looked askance at. Another, still alive, the inheritor of a great name, and later a prominent statesman, was kicked from pillar to post for his personal habits and known as " loony . . ." or sometimes by a more opprobrious epithet. A third, heir to a barony and a vast fortune was despised as " dirty . . .". It was the unexpected discovery of this spirit of social equality that so impressed the trade union inquisitors who descended on Eton after the Socialist Government came into power.

It is another question for how long the public schools as a whole, in the form in which we have inherited them, will be able to stand up to the predatory legislation imposed on the country by Socialist Government and to war-time taxation continued during years of peace, amounting to wholesale spoliation of the middle-classes that are the backbone of the public schools. Vote-seeking Conservatives and Liberals, fearful of maintaining their true principles lest they be denounced as enemies of progress, would seem not to notice that this tendency is precisely the same as that advocated by Trotsky on June 29, 1918, when he declared : " First, the bourgeoisie shall be placed upon the register, then it shall be held in a vice. . . . We shall put the bourgeoisie in such conditions that it will lose all wish to be bourgeoisie ! " The English middle-classes have already, by virtue of massive reduction in their income and the lopping of their capital by its nationalisation without adequate compensation, forfeited much of their fruitful freedom of action. They are now threatened, through the mouth of Mr. Emmanuel Shinwell speaking in March 1949, with seeing their remaining capital distributed among the rest of the nation. What place there can be for our traditional public schools in a world reduced to members of trade unions and governed by a locust swarm of

formula-inspired bureaucrats, every man must judge for himself.
What is certain is that civilisation, as we have known it in
England for at least seven centuries, would be violently uprooted
by their destruction or at least radically altered by their degrada-
tion, under the surveillance of lackeys of a Socialist Whitehall,
into an ante-room for universities reduced to the level of tech-
nological colleges.

I went to Eton from two private schools, the first very good,
the second to my mind very bad. Wilkinson's, my day school
in Orme Square, Bayswater, was owned and run by a man of
that name, a scholar and a gentleman with a genius for teaching.
Before I left Wilkinson's at the age of eleven, I knew more
mathematics—a subject at which I was always conspicuously
bad—than I learned till I was in Upper Fifth at Eton and not
very much less of the rudiments of classics. Years later I had
the delight of meeting Wilkinson at the Savile Club and telling
him how happy I had been with him. Wilkinson was only
sixteen years older than me, but to nine years twenty-five seems
a hundred. In the summer he taught his boys cricket on
Wormwood Scrubs, while in winter a delightfully volatile
assistant master named Payn coached us at football in Kensington
Gardens. Wilkinson hardly ever punished the boys ; Payn
would throw a ruler at dunces or lawbreakers but always
managed to miss. In winter too we had the joy of snow-fights
with " the cads " or neighbouring boardschool boys : a primitive
form of the still extant " town and gown " riots at the universities.

Unhappily London was thought to be bad for a digestion
always very poor till I went to Eton, so I was sent to a board-
ing school. My digestion did not improve and I was most
unhappy at the new place. The boys were underfed and overworked, and bullied by assistant masters who all were given the
right to use the cane. The headmaster caned frequently and
viciously. Parents are the last people to know what goes on at
private schools. But the food was so bad that my parents became
alarmed at my growing pallor. My father insisted on a thorough
investigation and reform. The headmaster blustered that if F.P.
were dissatisfied he could remove me from the school, vainly
imagining that no parent would have the pluck to take such a
step, for his school was one of the most highly reputed in England.

He little knew F.P., who promptly came down to fetch me back to London. Then the headmaster caved in at once. Amends were promised and there was a marked improvement ; and when a little later a revolt broke out at putrid meat being again served he did not dare to resist. Thanks to highly specialised cramming the school regularly won many scholarships at Eton and Winchester. In my judgment the method was thoroughly unsound and two boys, even during my short sojourn at the school, suffered so severely from over-cramming that, though they won scholarships high on the list, one after entering his public school remained completely idle for the rest of his life, and the other on leaving it had a total brain breakdown.[1]

The headmaster of this cram-shop said that, if he had had me under him for one year more, I should have been certain to get a scholarship at Eton. Much as I should have valued the right to put K.S. after my name, in company with my father, two cousins, and two brothers-in-law, I never regretted escaping from his clutches. As it was, I was one off the list. An unexpected vacancy in College occurred during my first half at Eton and there was a question whether it should be filled by taking me in : but the printed list won. So I went to Cornish's. Francis Warre Cornish was a lifelong friend of my father's, though senior to him. He was, I believe, a beautiful classical scholar and a man of the highest aims ; but he was totally unfitted to be a housemaster. It was characteristic of my father to send me to Cornish's, though it was known he must soon retire and though H. E. Luxmoore, a younger man and a very successful housemaster, was willing to make room for me. Luxmoore and F.P. were acquainted through Eton and Oxford friends, but the matter was determined by the extra pull of intimacy with Cornish and with his family. Mrs. Cornish was one of the three lovely and gifted Miss Ritchies. The eldest, a truly imposing beauty, married Douglas Freshfield, a wealthy solicitor and among the most celebrated of Alpine climbers :

[1] The headmaster in question died a good many years ago and, for all I know, the system he imposed may have been altogether reformed. To avoid any misapprehension I should perhaps add that my school was emphatically not the admirable Dragon School at Oxford which for over half a century has achieved great scholarship successes by different and seriously preferable methods. As my son went to " The Dragons ", I am in a position to know.

his books have remained classics on the subject. The second, by name Emily but generally known as "Pinkie", almost equally exquisite to look at, was supposed to lead a heartbroken existence for unrequited love of Tennyson and seemed to cultivate that legend by a certain pensive aloofness from things of the world; but she got about a good deal to teas, dinners, and concerts and I believe thoroughly enjoyed life. The third sister, Mrs. Cornish, was less tall, less willowy, but individual in her mind even to the point of eccentricity. The Ritchies were cousins of Sir William ("Willie") Richmond the painter, and their brother Sir Richmond Ritchie married Thackeray's daughter, so there were links of friendship all round between F.P. and Cornish. For some unknown reason the boys in the house had labelled Mrs. Cornish "the Banana". The stories told of her were endless. I can vouch for three of them, typical of the rest. She was chanting with idyllic enthusiasm how she had seen "an ox, standing in a lush water-meadow bright with golden buttercups, that grand beast moving his head majestically from side to side and swishing his tail"; then ended suddenly in quite a different tone, "so unlike the fox, is he not?" Mrs. Cornish was a wholly fascinating person. Her behaviour was as tangential as her conversation. One evening she was walking down the hill from Windsor where she and Cornish had been dining at the Castle. A soldier came up the hill on his way back to barracks. Mrs. Cornish, as indeed very often, was feeling full of good will to all men. "Good night, Mr. Soldier!" she called out. To which the man, not seeing in the dark the figure or age of the person addressing him, shouted back: "Wot 'oh, ducky!" Mrs. Cornish flung herself round her husband's fragile neck, upsetting his hat and his always ill-balanced eyeglasses, with a shriek: "Save me, Frank!" During my first half at Eton, where a term is so named both colloquially and officially, Cornish was appointed Vice-Provost of the College and gave up his house to reside in the beautiful Cloisters. The Vice-Provost, the Provost, and the Headmaster always had large parties for the fireworks that end Fourth of June celebrations, their drawing-rooms and gardens immediately overlooking the display. One Fourth of June a deluge of rain suddenly came down at the height of Mr. Brock's scintillating inventions.

The guests, all dressed up to the nines—organdie, lace, and wide-brimmed hats ; toppers, buttonholes, and fancy waistcoats—dashed for shelter, and a score of half-drowned rats poured into Mrs. Cornish's drawing-room. But they almost forgot their plight at the spectacle of Mrs. Cornish, sitting in an armchair in the middle of the room and declaring to all who would listen that "Lohengin is *pretty*—oh, yes ! pretty—but MERELY pretty ! " Far more than a flood was needed to distract Mrs. Cornish's mind from momentary concentration on Wagner to the reality of her guests' needs. Cornish himself is taken off in a sprightly portrait in *A Day of My Life*, published while the author Nugent Bankes, who signed it " Enby ", was still at Eton, the most brilliant sketch of life in the school ever written. The cruelty of the portrait is the natural, unconscious cruelty of youth, and the whole sketch, though long since out of date in its facts, is still intensely amusing to an Etonian.

Cornish's was what was technically known as a " bad " house. That is to say, discipline was almost totally absent from it but, during my one half there, I never saw anything more than want of discipline. Bullying was as much absent as discipline. On Cornish being appointed Vice-Provost, my father applied to Luxmoore to take me into his house. Luxmoore, I learned later, was very loath to accept a boy from Cornish's, fearing to take with him a breath of that want of discipline or worse. However, he relented and Luxmoore became my tutor—in Eton parlance m'tutor. Luxmoore, who lived to be the G.O.M. of Eton, where he was given a house long after he had ceased to be a housemaster or after that to take a division in the school, was the nearest thing I have ever known to a saint. He was unselfishness personified ; nor could devotion to highly enlightened ideals go further than his. Like the great saints of history, St. Vincent de Paul or St. Theresa say, my tutor was an extremely practical person. Stern, and feared by those who did not know his deep kindness, with the head of a Roman emperor and thick greyish white hair, there was no trouble he would not take for his boys' welfare, physical and spiritual. He was a good division master—I was " up " to him for three halves in Division III—but it was in his house that he shone. He had come under the influence of Ruskin at Oxford and himself was an exquisite painter in water-colours. His collection of Eton scenes, *Eton from a Backwater*, is a priceless monument to the beauty of the place, and his rare *Eton Housetops* by " Sparrow " more commonly known as *Sparrow on the Housetops*, a description of Eton architecture as humorous as it is luminous, makes a fitting pendant. Luxmoore's drawing-room, where on Sundays he welcomed his boys, and not only his, to hear him read and to talk, was full of beautiful books and furniture, and he was the only man I ever knew to use reading lamps lit with colza oil, that gave a light softer and more enfolding than any other. He was the one master in the school who led boys towards a feeling for beauty ; this he did deliberately, systematic-ally, but solely by way of suggestion and illustration and never by dogmatic assertion or a superior attitude. When we played a housematch at the Field game, the Eton football whence " soccer ", more spectacular but far less amusing to play, was evolved, however bad the weather my tutor was on the spot with his butler, Sayr, and a large can of the best bitter to refresh his eleven at the end. My tutor drank very little himself, but was a firm believer in the virtue of British beer and British beef, of which there was always a plentiful supply, cold, at supper for the senior boys. Sayr, mentioned in an earlier chapter for his Abraham Lincoln beard, distinguished himself during the great floods of 1894 by appearing in bathing drawers and swimming past my tutor's front door in 2 or $2\frac{1}{2}$ feet of swirling, dirty water, just to be able to say that he had done so. Without being out-standing at games, Luxmoore's made a fair show at them. Vivian Nickalls, the champion sculler and brother of his yet more celebrated elder Guy, had been in the house. So had George Duckworth, an Oxford blue. My tutor's had once played a draw in the final of the football house match, and in my last year we nearly did the same against Mitchell's. " Mike ", as R. A. M. Mitchell was universally known, had been one of the best bats in England, W. G. always excepted, and had gone to Eton to improve, less the standard of learning, than that of cricket. He certainly did so. Mike's always contained a goodly percentage of boys in the Eleven and the Field, and it was rumoured that lower boys at Mike's who got beaten in matches were in for a hot time from their seniors. Mike's was easily the most athletic house in the school, but not renowned for much else. In my last half they won, as they so often did, the cricket house cup, after beating my tutor's not too handsomely in the ante-final, Arthur Hazlerigg, afterwards Captain of Leicestershire and Lord Hazlerigg, making 50 not out for the last wicket, while myself with much trembling made 32 before being bowled by Mike's youngest son. Luxmoore's real glory at cricket was when Philip Cobbold was captain of the house and the best bowler in the school, just as at the University he became accounted one of the best slow bowlers in England. It was after him that my tutor named " Philip's Pool ", a delightful private bathing-place he made in a backwater surrounding the garden he miraculously called into being on an eyot opposite his house, an abandoned waste adjoining the Eton gasworks. For besides his other talents Luxmoore was one of the best flower gardeners in England ; the enchanted spot he there created has been kept up by Eton since his death as a memorial to him. None could be more fitting. Luxmoore died in old age one Armistice Day, of the emotion wrought in him by the thought of his boys who had fallen in the first World War. Happily for him, as it was happy in my father's case too, he did not live to see the second.

Great housemaster and tutor though he undoubtedly was, Luxmoore did not touch the highest level as a teacher. There were indeed only three men in the school in my time of whom this could be said. They were Francis Hay Rawlins, the philologist, brother of Rawlins, K.C., M.P., who had formed the abortive hope that my father would become the biographer of Sir Bartle Frere, and author of a well-known Latin grammar, Hurst who came in my last year with high mathematical honours from Cambridge, and from Oxford C. H. Marten, later Sir Henry Marten, K.C.V.O., Provost of Eton, and tutor to Princess Elizabeth and Princess Margaret, who transformed the teaching of history in the school. Both Rawlins and Hurst, though they could not make me good at subjects for which I had no aptitude, succeeded in making me feel their fascination. Rawlins ought to have been appointed headmaster after Warre, who was succeeded by Edward Lyttelton. My tutor told me how Lord Cobham, Lyttelton's brother and one of the Governors of Eton with whom the election lay, rushed out of the room where the decision was taken crying " We've got him in ! " Even Hugh Macnaghten, a cousin of my mother, who took Sixth Form when I was in it and was the most accomplished Eton classical scholar of his time, did not touch Rawlins's mark as an inspiring teacher. Hurst did not stay long at Eton but went to the Bar where for his massive form he became known as " Bull " Hurst and was undoubtedly destined for a successful career when he died not far from the age of forty. Apart from the glimpse he gave me of the grandeur of mathematics Hurst had a curious influence on me. He asked me where I was going after Eton. I said, to Trinity, Cambridge, to read history. Then he said : " Oh, you've got a great man there, Lord Acton." This was the first time I had heard the name of one who was afterwards to mean much in my life. Something in the way Hurst spoke struck me profoundly and inspired in me the conviction that I was going to find the master whom probably all boys unconsciouly seek. · Marten's teaching had already made history live for me. He dealt largely with economic history, then just coming into its own, but made every historical subject so vivid that boys under him realised the continuity of life in the past with that of the present and the importance to everyone of knowing whence they had sprung and of what stuff was made the commercial, political, and industrial world in which we all live. It may prove a boon to England that Sir Henry Marten was at hand to teach history and constitutional practice to the heiress to England's throne.

Philip Cobbold, of the great banking family from East Anglia and as aforesaid one of the best slow bowlers of the day, was for a short space my fagmaster. It may not be amiss to say a word on fagging at Eton, a custom often misunderstood by the uninitiated. Those who have passed through it will not need convincing that no better system could be devised for giving boys that sense of discipline which alone can lead later to a capacity for leadership. I do not mean that all former fags are capable of taking the lead in after life ; but it is sure that fagging for elder boys, that is, being at their service for certain, by no means onerous, personal duties for a year or more, inculcates promptness, accuracy, and willingness to carry out reasonable orders, and that this in turn leads to reasonableness in giving orders and ability to see them carried out. The system, from my time onwards at least, was based on the recognition of differences in power and responsibility and, within that framework, of equality between him who gives and him who obeys orders. It was achieved without the slightest presumption, pretentiousness, or arrogance, with a total absence of bullying, and with punishment inflicted only for serious negligence. Fagging has also the advantage that lower boys have a direct incentive to work hard and so get into Upper School when they will be fags no longer. It is an inspiriting moment when one of the seniors yells out : " Boy-oy-oy-oy ! " and all the fags in the house rush to his room. The last one to get there has to run the errand required.

Like the rest of the world Eton has undergone changes in the last half-century. But unlike most things in the world changes at Eton have only been for the better. Vast new playing fields were acquired through the generosity of old Etonians, so saving the school from threatened encroachment by industrial Slough, and a fine school hall and library were built. Many of the old houses were rebuilt and re-equipped ; others came into being. Besides these are new schools and laboratories, among which special mention should be made of the magnificent Art School with large facilities for the study of drawing, painting and sculpture. Education has grown in freedom and in breadth. Yet Eton now seems more compact as well as more complete than when I was there. Two internal changes of far-reaching and beneficent character have been introduced. The first is the rule that housemasters may retain their houses for a limited period only. Formerly a man might drag on, less and less competent, until forced by ill health to resign or released by preferment. Not all did so, certainly, but the possibility existed and was the cause of occasional " bad " houses. Now none of the housemasters is above middle-age, and there is far more general communion between them and their boys than was often the case under the old system. The second change is the institution, within the house, of " the library ", a committee of the senior boys that takes charge of internal discipline and sees to the various arrangements required among themselves by the boys. Of old this, or most of it, was actually done by the senior boys grouped under the Captain of the house, and any boy in Sixth Form, the Field, the Eleven, or the Eight would naturally have and use influence in his house. But the definiteness of having now a formally constituted authority to which new members are co-opted as the upper boys leave the school appears to me to have been accompanied by a serious advance in reliability, responsibility, and organising ability. Another notable change has taken place in the attitude towards work. In my time there was plenty of work done. The notion often to be found in silly books that Eton is a school for ignoramuses and idlers was always ludicrous. Any boy who wanted to work could work ; many worked very hard, and good tutors and division masters gave them every encouragement. The successes of old Etonians at the universities and in the professions is proof positive of this. But of old it was possible not to work. The pressure put upon idle boys was spasmodic. Now it is made very difficult for any boy to waste his time. The net result of all these changes is an air at Eton of alertness, solidarity, active contentment, and modernity, besides a noticeable increase in personal ambition among the boys, that affords a striking vindication of the efforts of those who have guided Eton's fortunes during the last generation and a half.

CHAPTER VIII

CAMBRIDGE

TO go from school to the university is as for a chrysalis to find itself a butterfly and discover the use of wings. Not so much the acquisition of greater freedom of action, pleasing though this be, but the realisation of a mental realm beyond the bounds of previous imagination makes this step the entrance into a new life or, to be more accurate, into life of the mind as it really is. The legend of the happiest days of life being spent at school can hold water only for those who are good enough to shine at athletics at school and yet not good enough at the university, and who have little or no other interest in life. It is not by the way exclusively boys who are good at games that turn out the best at them afterwards; for Eric Crossley, the son, so to speak, of Crossley's Gas Engines, who was at Luxmoore's with me and went up to Cambridge the same year had barely shewn more than usual athletic prowess at Eton; at Cambridge he quickly became a double Blue. Nor is it true that athletic ability precludes success in the schools at the University. Among those up with me were Mackay, scholar of Trinity, a lawn tennis Blue, or rather half Blue as it was then, and a prominent Wimbledon player, and Walter Morley Fletcher, amateur hurdles champion, a Fellow of the college and afterwards assistant Professor of Physiology. Among the judges there have been a dozen rowing Blues, one Cambridge quarter-miler became Bishop of Norwich, an Oxford three-miler Lord Chief Justice, and Lord Justice Chitty had in his time been called the best wicket-keeper in the country. I had been happy at Eton, but nothing there could equal the warmth, the vividness, the variety, and the expansion of life that awaited me at Cambridge.

Pollocks have been an Eton family for three generations; but they have been at Trinity for five. Not that the slightest favouritism was shewn me on that account; favouritism did

SIR FREDERICK (W. F.) POLLOCK ("GOOD SIR FREDERICK")

From a drawing by Samuel Lawrence

not exist at Cambridge, and besides there had been too many Pollocks at Trinity for one more to evoke any particular interest, the more so as I did not go up with a scholarship, but won mine in my second year. Everyone had to drive his own plough, and no more attention was paid even to the great-nephew of Macaulay, one of Trinity's and England's most shining lights, than to any Jones or Robinson till he had proved his own worth, as he very speedily did, with what success the whole world knows. In this Cambridge had the advantage of London, where heredity was a thing to be reckoned with and the heritage might be heavy. The unfortunate Pen Browning, son of Robert and Elizabeth Barrett Browning, was so pestered by literary snobs that he removed to Dinant in Belgium. On Mabel Robinson asking him why he had chosen such a tiny, irremediably provincial spot for a home, he answered : " Because it's the only place I have found where Browning means no more than Brown." To those with eyes to see, the university opens new horizons. Yet they are not disclosed all at once. The freshman has not the sensation of having, like Cortez silent upon a peak in Darien, a new, uncharted ocean before him. Rather it is the sensation of being plunged into an unknown stream and having to learn to swim with or perhaps against it. It is only when the motions of swimming have become easy and in the end swimming itself second nature that your undergraduate can begin to recognise the thrilling nature of such waters or the virile delight to be got therefrom.

It is impossible for the older to make the younger generation understand how easy, how spacious was life for everybody before the war of 1914. I say deliberately, for everybody. Real prices were lower in comparison with wages and salaries for the working man as well as for the middle classes. Nor is it a question of prices merely. Not only were all commodities required for the high standard of comfort attained at that date cheaper, but the quality of the commodities themselves was higher. This is true of all food and drink, and particularly of the British workingman's drink, beer ; of all foods, of tobacco and the pipes to smoke it in, of heating in one's home and of clothes to cover one's body. As regards price, it is true of all entertainments and of all books, and if the former do not always form an essential part of a young man's life, the latter do. The printing of books, moreover, was without stint ; if you wanted a book, you just ordered it. Dreadful Dora, whose oppressive hand has been spread yet wider in the last war and by scabrous Socialist snoopers in today's uneasy peace, had not yet been born. How can those who have never known an era of simple plenty comprehend this ? The answer is that they cannot. A young man of twenty remarked last year that he had never been able to go into a shop and buy eggs. So without trying to be persuasive on the subject I state as a fact that this ease of life and the sense of spaciousness that flowed from it had a vital influence on Cambridge, as of course on all universities, for undergraduates at the beginning of this century. It was an accepted fact that a man who aimed at getting a first class in his tripos must read during his three years' course as it was then for a minimum of eight hours a day, not including lectures and by no means letting up altogether in vacation ; in fact a great deal of reading was done in the Long Vacation term, when residence was optional and there were no distractions to hamper the studious such as Chapel, lectures, and social duties. " Reading " at Cambridge comprises work of all sorts for an examination : a man " reads " for his mathematical or Natural Science tripos as well as in classics or history. But reading for examinations, though a most important factor, was far from being the whole basis of university education, in which an equally essential part was played by the constant intermingling with your fellow-undergraduates, your elders, and the dons. Whereas masters at a school are a race apart from the boys, even for one who happened to be under a housemaster of superlative quality like Luxmoore at Eton or Bowen at Harrow, Cambridge dons treated undergraduates on an equality, always ready to help, to advise, to entertain, but never, never patronising, hectoring, or rebuking effort however childish. Once at A. W. Verrall's I heard an undergraduate declare : " I think Marie Corelli the greatest of all novelists." Verrall answered, quite simply and politely : " Well, if you think so, of course you're quite right to say so." Pulverisation of the poor wretch might have put him completely off all taste for literature in the future : treated as one who had the right to an opinion, even to such an opinion

he might—who knows ?—learn better. Association with seniors
—I do not mean Senior members of the University, i.e. Masters
of Arts, but men senior to yourself, second year men when you
are a freshman, then third year men, then Bachelors of Arts,
and all mixed up together—and with dons was carried on often
by invitations to breakfast, rarely by luncheon-parties, except
those at the houses of married dons, but on a lavish scale by tea-
and coffee-parties of an evening, when you could drop in to any
friend's, unless his door was " sported ", that is, the outer door
of his rooms shut : the door, for those who know it not, fastens
with a spring lock and can only be opened from outside with
a key, and the full phrase is " to sport your oak ", but I doubt
if I ever heard it used. There you might find one or two or
half a dozen other men, drinking tea or coffee, eating buns, and
discussing all things in heaven and earth. In an age when
everyone accepting an invitation fears to devour his host's rations
and at least knows he must return it without having the where-
withal to do so, this exhilarating communal hospitality that
existed in college when the gates were shut for the night can
no longer flourish. Tobacco and cigarettes were as free as
drinks piping hot from the hob of a roaring fire : now fires
roar no more and tobacco costs 4s. an ounce or upwards. Dons
would have regular days when they were at home to all and
sundry. St. John Parry, a much-beloved tutor at Trinity in
my day, and thereafter Vice-Master, always had a crowd in his
rooms on Sunday ; and his benign influence was even bettered
by that of Denis Winstanley, my exact contemporary who
succeeded Parry in his office and besides having a finer brain
than Parry earned a wide reputation as an inimitable raconteur.
On Sundays too Anthony Ashley Bevan, celebrated Arabian
scholar, had a constant supply of delicious chocolate brewed
by himself and in his precise, somewhat old-maidish way led
the talk on to elastic speculation of all kinds, enjoying an occasional shock as when F. M. Cornford, who later carried on the
torch lit by Jane Harrison, the great classical philosopher, was
championing the cause of complete truth in art. His theme
was Greek sculpture and the essential purity of Aubrey Beardsley's
drawings then greatly shocking the philistines and how the artist
should reveal the whole truth of the female form. On which

Stuart, the College chaplain and a very enlightened man, put in : " Have you ever seen the *whole* truth of it portrayed ? " Cornford was obliged to confess that he had not. Guy Le Strange once told me, apropos of Bevan's curious streak of prudery, how he had spent an evening with Bevan and with Vambéry, a Hungarian orientalist of fame, and how Bevan became greener and greener as the Hungarian amused himself by pouring forth a stream of wholly unprintable Eastern tales. And on great occasions there were gatherings at Henry Jackson's, the Socrates of Trinity, who kept open house especially on the night of the Commemoration feast. Among the younger men, B.A.'s when I went up, always ready to promote talk among their juniors, were George Macaulay Trevelyan, already enjoying among his friends the fame that became his throughout the world as historian and still later as Master of the College, G. E. Moore whose thin volume *Principia Ethica* shook the established schools of philosophy by its daring insight and simplicity of thought, and Walter Morley Fletcher, his brilliance as doctor and physiologist enhanced by athletic renown. It was Fletcher who found an annihilating retort to the pretensions of Christian Science. A relative of his who had become converted to Mrs. Eddy's pseudo-religion was holding forth on the falsity of all medical and surgical treatment. Fletcher said : " If you're sincere in what you say, why do you undergo a surgical operation yourself ? " " Never, never ! " blustered the other. " I shouldn't dream of doing such a thing." " Well," returned Fletcher, " you shave, don't you ? " After this no more could be said of the futility of surgery. Old Trinity men, not long gone down, often came up and joined in the mental sparring, among them R. A. Wright, later Lord Wright and one of our greatest judges, C. P. Sanger whose early death prevented his attaining similar eminence and joined to his brilliance in the law a still greater intellectual variety, W. W. Greg, that unparalleled student of Shakespeare, and Bertrand Russell, already known as an exceptional mathematician, now one of the leaders of the world's thought. Russell, who was of a contrary disposition though of the sweetest temper, loved an argument. One evening at Trevelyan's he was descanting on the foolishness of athletic exercise and the excessive importance attributed in

England to games. "Look at me," he said, "I never take any exercise, and my body's perfectly healthy." On this I put in : "Ah ! But is it beautiful ? " I was quite unprepared for the roar of laughter that greeted this sally. I was full of a theory of my own, in which I still believe there to be something, that games and sports have value in proportion to the beauty intrinsic in them and that an unconscious sense in their devotees of this beauty is one element in their popularity : how else indeed do you explain the intoxicating reputation with the crowd of artists like Jim Driscoll and Jack Hobbs, than whom may have been stouter boxers and bats but none more elegant ? I was far too much in youthful earnest to want to poke fun at Bertrand Russell ; nonetheless the wind was quite taken out of his sails.

Besides these delights at Trinity there was another special to the place and that was the chance to form a respectable gastronomic taste. Not that the daily cooking in college was out of the ordinary. It was sound enough and leagues apart from the state of things guyed by Sir George Trevelyan in his sparkling parody *Horace at Athens* where the hero complains of the fare served in Hall as

> Veal void of stuffing, widowed of its ham,
> Or the roast shoulder of an ancient ram.

And again

> Veal that is tottering on the verge of beef.

But Commemoration dinner was a marvel not to be forgotten. I remember an Audit luncheon at King's where I was a guest and the food had been specially selected and offered by the College tenants : there were fat oysters, luscious turbot, cold plump partridges, and a finer madeira than I ever tasted elsewhere. But Trinity at its best was unbeatable. Even the vegetables—rare phenomenon in England—were good. The sole was perfection, and nowhere could rounds of beef and turkeys be better roasted. The acme of the feast was the sweets. The Trinity kitchens had two jealously guarded secrets : one was the " hard " sauce served with plum pudding, the other *crème brulée*. Various Cambridge colleges had recipes for the latter but nowhere was the Trinity *crème brulée* equalled. It consisted—for it lies murdered by post-war restrictions—of what I think the

French call *crème bacchique* as a foundation or of the delectable and equally defunct Russian *gourievskaya kasha*, and on top of that a thick layer of caramelised sugar. Easy for cook to make, think you, out of any reputable cookery book? Not so. For in the foundation *crème* was just something, and in that ice of thick smooth sugar was just something else, which raised the dish to the standards of Elysium. What were those somethings? Marsala? sherry? brandy? maraschino? You may take your choice and yet be wrong, for it will not be known till that day when all secrets are revealed. "Hard" sauce was of course a brandy and butter sauce. Its peculiarity was that after being served to a hundred diners it did not melt but still stood up stiff to be cut. I never saw this but at Trinity. Also plum-pudding was served with a second sauce, semi-liquid this, to be used at the same time, and subject to correction I suspect it to have been made with cherry brandy. Before dessert and speeches at Commemoration two huge silver loving cups went round the Hall. They were filled with that potent, delicious drink, another Trinity secret, known as Audit ale. As the loving cup reached your neighbour from his right hand, you stood up while he drank; he passed it to you and while you drank remained standing, your left hand neighbour rising at the same moment. Thus three men were always on their feet, the middle man drinking from the cup so large that both hands were needed to hold it, the other two (so the historic custom was explained) ready to guard the drinker from sudden assault. It was an impressive ceremony. Trinity's cellars were renowned. If King's beat us for madeira, our claret, port, and when I went up champagne were in the highest class. For the two former a palate needs long and careful training, such as could be begun by young Fellows of the College in the Combination Room; but even a freshman could recognise the perfection of the champagne served at college feasts. When I went up it was Ayala; I am sorry to say that I do not know the year, but I never tasted any so good till the Pol Roger of 1928. On my first appearance in the Combination Room at Trinity the Fellows were still drinking the almost mythical 1834 port. Soon it was reserved for grand occasions only; then it ceased. I was present on a memorable evening. It was known that the last bottle of the '34 port was to be drunk and the attendance was higher than usual. Exalted hope of participating in a unique historical occasion possessed the juniors' souls, while seniors reflected tragically on the glories of the past. The butler, who at Trinity rejoices in the official title of the Manciple, put the decanter on the table in front of the Vice-Master, Aldis Wright, saying with a sob in his voice : " The last bottle of the '34 port, sir." Out of respect for so noble a vintage, no one touched his glass until the decanter had gone round the table and all the glasses were charged. Expectation was poignant. Then the Vice-Master raised his glass and put it to his lips. Then he set it down. " Corked," he ejaculated with disgust amid general stupor. If ever ecstasy was debunked, it was then. Afterwards I asked Aldis Wright, an acute connoisseur of port, whether he thought the '34 port was better than the '57 which succeeded it or the '68 that soon followed. " Not a bit," he barked in his dry, emphatic tone.

Erant fortes ante Agamemnona. Doubtless after him too. Memory is apt to exaggerate the excellence of what one has known at the expense of perhaps equal virtue outside its ken. No one can know succeeding generations at the university as well as he does his own. Yet I cannot but think that my years at Trinity produced an unusual crop of talent. I am happy in having been up with a dozen men who made a mark in after life that will never be effaced. To take my own subject first, the Trinity Historical Society, founded by Lord Acton, begot three historians of the first rank : G. M. Trevelyan, G. P. Gooch and Denis Winstanley. Of Trevelyan I need do no more than speak his name : his works take rank with the classics of our historical literature, his influence as Regius Professor of History and as Master of Trinity has been profound at Cambridge and far beyond the banks of Cam. George Gooch was Lord Acton's favourite pupil. Even at that early age his learning was exceptional and his mind sought ideas behind the facts of history. Acton, I have been told, was violently angry when Gooch was not awarded a Fellowship. His failure was due to the opposition of Archdeacon Cunningham, a powerful voice among the electors ; Cunningham said that the dissertation submitted by

[1] Denis Winstanley.

Gooch showed no signs of original thought but was a compilation merely. Wherein Cunningham showed his own want of originality, being indeed a very matter-of-fact man. Honours of every kind, and an honorary Fellowship at Trinity have since made ample amends for this rebuff to one of the most accomplished historians of the last half-century. Since it is perhaps less well known than his works on European diplomacy, British foreign policy, and Frederick the Great that are written with no less grace than penetration, I will mention Gooch's *Annals of Politics and Culture*, a compendium of facts and dates of decisive originality that has been a valued companion to me throughout the years. " Oh dear," sighed Montagu Butler, then Master of Trinity, on Gooch not winning the Fellowship that was his due, " I do hope we are not refusing another James Anthony Froude," who had also been an unsuccessful candidate for a Fellowship at his college. On this it was later remarked that whatever Trinity was refusing, it was certainly not another Froude, one of the least accurate of historians. Some surprise may be felt at my joining Winstanley's name to these two most eminent historians. True, his work *Unreformed Cambridge* and its successors deal with a restricted subject, but it broke such fresh ground, letting in a flood of light on curious and important phases of university history, which after all goes to form a large part of the intellectual life of the nation, that it deserves the compliment. On my once asking him what he thought of the *Dictionary of National Biography*, Lord Acton answered concisely : " It doesn't get us any further." Apart from the astounding scope of knowledge revealed by this remark—an ordinary man indeed can barely imagine any searcher for biographical truth finding that the *D.N.B.* did not get him " any further "—it invites the obvious inference that one main object of historical study is precisely to " get us further ", i.e. to reveal new wells of knowledge concerning the past. Winstanley's researches, related in an extremely pleasing and human way that was very much his own, do distinctly get us further on the path of knowledge of the past and of our fellowmen. On this ground therefore his name must be coupled, though on a lower plane, with those of two of the finest historians Cambridge has produced.

Among contemporaries there were but two others about

whose achievements I am competent to hold an opinion of my own. They are A. A. Milne and Desmond MacCarthy, happily both still alive to carry on the long Trinity tradition of literature in which the top lights were Dryden, Byron, Tennyson, and Thackeray. No one, I suppose, will challenge MacCarthy's position as the most delicate and most understanding literary critic of his generation. At Eton he had been at Miss Evans's, the last of the real " dames' " houses : I say, real, because after her and indeed earlier too mathematical masters who had houses but were unable to be classical tutors were known as " dames ", two well-known such men in my time being " Hoppy " Daman, so called from his peculiar method of pedestrian progression, and " Old Mo ", the inevitable nickname of Moseley who inherited the remains of Cornish's house. Like many from Evans's, MacCarthy in early days at Cambridge was of a sporting disposition and went in for riding. He had an heroic story of a semi-mad undergraduate who in MacCarthy's own rooms at Trinity calmly declared to a mixed audience that MacCarthy was his illegitimate brother. This impudent fabrication so enraged the future Doctor of Letters that he snatched a hunting crop from the wall intent on summary vengeance ; but, as he plaintively related, " It's so difficult to horsewhip a man in an armchair," the lunatic having taken refuge in one of those low and immensely deep wickerwork easy chairs that adorned all Cambridge rooms. Of A. A. Milne it is equally unnecessary to speak. His wonderful creation of " Pooh " and that noble company has gone the round of the globe. But for conscience' sake I must record my opinion that Milne's play *The Dover Road* is nearly as perfect a specimen of a comedy as exists in the English language and by itself entitles its author to a high place among dramatists. Those who saw it acted by Henry Ainley and Allan Aynesworth had a rare treat.

Besides others already mentioned incidentally—Moore, Fletcher, and Cornford—a bevy of notable men sprang from those years at Trinity, among them Sir Henry Dale, the leading European physiologist and P.R.S. during the years of the late war, G. H. Hardy acknowledged by others if not by himself the foremost pure mathematician of his generation, E. W. Barnes, Bishop of Birmingham, learned mathematician and notably controversial theologian, the Earl of Lytton, sometime Governor of Bengal, Sir James Jeans, applied mathematician and populariser of recent astronomical discoveries, a fine musician too, and St. John Filby, greatest of modern, perhaps of all, Arabian explorers. Austin Smyth, a very fine classical scholar, would have done more in the world save for the invincible modesty that led him to the quiet post of librarian to the House of Commons. Smyth had written an introduction to the *Agamemnon* of Æschylus intended to be published with a new edition of the play. He sent it for an opinion to Walter Headlam of King's who enjoyed the reputation of an outstanding Greek scholar. Headlam lost the MS., which was discovered amid a welter of papers only after his death. Headlam, however, besides mislaying Smyth's MS., had totally lost the title-page with Smyth's name and the covering letter sent him with it. So here was supposed to be a new introduction to the *Agamemnon* by Headlam himself and as such it was published with rejoicing by the University of Cambridge. Smyth behaved with exemplary, indeed excessive forbearance. An apology was of course forthcoming, but Smyth might well have insisted on ampler publicity for his work. He was a gay, witty companion. Once travelling in Austria we met at Salzburg Donald Tovey and the inevitable Miss Weisse. This earnest-minded lady, German born, spoke impeccable English. But there were turns in our tongue that escaped her and now at luncheon in the crowded Speisesaal of the Elektricitäts-Hotel (electric lighting in the Salzkammergut was still young), suddenly let off in all innocence an impropriety enormous enough to have made a Restoration dramatist blush. Smyth, Donald, and I felt, as the saying is, like nothing on earth. From this earth, like Hardy, Jeans, Victor Lytton, Fletcher, Cornford, Waterlow, and Winstanley, Smyth has now passed. Time's wingèd chariot ceases not its hurrying.

A certain rebellious streak in me came to light at Cambridge. If you were on academic business—lectures or Chapel—and after dark, you were compelled to wear the regulation cap and gown. Otherwise there was no prescribed garment or head-gear. It may seem strange, but until my time no one had ever gone hatless in the streets of Cambridge or capless down to the football field or lawn-tennis court. I started doing just this.

Elder men, and the dons, were horrified. It was a positive revolution. But the hatless creed made its way and became an established faith. " So you belong to the no-hat brigade ? " diehards would scornfully accost you. The no-hat brigade swelled until half a century later it is almost the exception for a man to wear a hat save on formal occasions. Soon only cads will wear hats. Another trouble was the football clubs. There were in Trinity three soccer clubs : Trinity Etonians, Trinity Harrovians, and the Rest, which last having the pick of men from Charterhouse, Marlborough, and the other soccer schools was far stronger than the two first. From the point of view of the ordinary undergraduate their weakness was that all three existed primarily for playing matches. I wanted to be able to play simple games. So with G. H. Hardy, H. M. Joseph, afterwards a very well-known doctor and skilful, and one or two others, I formed a club of our own for this purpose. We called it the Nomad Scythians. Again the idea caught on. We hired a field and, with a membership that speedily grew to be over three-score strong, it was rare that we could not get three good games a week. Again the proceeding was thought quite revolutionary. A solemn meeting was arranged between the Scythian ringleaders and the great men of the established clubs, who thought that by appealing to our better feelings and offering advantages to certain among us they might break the movement up. But we held firm, and within two years the Scythians, dropping their first name, had a printed card with " The Trinity Scythians " on it, colours of their own, and were actually playing matches against other college second elevens. Once we even played a match against the Athenians, an inter-college club considered as anteroom to the University eleven. The Athenians had three blues playing and beat us easily 4-love. The moral victory lay with the club that had been despised as a set of ragamuffins and I know not what. But the Scythians' first aim remained to provide games for those who wanted to play them, and for over twenty years the Scythians went on doing it. Hard-working undergraduates and Bachelors formed their backbone. It was inspiring to see Walter Fletcher, one of the fastest men in the world over hurdles, racing after the ball only to miss it clean, and George Trevelyan devoting all his earnestness to a fierce kick at the ball, sometimes in the wrong direction. Joseph and I were the regular centre forwards ; Hardy an accomplished full-back.

The third revolution in this miniature series that I put through concerned Chapel. One of the great achievements of nineteenth-century progress was the admission of Catholics to the University. This was followed in due course by the exemption from obligatory attendance at College chapel of all Catholics and dissenters from the Church of England. I did not consider myself a member of the Anglican persuasion, so refused to go to Chapel. Hauled before the Junior Dean I gave my reason. Why was I not a member of the Church of England ? he asked. Was I a Catholic ? Of course not ! Was I a member of any known sect ? No ! Had I not been confirmed ? This time it was for me to answer : No. Indeed ! Why not ? Because, I said, I could not honestly repeat the Athanasian creed. But the Junior Dean was not stumped yet. Had I not been baptised ? Of course I had ! Then I was *ipso facto* a member of the C. of E. and must go to Chapel. My answer was simple : if I had been baptised, it was without my knowledge and without my consent, and without consent no one can be a member of any body. The Junior Dean threatened me with " gating ", with being " sent down ". An appeal went to higher quarters, with the obvious result. Once freedom of conscience was admitted, it was impossible to force an objector who had not otherwise than as an infant been admitted to the Church of England to attend its services. So thereafter I went to Chapel only when I listed, as I have often attended service in other places of worship. The Junior Dean was ill-advised to push the matter to an issue. Had he accepted my personal explanation, there would have been no fuss, no decision at all. As it was, a precedent had been created. Before the 1914 war compulsory Chapel was altogether dropped.

Cambridge at the beginning of this century was blessed with a real splendour of professors and dons. In economics Marshall and Foxwell, in pure mathematics Forsyth, in surgery Marsh, in art Waldstein, in physiology Michael Foster, in astronomy Sir Robert Ball, in archæology Sir William Ridgeway, in Latin Mayr who, it was said, had not only immortalised Juvenal but buried him in a vast edition of the poet's works, in Greek Verrall and Jebb, in eastern tongues Cowell and Browne, in biology Shipley, were all household names in university circles ; and professors of note not only shine in their own subjects but spread a great luminosity through planes having no direct contact with their orbits. Some of these reputations did not maintain the same height in after-years. Forsyth, then classed as one of the first four living mathematicians, was later greatly deconsidered : Hardy once told me that his position was afterwards as much over-decried as it had previously been exaggerated. Yet Forsyth was a notable figure. He was the son of a Scottish crofter, who had risen purely by his own brains to become Regius Professor at Cambridge. An innate nervous tension accentuated by a certain inferiority complex in the society of men sprung from easier surroundings gave Forsyth the appearance of fierceness but, once the shell was pierced, he was accessible and even forthcoming. He had an uncommon physical gift in a pair of the darkest, most piercing eyes you could ever find : I have only seen the like in that champion chess player, Capablanca. Forsyth could look straight at the midday sun at the height of summer without blinking. He startled the university world by running away with my cousin Marion, the wife of Professor Bois of London University, a physicist highly regarded for his feat of weighing the earth, and resigned his chair at Cambridge to find reward in an ideally happy marriage and a professorship of almost equal importance at the Imperial College of Science. Waldstein of King's, Professor of Fine Art, was another man impossible to overlook. Later he modified his name and blossomed into a new phase of life as Sir Charles Walston. His detractors hinted that Waldstein's knowledge of art was like a dealer's. But the fact remained that his enthusiasm for painting and sculpture was an inspiration to many and he was right in maintaining that Herculaneum, when excavated, would prove a storehouse of Greek and Roman sculpture of the highest quality. I enjoyed Waldstein's company not a little. He had real imagination and I always found him an encouraging influence. Once when Waldstein was reading a paper to a learned society, Archdeacon Cunningham was heard to explode : " I wish that confounded American-German-Jew would go back to his respective countries and stay there ! " Which Waldstein repaid at a lecture of Cunningham's by flinging himself out of the room, stuttering : " Devil ! Hogwash ! Damn ! " Waldstein was undeniably a snob, vying in this with Oscar Browning, also of King's. On the death of a royal princess Waldstein went into deep mourning. Now it seemed he had finally bested O. B., as his rivalry for royal acquaintances was widely known : not, by the way, *the* O. B., a mistake often made after his death. O. B. was not visible for several days. Waldstein triumphed. But then the discomfiting truth leaked out : O. B.'s grief was such that he had taken to his bed.

That bombastic personage O. B. was, for a history lecturer, the most slipshod of men. My first contact with him was the receipt of a postcard with the words : " Why have you not answered my invitation to luncheon ? " I replied, also on a postcard : " I have received no invitation from you to luncheon." Which was the fact. Once O. B. wrote a life of Peter the Great in a hotel at Cannes, without any books of reference : it was a thoroughly bad book. His was a brilliant brain ruined by excess of facility. He could master all subjects so easily that, despite the best intentions, he ceased to be master of any. The speed at which he galloped through work ended by his getting nowhere. Verrall told me that he had seen O. B. writing and that O. B. wrote physically as fast as he, Verrall, could think : anyone who knew Verrall's power of quick, clear thought could guess what this meant. Oscar Browning was a genial host. The evenings in his rooms at King's rivalled those at " Monty " James's, where the future Provost of Eton, one of the most learned men in Europe and the leading authority on the Mediæval Church, thrilled a younger generation by telling those eerie tales afterwards published as *Ghost Stories of an Antiquary*. It was of kindly, fat, esurient Oscar Browning that J. K. Stephen, lamented after death as truly as he was admired in life, Leslie Stephen's nephew and follower in the Cambridge line of light classical verse writers led by the inimitable Calverley, wrote the quatrain :

> O. B., oh be obedient
> To Nature's stern decree !
> Or else, instead of one O. B.,
> You will be too obese.

I saw J. K. S. once only. That was when I was at Wilkinson's, the two being warm friends. I was no more than nine, but was struck by J. K. S.'s handsome face, herculean frame, and wild look. He had been hit on the head by a windmill sail ; the blow gradually deranged his mind, then killed him. Another of his squibs never, I fancy, printed was against a winner of the University Prize Poem with an effort that he was alleged to have stolen :

> Lo ! I am — — ; you look a bit disgusted !
> I too have known the taste of self-disgust.
> Lo now ! I am not asking to be trusted.
> Lo ! you may kick me if you really must !

Cambridge, as strangers to it may by now have realised, was a place where hard knocks were given and taken. None was keener for the fray than Sir William Ridgeway, illustrious as author of the only book published by the University Press ever to be reviewed in the *Sporting Life* otherwise the *Pink 'Un*, bawdy, scurrilous, clever rag that it was. Ridgeway's book, entitled *The Origin and Influence of the Thoroughbred Horse*, was that noble animal's scientific story back to prehistoric times. No other review, it was said, gave the author such pleasure. Ridgeway nearly killed poor Walter Leaf, a scholar who had early left university life to blossom forth as a director of the National Provincial Bank, by insulting him in print in the course of some quite academic argument as " a lickspittle of the German school ". Leaf fractiously replied that his assailant " must be a practised polemist ". Polemics was one of the chief joys of resident seniors. Sometimes a dealer in the bludgeon school was overcome by a rapier. This was the fate of Walter Headlam who fell foul of Verrall over one of the latter's publications that Headlam slanged with outright abuse. Verrall wrote so elegant and restrained a reply that Headlam's friends had to throw up the sponge. Headlam went about muttering : " Well, I may not know " . . . this and that . . . " as well as he does, but I think I do know what an Athenian gentleman did when he was drunk." Arthur Verrall, patient as a saint under the crippling pain of the arthritis that ultimately killed him, was in Kipling's word a devoted " Janeite ". He virtually knew Jane Austen by heart. He was one of the most brilliant talkers as well as writers of our age ; and his book *Four Plays of Euripides* shows in him, it is barely too much to say, not only a great critic and scholar but a man with the soul of a first-rate dramatist. Verrall and still more Mrs. Verrall were interested in the movement for psychical research, the main impulse for which at Cambridge was given by Frederick Myers, brother-in-law of Lady Stanley ("Dr. Livingstone, I presume ? "), and Professor Henry Sidgwick the philosopher. Sidgwick had gone in for séances and was one of the dupes of the medium Eusapia Palladino whose fraud was exposed by Maskelyne, the celebrated conjurer. Verrall's interest was mainly to establish some certainty in the matter of thought transference. He and his wife made the following experiment. He thought of a certain thing known to her and went on thinking of it ; she was to attempt by transference of his thought to her mind to discover what it was. The thing chosen by him was a line of Greek well known to both of them. After several months of vain endeavour the attempt was abandoned, Mrs. Verrall not having come within a mile of the desired goal. Verrall's interest in psychical research grew distinctly cooler.

There was one senior at Cambridge in my time of whom it would be wrong indeed not to speak. Though not a don, Albert Dew-Smith, commonly called Dew, was made a member of the High Table at Trinity. His official work was the grinding and polishing of lenses at the Cambridge Observatory and of laboratory microscopes, at which he was reputed to be unrivalled even by the best Germans. But his claim to fame lay still more in his having been the model for R. L. Stevenson's Attwater in *The Ebb Tide*. Six foot three, a grand, mysterious appearance and a carefully trimmed pointed beard gave semblance to a legend that was true. Dew was also the best portrait photographer that has ever lived, superior even to Mrs. Cameron ; his portraits of Joachim and Stevenson, as well as of a host of Cambridge worthies, will live so long as their names and memories survive. He had an exact knowledge of precious stones and used to carry sometimes a handful of the minor varieties loose in his pocket. To top all, he had married Alice Lloyd, once of Hind Head, who by her *Soul Shapes*, *Tom Tug and Others*, and *The White Umbrella*, and by her contributions to the *Pall Mall Gazette* then at the zenith of its career under Harry Cust, the handsomest editor London ever saw, had in a few years collected a record public of " fans " for her grace and fancy. The Dew-Smiths lived at Chesterton a few miles outside Cambridge in a lovely house and a lovely garden, always open to those that prized the welcome to be found there. Alas ! no one will ever read again so clever or intellectual an evening paper as the *P.M.G.* ; nor probably ever see so curious a character as Dew, nor— quite certainly—ever meet a writer of such elfin wit as Alice Dew.

Under the impulse of Lord Acton the historical school at Cambridge touched a level undreamt of with his predecessor Sir John Seeley, who despite two books with a touch of genius in them was in reality a second-rate historian. Acton, whose appointment Cambridge owed to the inspiration of Lord Rosebery, was far from being alone. Outside Trinity (though a Trinity man too) was F. W. Maitland whose genius, to repeat my father's word of him, was not only for law but for history, and his acolyte the Rev. J. N. Figgis of Cat's, more formally St. Catherine's ; also Professor Gwatkin, a pundit of late Byzantine and ecclesiastical learning, who saving his cloth—he was D.D.—positively revelled in scandal at the court of the Emperor Justinian ; and again Sir Adolphus Ward, Master of Peterhouse, with German history at his fingers' ends, a charming and considerate person, for all that Acton in a moment of irritation had called him " a high-stepping hearse horse ". At Trinity were Cunningham, another D.D. and Archdeacon of Ely, and Stanley Leathes, formerly Captain of the School at Eton. Cunningham, whose *magnum opus*, *The Growth of English Industry and Commerce*, created a revolution in our historical tendencies, appeared to me ideally to illustrate the classical definition of an archdeacon as " one who fulfills archidiaconal functions ", for it would be hard to imagine anyone less traditionally clerical than Cunningham with his tremendous horse-laugh and his disdain for all, in his view, inferior intellects. Leathes, who later was a K.C.B. and senior Civil Service Commissioner, applied a welcome spice of levity in his teaching. He once began a lecture with the words : " Gunpowder was invented in the fourteenth century A.D.—or perhaps B.C." He, together with Sir Adolphus Ward, inherited the editorship of the mighty *Cambridge Modern History* planned by Acton, who died before its publication began. Of Acton himself I must speak separately. He towered among these eminent men like the Jungfrau herself among the peaks of her fortress range. Leathes's father had been a well-known dean, disliked for some reason or other by Montagu Butler. Leathes, when senior B.A. at Trinity, had to make a speech at Commemoration, a custom afterwards dropped. As he sat down, Butler, all smiles, called out in his most dulcet yet penetrating tones : "Just like his dear father—flippant and dull."

Dr. Montagu Butler, Master of Trinity, during my six years' residence at Cambridge, provided a background of endless delight. Tall, large, gracious, courtly, he was, as my father has testified,[1] the best-beloved Master of the nineteenth century. His peculiarity was that no one could feel sure whether, by exercise of his mellifluous charm, he was not making ferocious game of someone. My own belief is that he got vast enjoyment from saying or doing unexpected things in seemingly innocent fashion. On one occasion he held up a university procession, apparently wrapped in deep thought, to come out of his abstraction with the words : "Now, what *was* the name of that perfect gentleman who died of bleeding of the nose ? " In speaking he made use of a slow, uncommon emphasis on a word here and there. In a London bus he once electrified the passengers by calling from one end of it to the head of a different Cambridge College he recognised at the other : "Master of *Jesus* ! Master of *Jesus* ! Is that *you* ? " The greeting, natural enough at Cambridge, was staggering to Cockneys. No one really ever knew, was Montagu Butler a sweet, simple old gentleman, or a slightly malicious wit with a schoolboy's delight in making people's flesh creep. Did he, to take another instance, once really go to sleep during the lesson in Chapel, to wake up at the end of it with a loud "Amen " ; or was this his covert way of showing how bad he thought the reading of the lesson had been ? Did he, when inveigled to take the chair at a religious meeting the propagandist spirit of which had been concealed from him—and he hated propaganda of all sorts—really mistake the speaker's meaning who adjured his hearers to say

[1] In *For My Grandson* (John Murray).

to themselves : " I may be a regular rotter " at this or that " but I can still do good to my fellow-men by," etc. etc. ? Or did the Master, who, moving a vote of thanks at the end, said beamingly and as by way of a grand compliment : " Whatever else we may think of him, at least no one will deny that he is a *regular rotter* at all good works," know precisely what he was saying, and mean it ? At the breakfasts that by custom the Master gave at the Lodge to relays of nervous freshmen, quite incapable of getting away decently when the meal was over, Butler would bend forward from the head of the table and chant, almost : " *Must* you go ? *Can't* you stay ? " His chanting speech produced intense pleasure at the High Table when he dined in Hall and read the Latin grace alternating sentence by sentence with the Vice Master. Butler, heavily sentimental, read with the modern Italian pronunciation and infinite emphasis : " *Oculi* in te *sperant, Domine.*" Aldis Wright, grim, stony, disapproving, snapped back in an uncompromising English twang : " Et tu das escam illis in tempore." And so on through the long grace. It is impossible for me not to think that the Master enjoyed provoking the contrast. He was quite capable of scoring off himself too. At one Commemoration, where the Master always made the speech of the evening, the chief guest, Lord Goschen I think, had put a question that Butler did not think fit to answer and evaded by quoting Longfellow's

> Cautiously replied the beaver,
> With discretion made he answer :
> " Give me time to ask the others,
> Let me ask the other beavers."

A roar of applause went up from the assembled M.A.'s, Bachelors, and especially from the undergraduates, instantly struck by the resemblance of the Master with his streaked spade beard to a benign beaver. Did the Master, in choosing the quotation, alone ignore the resemblance ? I think not indeed. For those he thought wanting in due respect to the College the Master had no mercy. To be a Trinity—a " *Ter-r-rinity* "—man, as he pronounced it, was in Butler's eyes a privilege beyond price, and one who did not recognise this was an infidel. The Principal of London University, Rucker, was a guest at one Commemoration and proposed the health of the College. Unhappily for him, he spoke too much about London, then chiefly known as an examining body, which irritated the Master as propaganda, and too little about Trinity, which for the Master was positively criminal. Butler rose to reply. With his most glowing smile and honeyed voice he turned to Rucker and pronounced these words : " *Oxford* we know, and *Durham* we know. But what are *these* ? " Not one other syllable did he utter about London, or about Rucker, who turned purple and nearly sank through the floor.

" Whatever we may think of him ", was a favourite formula with Montagu Butler on the war-path and about to scarify an unexpected victim. He bore a grudge against Edward VII who when Prince of Wales had insisted on smoking at the Lodge, a habit abhorrent to the Master. On Edward's accession the Master, in proposing the King's health at Commemoration, broke the unwritten rule against speaking to the toast and delivered an eloquent, slightly florid oration in praise of the new sovereign, working up to the climax : " Whatever *else* we may think of him "—shades and echoes of Tranby Cross !—" at least *no one* will deny that he shares the tastes of *all* his people." Tableau, in which the only person apparently unconscious of a double meaning was the Master himself. He used the same technique far more openly on Lord Halsbury, then Lord Chancellor, being the principal guest at the feast ; as such he had the task of proposing the College's health. Lord Halsbury, whether drunk or simply in a vile temper, got on his feet and after mumbling a few words plumped down again. Without showing the slightest sign of annoyance the Master in replying, as if to a properly proposed toast, this time in his most florid style, flung heavy compliments at the Lord Chancellor's head and finally in his sweetest way poured forth this blessing : " Whatever *else* we may think of him, at least no one will deny that he *never* forgets a *friend*." This time an almost audible thrill went through the Hall. It was just after Halsbury had raised to the Bench Grantham, Ridley, and Darling, in three of the most blatant political jobs within memory. Actually Darling turned out a very fair judge, but he had no more claim to a judgeship, save one arising out of party politics, than had Ridley, the Home Secretary's brother, who was a disastrous failure on the Bench. And this, it will be noted, was an impromptu on the Master's part, since he could have no idea beforehand that Halsbury would behave with such scandalous want of courtesy. There were, in the vernacular, no flies on Montagu Butler, the well and rightly beloved Master of Trinity.

CHAPTER IX

LORD ACTON AT CAMBRIDGE

WHEN Acton died, F. W. Maitland wrote an article on him in the *Cambridge Review*, which unless I am mistaken has never been reprinted. This is a pity. Maitland's judgment merited preservation in some more accessible form, for it was genius writing about greatness. One passage I have quoted below. Another runs:

"Really one must live in Little Peddlington and never transgress the parish boundary if one is to inform the British public (see a letter in the *Daily News* of July 8, 1902) that Lord Acton and his 'hoarded knowledge' counted for nothing in the Europe and Christendom of the nineteenth century."

Maitland goes on: "At last came the great opportunity" for which Acton had waited so many years, the planning of the *Cambridge Modern History*:

"at last and too late. We saw with wonder how eagerly it was seized, and how a project that might have been pedestrian, took horse, took wings and soared. All modern history—the scheme was large enough. Twelve stout volumes—there would be room for minutely truthful work. Stored knowledge, big thoughts, an acknowledged primacy, polyglot correspondence, ramifying friendships, the tact of a diplomatist, the ardour of a scholar, all were to be subservient in a noble cause to the greater glory of truth and right: to the greater glory, be it added, of a Cambridge he had learned to love. It was Napoleonic, I know no other word, and yet it is not adequate. I felt as if I had been permitted to look over the shoulder of a general who was planning a campaign that was to last for five centuries and extend throughout the civilized world. No doubt there was some overestimate of health and endurance and mere physical force, some forgetfulness of the weight of accumulating years. We feared it then, we know it now. But of such mistakes the brave will be guilty. And about mental power there was no mistake. With whatever doubts I had gone to his rooms, I came away saying to myself that if contributors failed, if the worst came to the worst, or perhaps the best to the best, Lord Acton could write the twelve volumes from beginning to end and (as the phrase goes) never turn a hair. But it was too late : too late by ten or fifteen years."

In what follows, which was indeed written not long after Lord Acton's death, I have tried to write of him as I saw him and to recapture the enthusiasm that his unique personality evoked in almost all who came into contact with it. Whether I have succeeded or not, I should perhaps ask pardon. Failure to transmit to others an impression of a great man is to do him a disservice. Success in the present case may now be thought somewhat youthful. German has an useful word, *schwärmen*, which means to conceive or to display baseless or excessive enthusiasm for somebody. The Fatherland of shoddy sentiment was full of *Schwärmerei*, generally for opera singers. If any reader thinks me *schwärmerisch* about Acton, I refer him to Maitland and submit that the effect is produced by my clumsiness of expression, not by any tinsel in the object of my description. No one can ever have lived less liable to provoke false emotion than Acton. It would be presumptuous in me to claim the power of pronouncing an adult judgment on such a man : I can write of him only as he appeared to the undergraduate and B.A. that I was during the four years I knew him, sat at his feet, and saw him constantly in private.

This Regius Professor of Modern History in whom Hurst, the mathematical master at Eton, had aroused my interest, was a striking figure. He spoke and wrote perfectly four languages and was versed in half a dozen others. He was descended from one of the noblest families in Europe, his full surname being Dalberg-Acton : when the mediæval Emperors of the Holy Roman Empire, so-called said a scoffer because it was neither holy nor Roman, took his seat in conclave, a herald cried out : " Is no Dalberg there ? " Since, were a Dalberg present, he had the privilege of sitting on the emperor's right hand. Acton came on both sides of an ancestry of statesmen, soldiers, and diplomatists. He had sat in Parliament. He had converted Gladstone to belief in Home Rule for Ireland. From his cradle he had mixed with men busy in shaping the world's fortunes. Before he was thirty he was recognised as one of the most learned men of his time. He was a Catholic and theologian no less than historian. One of the things that most intrigued the world about him was the comparatively small output of his mind. A personal friend of his recorded his wish that Acton " had more frequently consented to dash off light work in a quick, unstudied way ". He was compared with Döllinger, his friend and master, of whom he said : " Everyone has felt that his power was out of proportion to his work, and that he knew too much to write," and again : " Twenty years of his historical work are lost to history." And Döllinger is said to have observed of him that, if he did not write a great book before he was forty years old, he would never do so. He did not write a great book ; though he inspired more than one, he did not write any book at all. It was frequently said that he could not write.

Now it is precisely that capacity for not writing which, I venture to say, marks Acton as pre-eminent among scholars and among men. It was not true that he could not write. On the contrary, he was a master of language, rich, eloquent, and pointed. In dramatic power of constructing sentences, he was not surpassed by many. He knew how to choose the exact word which would most stimulate the mind. His thought was compressed into words with a closeness that can be likened only to that of Dante. It was not that he could not, but that he would not write. Nor was it true of him that " his power was out of proportion to his work." Beneath a world of learning, under the weight of which another might have been honoured for sinking, Lord Acton's tread was elastic. As an arch of Michelangelo's building springs under the load it bears, with such grace that it seems to stand without any burden, such was the ease with which Acton appeared to carry his knowledge. But, in the pursuit of his ideal, he would not give his soul to the world. The attainment of the present never satisfied him. His aim was at nothing short of perfection, and, so far from being a source of weakness, it is exactly that fact from which we can most gain strength.

By what he wrote, as well as by what he did not write, Lord Acton held his ideal high above the standard of the multitude.

What he performed, he was sure of having done well. His criticism had made it an achievement on the value of which he could rely, a work of long time brought at last to perfection. Only, the example of the sacrifice of so much toil to his ideal is greater than what he actually accomplished. Good as was what he could do, it was better left undone if it was not the best. And it was just this striving for the best, and rejection of everything short of it, this self-knowledge and self-confidence, this steadfast view of the ultimate goal, this indomitable self-restraint, that are the legacy and the supreme lesson given to us by one of the richest of human minds.

It must be remembered, too, that Lord Acton was deeply occupied in other ways than in study. While he was storing a wonderful memory with countless facts, not a few unearthed by him from long oblivion or secret papers, he was himself engaged in the making of history. Before ever he became professor at Cambridge, he was a leader in one of the greatest fights in the cause of liberty seen by the last century. He was also for some time Lord-in-Waiting, and did secretary's work for Queen Victoria. It was he who in the year 1875 wrote for her a letter to the German Emperor, to restrain Bismarck from the military projects against France, which he was believed to be renewing. " It was a very strong letter ", he said to me : " I wrote it myself." In his Memoirs, the Chancellor denied that he had harboured any such projects ; but Acton evidently thought otherwise. The full truth of the long struggle within the Roman Catholic Church cannot yet be known ; but assuredly the part that Lord Acton played in it was a hard one and an honourable. That marvellous self-restraint that has robbed us of his learning to give us his example, that caused him to bring to an end the *Home and Foreign Review* that he had founded and edited rather than run the risk of creating schism in the Church, sealed his mouth on the subject afterwards. Only perhaps in an occasional passage there may be detected a deep undercurrent that tells his opinion of the Vatican Council. Flushed with the triumph of his partial victory, Cardinal Manning did not hesitate to make known his opinion of Döllinger, Acton, and their associates. " In truth ", he said, " the main characteristic of these men was vanity—intellectual and literary. They had the inflation

of German professors, and the ruthless talk of undergraduates."
When Manning's spiteful hostility is discounted, that is perhaps
not a bad tribute.

Two sets of lectures, one on the French Revolution, the other
on modern European history, made up the greater part of Lord
Acton's writing at Cambridge. They had little in common
with most lectures that are heard. Each lecture was carefully
written out, and was in style a finished essay. It was finished in
style alone ; for the little alterations in the manuscript showed
how the writer's mind never failed to master new facts that had
come to light since the last delivery, and never ceased to weigh
and turn over and over a statement to which they were related.
"The most generous of book-lenders," Sir Mountstuart Grant
Duff called him ; and the generosity was great indeed, for he
lent, not only books, but those precious papers, the outcome of
a life's work, to students and pupils who asked for them. All
this was different enough from the ways of the general. But
there was a greater difference to be marked between Acton's
lectures and those of others. For his personality exerted in
some sort a spell upon his hearers. As he entered the room,
his sturdy figure carrying erect a head of singular majesty and
beauty, the hum and unrest died away. Something seemed to
draw over the spirits of those waiting, something subtle, marvellous, indefinable, something that created of itself a deep stillness,
charming care from the mind, stretching and raising the faculties,
till they seemed to pulse faintly in a rarer height, exciting them
and at the same time soothing.

> Sage he stood,
> With Atlantean shoulders fit to bear
> The weight of mightiest monarchies ; his look
> Drew audience and attention still as night
> Or summer's noon-tide air.

Partly, perhaps, it was the sense of the privilege in seeing the
working of a great mind, partly the solemnity that men might
feel who were brought to view with their own eyes the fount
of truth itself. For Lord Acton might have used of himself
the words of his illustrious contemporary Fustel de Coulanges :
"Ce n'est pas moi qui vous parle ; c'est l'histoire qui parle par
ma bouche."

And those who came did not only attend some skilful dissection of the motives of historic men, or some illuminating dissertation on the body politic of Europe. The lecture began— often enough with a very bombshell, such as the fiery sentence : " Freedom degenerates unless it has to struggle in its own defence,"—then developed into a fuller and a more rich achievement. There was a magnetic quality in the tone of his voice, and a light in his eye, that compelled obedience from the mind. Never before had a young man come into the presence of such intensity of conviction as was sounded by every word Lord Acton spoke. It took possession of the whole being, and seemed to enfold it in its own burning flame. And the fires below on which it fed were, at least for those present, immeasurable. More than all else it was, perhaps, this conviction, that gave to Acton's lectures their amazing force and vivacity. He pronounced each sentence as if he were feeling it, poising it lightly, and uttering it with measured deliberation. His feeling passed to the audience, which sat enthralled. There was one lecture, to take a single instance, on the travels and discoveries which began the modern world. It was not descriptive merely, but filled the mind with living images, with the wonder of all men at the heat and wealth of the Spice Islands, where the ships lay lazily to be filled with cargoes of fabulous value, with the wonder of the world to see subverted all its old notions, and the birth of a new reign, and new conditions of production, wealth, and power. The warmth and glamour of the East, the terror and fascination of the pathless Western seas, were drawn together and set in a splendid picture by a superb effort of imagination. Over the Renaissance, the Reformation, the ages of Louis XIV, and of Peter the Great, Lord Acton's power was the same. Every here and there his depth and gravity were thrown into relief by touches of delicious humour, such as the picture of Luther at the Wartburg disguised as a country gentleman, and that of Columbus striving not to be mistaken for the man who had discovered America. More grim were the lectures on the French Revolution, more exciting perhaps, necessarily more detailed, but not more thorough. It was the unfolding of one of the world's greatest dramas, of which the crucial moments became in Acton's hands tragic, almost agonising, but without a touch of theatrical effect. At the end of one of the lectures the Master of Trinity, sitting behind me, bent forward and said : " Very terse, is he not ? " For this distinguished man, Acton's senior, himself wise and learned, came regularly during the whole of a term to sit at Acton's feet on a hard student's bench. Nor was Montagu Butler alone among Seniors to come. To attract such an audience, Acton's lectures must have been good indeed.

Poetry, says Ruskin, is " the suggestion by the imagination of noble grounds for noble emotions ". With this idea, it has been said that history is " the suggestion, by the narration of fact, of noble grounds for noble emotions ". Expounded by Lord Acton, it was certainly this ; but it was something else as well. In the course of the last century and a half, the conception, as well as the knowledge, of history has been greatly changed and expanded. How wide the expansion has been, and how manifold the change, we can learn best from Lord Acton and from Professor Maitland. Striking instances occur to everyone. Macaulay wrote with one eye on modern politics, Mommsen for the glorification of power, Taine as a pathologist, Ranke with his judgment in suspense. More recently, there have been, and are still, many to enforce on us by precept and example the methods of less eminent German historians, and to urge on us that history must be divorced from literature, and immersed in the exposition of documentary evidence. That, as I have tried to show, was not Lord Acton's way ; and, while we are sometimes oppressed by those who would debase history from its place among the arts, he carried the conception of the art of history into a region never before reached, and raised it to a stature more lofty than was known to his predecessors.

To many this claim may seem fantastic ; perhaps Lord Acton would have rejected it for himself. But, for all that, it should not go unstated. " It may seem to some," again to quote from Maitland in the *Cambridge Review* :

" it may seem to some a plain untruth that he was more deeply interested in certain great problems of a philosophical kind than in any concrete presentment of material facts. They may well have thought of him as the man who, with wonderful exactitude, knew and enjoyed all the byplay in the great drama—at home, no doubt, upon the front-stairs, but supreme upon the back-stairs, and (as he once said) getting his meals in the kitchen ; acquainted with the use of cupboards and with the skeletons that lie therein ; especially familiar with the laundry where the dirty linen is washed ; an analyst of all the various soaps that have been employed for that purpose in all ages and all climes. Disclaiming all esoteric knowledge, and reading only what all may read, I cannot think of him thus. When he was observing, recording, appreciating the incidents, the by-play, he was intent on a main plot difficult to apprehend : ' fatalism and retribution, race and nationality, the test of success and of duration, heredity and the reign of the invincible dead, the widening circle, the emancipation of the individual, the gradual triumph of the soul, over the body, of mind over matter, reason over will, knowledge over ignorance, truth over terror, right over might, liberty over authority, the law of progress and perfectibility, the constant intervention of Providence, the sovereignty of the developed conscience.' Plenty of men are troubled about these matters ; plenty of men make theories, ' alluring theories ' about them ; but then they are not the men who know the back-stairs and get their meals in the kitchen ; not the men who have toiled in the archives, hunting the little fact that makes the difference."

This was Lord Acton's view of history, and from it there passed into his work—his written historical work—a quality hitherto unknown, a characteristic hard to define, which can only be considered as an entirely new step taken in the realm of historical thought.

Two things are necessary for an historian : to discover the facts, and to appreciate their significance. The former is hard enough, and many are they who never emerge from the study of obscure and fundamental technicalities. Acton spoke with reverence of this work, for he was a master of it, and knew its difficulty. He had worked in thirty-nine archives. His transcripts filled three large cases. When the Marchesa Campana de Cavelli had completed her great collection of documents relating to the exiled Stuarts, she sent him the work, two stout folio volumes, with the remark that she owed it to him, since every paper which she had transcribed was marked as having been first copied for him. He spoke with admiration of the " light and dexterous touch " with which Ranke scrutinised and dissected historical evidences. His own touch was no less sure. But if this is difficult work, the other necessity of the historian is infinitely more so. To tell a story of discovered fact, when the fact is discovered, is not in itself to show " an energetic understanding of the sequence and real significance of events ". " It is playing at study ", said Acton, " to see nothing but the unmeaning and unsuggestive surface, as we generally do." The events once known, they can be made by a man of insight and cunning power to tell the story of the mind, to show their relations to men and interaction with them, to lead from the history of occurrences to the history of ideas which mould and lie behind them, to appear as the links in a long chain, and as straws floated on the stream of some great movement. This is to write the history of a particular era, of a particular nation, of a particular tendency. The historian must be a psychologist ; it is his business to understand men's minds, and trace the course of their thoughts and motives ; for it is the mind of man which gives shape to the course of events. Even in this there are many who fail to achieve success, by reason of prejudice, want of application or power, or deficiency of knowledge. The few who do not fail, or for whose shining qualities partial failure is condoned, are the historians whom we acclaim as the best.

But take another step, and we come into a region where far fewer, very few indeed, have attempted to tread, and where but one has marked a clear path. Pass from the realm of particular to that of universal history ; and how infinitely greater are the difficulties to be overcome. He who would grapple with them must be proved in all the lower walks. He must be above prejudice, above party, above religion, above nationality. He must have at his hand and in his head an almost boundless wealth of knowledge. He must have the keen eye to trace events to causes far remote, and a keener suspicion to spy the least weakness in the train. He must have sympathy for all men, and a stern sense of justice. Above all, he must have the mind of a great constructive artist, using head and heart alike, to set in ordered array his vast field of material, and to draw from each part its proper meaning, in due proportion to the whole. For here the historian deals with the psychology of nations. No longer individuals, but powers and authorities of organic growth, have become the units for him ; and he must analyse the soul, not of one man, but of the mass. He deals now, not with the individual aspiration and effort, but with general ideas. Only when he has impressed into the main channel all the streams and rivulets that meander over his field, can he feel that he is accomplishing his task. One discernible fact, one obscure feeling, one thin tendency omitted, one train of deductions, however slightly, false—and all may be in vain. The world, no less, is the realm of the universal historian ; but he must justify himself by its right use. Solemn streams of fact will not alone suffice. In this region Lord Acton was the pioneer, and supreme. He showed the real possibilities of universal history, as a distinct and the highest branch of the art. As a city of four million inhabitants differs, not only in degree but in kind, from one of forty thousand, so the world's history differs in kind, and not in degree, from that of its component parts. It has a unity special to itself, which cannot be divided without changing its whole nature. The idea for which men groped confusedly, Acton mastered and expounded for our understanding. He spoke once of Treitschke as the greatest of historians, and justified his choice by saying that he had the greatest power of generalship in marshalling facts. It may be doubted whether his own power was less than that of Treitschke ; and he towered above him in this, that he was beyond nationality and without rancour. The least product of his mind had the stability of a pyramid, of which the apex is touched by the glow of dawn, while the base lies wrapped in night. It seemed to be the point to which all his knowledge and forces tended at the moment : a construction of harmonious proportion and imperturbable firmness. Whatever he said had an evident solidity ; for it was drawn from a storehouse the depth and richness of which were unique. " We can never have too much knowledge," he said. Others have been rich in learning ; but the secret that Acton discovered was : how to combine the erudition of an archivist, the method of a scholar, the reflection of a philosopher, the impartiality of a judge, and the soul of an artist. These alone can give the prize of universal history. These he had, and he attained it. And, since he dealt with new realms, he spoke a language that was sometimes new. His style has been called obscure ; but is not so. Where there is difficulty, it is because the thought is difficult to follow, and not because the style is crabbed.

Those who knew him well before he came to Cambridge said that Lord Acton gained from his life there a certain freedom of intercourse that in earlier years was less marked in him. How great was the value of that intercourse to his immediate pupils, they alone can be fully conscious. Never was there a master more patient or more accessible, readier with advice and encouragement, or one whose encouragement was more inspiring. The absolute sincerity of his praise or rebuke left an impression of ineffaceable strength on the mind of the learner. Praise was indeed seldom forthcoming, hardly ever unmixed ; but it was drawn on occasions when a lesser man might often have withheld it. Qualities, rather than accomplishments, earned the golden reward for young men ; ingenuity less than modesty of work, genuine pains, sincerity, largemindedness. " I don't like clever young men," Acton is reported to have said : not meaning that he did not like them to be clever, but that he did not like them to be conscious of cleverness and to take it for a subject of pride ; and his teaching was always directed to prevent his pupils from being, in this sense, clever. Generally a little raillery or a touch of irony sufficed ; but, though he never desired to exercise it, he had the power to be cruel when necessary, anything that smacked of vainglory or tinsel called it out with speed. A paper was once read before him by a pupil, on the subject of Austrian policy during the year 1815. It was a most careful and painstaking piece of work, portions of it based upon the Memoirs of Fouché. At the end Lord Acton rose and spoke in terms of high praise, correcting it lightly and adding where he thought it weak. As he sat down, he half rose again and, as if by an afterthought, remarked : " I think you made some use of Fouché's Memoirs : I suppose you know they are not authentic ? " The author of the paper was Denis Winstanley, then as young as myself, of whose later achievements I have spoken elsewhere. No more gentle or sympathetic way could possibly have been found to impart the impression Acton desired to give, without a touch of severity. Not long after, he heard a paper on another subject read by a man of far greater attainments, a brilliant and entertaining essay, but somewhat lacking in solidity. The half-minute of austere condemnation that followed its close could be likened to nothing but the bursting of a tropical thunderstorm. Not that Lord Acton discouraged accomplishments in his pupils. " It is a great demerit not to know Italian," he said to me when I was airily excusing my ignorance of that language.

The fault that perhaps most roused Lord Acton's scorn, and for which, in his eyes, there was no atonement, was the restatement of facts already known. Ignorance and omission might meet retribution in irony. " Like most things attributed to the Abbot Joachim," he remarked in a review, " the *Vaticinia Pontificum* is a volume not in common use, and decent people may be found who never saw a copy." His delicate method of imputing ironical intention to authors guilty of mistakes may often be found in his writing. This was a vein which came out strongly in conversation. Plain and pertinent questions met with plain answers ; but the solemn leg held out by merely respectable inquirers, Acton did not fail to pull. The waste of time involved in the offer of old stuff as new deserved nothing but sharp and direct strokes. In this sense Lord Acton once criticised a book by a pupil whose power he admired, and he refused a place on his shelves to a work of more encyclopædic character, passing on it the same judgment—" It doesn't get us any further." The object of this astonishing remark, as I have already related, was the *Dictionary of National Biography*. The patience with which he treated the smallest matter, and the way in which his mind seemed to run alongside of that of any who came to him, won instant affection ; he put questions to the least of his pupils with as real a desire to learn their opinions as if they had come from men of tried worth ; and the ungrudging advice which came from him in conversation on a line of study or controverted point was often followed by a letter on the following day, written amid the press of other work. This was the source of a potent influence, that was enforced by the candour and directness of his criticism. You had but to ask his opinion, and you received it straight. His criticism was always the most luminous imaginable, and it was in criticism, more than in immensity of learning, that his mind was strong ; and in the constructive vision of ideas yet more than in criticism.

Lord Acton's judgment concerning one historian has already been indicated. Others may be found to conflict with it. The spoken opinions of great men are seldom quite free from contradiction. At a dinner given by the Historical Society which he founded in Trinity College, he told the following story. " I was once with two eminent men, the late Bishop of Oxford and the present Bishop of London.[1] On another occasion I was with two far more eminent men, the two most learned men in the world—I need hardly tell you their names—they were Mommsen and Harnack. On each occasion the question arose ; who was the greatest historian the world had ever produced. On each occasion the name first mentioned, and on each occasion the name finally agreed upon, was that of Macaulay." Burke and Macaulay Lord Acton held to be the two greatest of English writers, and Burke at his best to be our wisest political thinker ; but, at a time when Macaulay's name is more often than not held up for rebuke by historians, it may not be unprofitable to remember so remarkable a consensus of opinion of five men, whose varied accomplishments at least cannot be accused of lightness or want of breadth. The preference generally given by Acton to historians not directly concerned with politics, such as Rashdall and Leslie Stephen, is well known. As they stood beside Sir Henry Maine's grave in the south of France, Fustel de Coulanges turned to him and said : " C'était le plus grand historien de notre temps." Acton's admiration for Maine was profound. At the only other dinner of the Trinity Historical Society which he attended, he named the three Cambridge historians whose work and methods were, in his opinion, most distinctive of all that was best in the university : they were Maine, Lightfoot, and Maitland. Some other historians at Cambridge did not earn such hearty approval ; but this was a subject on which Lord Acton was reticent. On one occasion Oscar Browning with whom, as professor, he had to work on friendly terms, sent him a book which Acton knew to be worthless ; he cut the leaves and left it on his table with slips of paper inserted here and there, that the author might suppose it had been read with approval, and so spare him the difficulty of delivering judgment. O. B. was enchanted.

[1] Bishops Stubbs and Creighton.

Throughout all Lord Acton's work, as throughout his life, ran the strong current of a passion for freedom and for right. "The method of modern progress was revolution," he said; and it was a method of which he approved. This belief was the outcome of moral principles, which he applied alike to history and to politics. In his Inaugural Lecture, he quoted from Burke words that might have been his own.

"My principles enable me to form my judgment upon men and actions in history, just as they do in common life; and are not formed out of events or characters, either present or past. History is a preceptor of prudence, not of principles. The principles of true politics are those of morality enlarged; and I neither do now, nor ever will, admit of any other."

Shortly before, in speaking of the historic cycle with which he was dealing, he said:

"Beginning with the strongest religious movement and the most defined despotism ever known, it has led to the superiority of politics over divinity in the life of nations, and terminates in the equal claim of every man to be unhindered by man in the fulfilment of duty to God—a doctrine laden with storm and havoc, which is the secret essence of the Rights of Man, and the indestructible soul of Revolution."

This doctrine he made peculiarly his own. Freedom in justice, liberty and not licence, the right to do good according to the dictate of conscience and of reason, were the things for which he strove. Few who did not hear him can have any idea of the fire and force with which he reprobated offences against the principle of liberty, or of the rigour with which he condemned breaches of morality in those whom he otherwise admired. The standard of right and wrong was the only one he admitted in judging actions. In applying it, he was without prejudice of country, or party, or creed. He could speak with respect of an enemy, and did not call him a scoundrel but on grounds on which he would have damned a friend. Once he called Nelson "that infamous man", thinking of the way in which he let selfish passion cloud his sense of duty. I asked him if he thought Bismarck a great man. He replied without hesitation: "A great man, and a great scoundrel." And once, when someone in conversation quoted words spoken in palliation of a piece of religious persecution, he broke out : " The man who said that would have murdered a street-walker in the Haymarket." Whether he meant St. Charles Borromeo who spoke the words, or Cardinal Manning who had approved them, I do not know. Perhaps both. So was the opponent who accused Lord Acton of " the ruthless talk of undergraduates " justified. For the weaker side, for any person, or party, or State, oppressed or persecuted, Acton seemed to have imbibed at his birth an almost Neapolitan fierceness of sympathy ; and the fierceness of that splendid passion, springing from the solid foundation of well tried principle, and weighted with the learning of the centuries was a thing, once witnessed, never to be forgotten.

The political creed that Acton held and inculcated was no easy one. " Liberty ", he wrote, " is not a means to a higher political end. It is in itself the highest political end." And again :

" By liberty I mean the assurance that every man shall be protected in doing what he believes his duty, against the influence of authority and majorities, custom and opinion. . . . It is bad to be oppressed by a minority, but it is worse to be oppressed by a majority."

Let us then be liberal, and above all to those in danger of oppression by the multitude.

But Lord Acton's Liberalism was a very living thing, more like to the Whiggism of Burke and of the men who drove out James II, or to the zeal of Mazzini, than to the colourless views that often pass under the name. What is it to be a Liberal ?

" A Liberal who thinks his thought out to the end without flinching is forced to certain conclusions which colour to the root every phase and scene of universal history. He believes in upward progress, because it is only recent times that have striven deliberately and with a zeal according to knowledge for the increase and security of freedom. He is not only tolerant of error in religion, but is specially indulgent to the less dogmatic forms of Christianity, to the sects which have restrained the churches. He is austere in judging the past, imputing not error and ignorance only, but guilt and crime, to those who, in the dark succession of ages, have resisted and retarded the growth of liberty, which he identifies with the cause of morality, and the condition of the reign of conscience."

This was the kernel of Lord Acton's teaching, and might be illustrated by many quotations. The mind, he urged, should always be fixed on the end, and not allow itself to be bewildered by the great achievements of past or present. Liberty is not to be gained by striking deeds ; and, he wrote, " if hostile interests have wrought much injury, false ideals have wrought still more " ; and the advance of liberty " is recorded in the increase of knowledge as much as in the improvement of laws ". Again we meet the sentiment : " The most certain test by which we judge whether a country is really free, is the amount of security enjoyed by minorities." Modern Socialists might take note. In one form or another, this principle recurs again and again, and it lay, beyond a doubt, very near to Acton's heart. His feeling for State rights, as something belonging to a living organism, was beyond the common ; and to see them trampled under foot was a thing horrible to him. He is believed to have sympathised keenly with the South African Republics at the beginning of the Boer War ; and when he was asked, on the night after the rejection of Gladstone's Home Rule Bill, what his feelings on the subject were, he answered :

" If I were capable of suffering, I should suffer now as I never did in my life. But I have no power of suffering since the surrender of General Lee's army. My sorrow was so profound then, that I think it has left me without the power of feeling ever since in political matters."

Lord Acton distrusted the formation and consolidation of great states. He wrote of the example of Washington and Hamilton with enthusiasm.

" It teaches that men ought to be in arms even against a remote and constructive danger to their freedom ; that even if the cloud is no bigger than a man's hand, it is their right and duty to stake the national existence, to sacrifice lives and fortunes, to cover the country with a lake of blood, to shatter crowns and sceptres and fling Parliaments into the sea. On this principle of subversion they erected their commonwealth, and by its virtue lifted the world out of its orbit and assigned a new course to history. . . . No people were so free as the insurgents ; no government less oppressive than the government which they overthrew."

But now it was very different.

"Legally, and to outward seeming, the American President is the successor of Washington, and still enjoys powers devised and limited by the convention of Philadelphia. In reality, the new President differs from the magistrate imagined by the Fathers of the Republic as widely as Monarchy from Democracy ; for he is expected to make seventy thousand changes in the public service : fifty years ago John Quincy Adams dismissed two men."

In the mid-twentieth century, the number is said to run into millions. And, combined with this, we have here the clue to Acton's grief over the surrender of Appomattox :

"That which made the conflict terrible, and included Europe in its complications, was, not the work of premeditating slave-owners, but of men to whom State rights, not slavery, were supreme, who would have given freedom to the slaves in order, by emancipation, to secure independence."

To Mrs. J. R. Green who once spoke to him of the petty tyranny exercised in small states, he replied : "That is the silly thing that vulgar people say." The same feeling found expression in the words :

"A generous spirit prefers that his country should be poor and weak and of no account, but free, rather than powerful, prosperous, and enslaved. It is better to be the citizen of a humble commonwealth in the Alps, without a prospect of influence beyond the narrow frontier, than the subject of the superb autocracy that overshadows half of Asia and of Europe."

Assuredly Lord Acton would have sympathised deeply with Mazzini's cry : "War is the greatest of crimes, when it is not waged for the benefit of mankind, for the sake of a great truth to enthrone, or a great lie to entomb." And I cannot think he was far removed in spirit from the poet who sang :

> By the golden-growing eastern stream of sea,
> By the sounds of sunrise moving in the mountains,
> By the forces of the floods and unsealed fountains,
> Thou that badest man be born, bid man be free.

Acton defined fullness of learning and solidity of criticism as the two means which most straighten and expand the historical mind. None has, assuredly, ever mastered and employed them to better purpose than himself. These were the foundations of his power, and are qualities perhaps within the reach of ordinary mortals ; but Lord Acton brought to aid them what is far beyond either. He added the imagination and the grasp of mind which are rare except in the greatest of historians ; the sanity, the wit, the passion, which are not rare only in the greatest of men.

CHAPTER X

THE YEARS BETWEEN

BEFORE the 1914 war Germany loomed large in English life on the map of Europe. Not only for her size and power. German philosophy, German music, German beer had a great hold on Englishmen. When that war broke out, a man in a Manchester club was holding forth to his friends on the strange feeling of finding ourselves fighting with the French and against the Germans. " Not strange to us," put in the chief engineer of Brunner, Mond's, a Scot whose ancestors had fought for centuries side by side with the French and had helped them to thrash the Hanoverians at Fontenoy. Despite recurrent irritation against the success of goods marked " Made in Germany ", the descendants of Frederick the Great, whose reputation was firmly established with admirers of Carlyle, held an ascendancy over English minds. It was an ascendancy, in my belief even at an early age and due possibly to my Scots ancestry, tinged with mirage. A good view of the real German character can be obtained from Queen Marie of Rumania's account of her education at Coburg in her *Story of My Life*.

I began visiting Germany when I was about fifteen and found Germans unsympathetic to me. An Englishman could feel at home in every country of Europe where I have been, but not in Germany, any Englishman that is capable of looking below the surface. The police state existed in Germany before Hitler, before the 1914 war. What is the basis of the police state? Nothing more nor less than the principle that everything is forbidden except that which is expressly permitted. That was from long ago the principle of German life. It is in direct contradiction with that of democratic life and of even more than one nation with small pretensions to democracy, namely, that anything is permissible which is not expressly forbidden. *Verboten* (forbidden) was one of the commonest among German words. The attitude engendered by the acceptance and enforcement of the *verboten* principle resulted in a sheepishness towards authority on the part of the German people that is responsible for modern socialism, largely a German production, and like that child of German mass mentality most unpleasant to anyone brought up in the principles of freedom. Heine's bitter gibe : " There can be no revolutions in Prussia— they are forbidden by the police," puts the matter perfectly for pre-war Germany. As Sir Stafford Cripps has vaunted the revolution achieved by the State in England, it must be presumed that State revolutions are the only revolutions permitted by Socialism and that England is well on the way in turn to become a police state.

To judge from the memoirs of Edward Speyer, a Frankfort man of business who made this country his home, the police state took root in Germany about the middle of the last century. Speyer came to England as a young man, then returned to Germany ; the atmosphere he found there was, he says, unbreathable, in contrast to that of liberal Germany after and indeed before the revolutions of 1848, inspired by the romantic ideals of Goethe, Schiller, Beethoven, and Novalis. The spirit of *Egmont* and *Die Jungfrau von Orleans* is as far from anything in Modern Germany as Schiller's ode to *Freude, Tochter des Elysiums* and the Ninth Symphony are from Hitler's " Kraft durch Freude " slogan. The earlier sentimental *Deutschtum* or Germanism changed under the influence of such diverse teachers as Hegel, Treitschke, and Nietsche to a horrid form of self-expression capable of swinging in an instant from boastfulness to whining. Arrogance in success, self-pity in adversity came to be among the leading German characteristics. Now there is a connexion between the emotions of pity and of love. For instance the Russian peasant has the same word for both : when he wants to say of a person " I love ", he says " I pity ". In Germans self-pity is nothing but a form of self-love ; and the self-pity that spilt itself over the world after Germany's defeat in two wars was nothing but a form of the overweening self-admiration to gratify which she inflicted them on the world. The typical German attitude is to lick your boots or kick your backside.

This exordium is merely to explain why, when after I had taken my degree I wanted really to learn German, I chose

Vienna rather than one of the prime favourites with English educationalists, Dresden or Hanover. I had already enough German to find my way about in trains and hotels and had discovered Germans to be lacking in two of the basic requisites of civilisation : they had the worst cooking and the most uncomfortable beds to be found in Europe. I cannot testify as to Spain and the Balkans, where I have never been ; but for the rest the observation is lamentably true. The only eatable dishes in an average German inn were roast goose and boiled ribs of beef: everything else was thoroughly nasty. Now a demand for good table fare and kind mattresses is not evidence of gluttony or sloth. We spend at least one-third of our lives in bed and more than a twelfth at table, and the repose and vigour we gain from the one and the other are necessary components of a life of reason and taste, two desiderata to which we must all aspire and in which Germans of the past two generations have been conspicuously poor. That without them Germans should earlier have been able to produce such an immense amount of capital work in almost every department of life is a tribute to their national strength, which no one denies. The fact that its stream almost dried up is a proof that admirable results cannot be maintained indefinitely once authority is substituted for reason and critical taste displaced in favour of hysterical enthusiasm. The change is very noticeable in music, once, however wrongly, considered in England to be a German appanage. While England, France, Spain, Russia, and Scandinavia have all given proof in the last sixty years of musical fertility as vivid as it has been varied, Germany has produced nothing worth while since Brahms, who was born in 1833. My appraisal of Germans, however, was personal and instinctive, not based on intellectual considerations of which I was as yet unconscious. Germans had an unpleasing habit when meeting others, foreigners included, in public places such as trains, of pricing every article of clothing on the company in comparison with their own. But the top was put on my dislike when once in a train between Munich and Bayreuth a gross, sweaty German stranger coolly, or rather feverishly, suggested that he might share my room at the hotel. Manners apart, most English people attributed to Germans a high standard of morals that was totally fictitious. When Gertie Lewis, the handsome, kindly elder daughter of the first Sir George Lewis, in his day a celebrated solicitor, married one Birnbaum, a wood merchant I believe, the officiating Rabbi in a moving address to the newly-wed couple who were off for their honeymoon abroad adjured them to hold high the standard of their race and not be tempted by the debauchery they would find in that sink of iniquity to which they were going. Most of the fashionable crowd in the synagogue assumed that the Birnbaums were going to Paris. Not a bit of it : their tickets were taken for Berlin.

Austria and the Austrians were a very different pair of shoes. A deep dislike of educated Austrians for North Germans, particularly Prussians, found its expression in a thousand *Wiener Witze*, little jests peculiar to the Viennese, redolent of lazy wit and gentle, but very gentle, spite. One ran :

Es giebt nur eine Kaiserstadt,
Es giebt nur eine Wien.
Es giebt anch eine Räuberstadt,
Die heisst . . . die heisst ? . . . ach, Berlin !

There is only one Empire City,
There is only one Vienna.
There is, besides, a Robber City,
That's called . . . now, what's it called ? . . . ah, yes, Berlin !

Austrians had a deliciously delicate tone in pretending they had forgotten the name of the hated Brandenburg capital. Austrians were full of gaiety. They were amiable, quizzical, slightly cynical, clean, quiet, smart, courteous, discreetly welcoming to the stranger, and loved to eat well and to sleep well. They justly prided themselves on the possession of good taste. They had the best red table wine outside France and the best coffee in the world. Some time before I went there, Vienna, most royally lovely of modern cities after Paris, had been dowered by its celebrated burgermaster Lueger with the best water supply, the best electric light, and the best tramway service in Europe. But it was not Vienna alone : the whole of Austria was a veritable land of Cockayne. Bohemia and Galicia might grumble against the paternal character of the Imperial Government, but they profited by the best administration to be found probably since the fall of the Roman empire. In particular the forestry department was far in advance of its opposite numbers elsewhere and roads were better kept up than any except the main roads in France. Especially outside Vienna one got the impression of greater virility than was perhaps often suspected in the Austrians. Their own poet Grillparzer's oft-quoted description of Austria as " Zwischen dem kind' Italien und dem Manne Deutschland "—Between Italy the child and Germany the man—does not, I have always thought, do justice to the Austrian character, which was something of its own and not merely a buffer 'twixt north and south.

Fustel de Coulanges, one of the world's really great historians has told us that there was a good deal of Gallic blood in the Danube basin. Which may account for Austrian *joie de vivre*, amiable wit, and decency of taste. Certainly the Viennese were pleasure-loving folk. Their pleasures were of an ideally simple order. They loved lounging in pleasant surroundings. The Prater, that vast park at Vienna's door, was crowded on summer evenings with happy people of every class, workmen and small bourgeois predominating, to sit in cafés, eat, drink in moderation, dance, and listen to music. Dancing and music filled a notable part of Vienna's life. Everyone who could gave and frequented private dances ; for those who could not there were vast halls where for a few kronen, a krone being worth 10*d*., anyone could dance till the small hours to a full band conducted by Johann Strauss, grandson of the famous waltz King, or one of his rivals. Bands were everywhere. The waltz of course was the thing. Nowhere, at no time, can so many have waltzed so well as in the spring of this century at Vienna. It was a joyous spectacle. Nor was the Imperial Viennese ballet to be despised, being the finest outside the Russian ballet, as yet sealed from the West. The weak spot of all Western ballets was the male dancing : what that could be we had to learn from Fokin, Nijinksy, Bolm, and Rumanov. Dancing was in the lifeblood of Vienna, and Austrian balletomanes were nearly as hard to please as those of St. Petersburg. Four exquisite ballerine reigned in their hearts—their names have long since gone from me—and over those, it was said, of certain Archdukes and princes whose brilliant uniforms and carriages made the Ring a fairy spectacle on Sunday after Mass as they drove round with these lovelies. Another Archduke

had for his lady the enchanting Selma Kurz, coloratura soprano
of the Opera, and one of the perfect half dozen of my lifetime,
the ideal Mozart heroine. Brilliant though the Ring might be,
the keynote of the Viennese streets was a pleasant, homely
gaiety. The people loved their Emperor and you might see
him almost any day strolling along the Ring, with no more
guard than a couple of plainclothes men at a discreet distance,
on his way to visit Frau Schratt, no longer his handsome lady
love of the 'eighties, but an elderly bourgeoise on whom Francis
Joseph still greyer, more elderly, dropped in for a chat and
relaxation from affairs of State. He always smoked a " Virginier ", one of those long thin cigars made of scraps of tobacco
packed in a surrounding leaf, with a straw mouthpiece to ensure
the draught : not the common Virginier, an article similar to
those sold in Italy and Switzerland, made of coarse Dalmatian
tobacco and vulgarly known as *Giftstengel* or poison-stalks, but
a special brand made of Havana tobacco. The Emperor's
tobacconist in the Kärtnerstrasse was allowed to sell them to
the public. Anyone might go in and buy a handful of " Kaiser-
Virginier " and very good they were as well as cheap. Until
the 1914 war, as I found out afterwards, you could get them at
Van Raalte's in Piccadilly Circus. Even more beloved than
the Emperor when I first went to Vienna was his granddaughter,
the only child of the tragic Archduke Rudolph, an intoxicatingly
pretty girl, then on the eve of the first in her series of disastrous
marriages that ended in her being a Communist outcast from
her family.

Francis Joseph had ceased to frequent the theatre, but the
Opera and the Burgtheater were very much his. £20,000 a
year or nearly that was the subsidy paid from his private purse
to the Opera, that was also rent free and could draw on the
vast resources of the Imperial furniture depository and the
finest armoury in the world. No wonder the Hofoper staged
the most sumptuous performances of our time and under the
baton of Gustav Mahler, the successor of Hans Richter, the two
finest conductors before Toscanini a corner of whose mantle
today has fallen on Charles Münch, attracted the most brilliant
singers. Schmedes and Slezak, the two magnificent leading
tenors, were rising to the height of their fame; Reichmann,

greatest of all Wagnerian baritones, Friedrichs the bass accounted second only to the almost legendary Fritz Planck—noblest bass voice ever heard, with the possible exception of Paul Robeson's—were already at the height of theirs; Fräulein von Mildenburg, the most electric dramatic soprano since the age of Malten and Rosa Sucher, has remained an unsurpassed Isolde and Brünnhilde ; of Frl. Kurz I have spoken ; Edith Walker was the most touching of all Brangänes ; and in Frau Gutheil-Schoder, also the best Eva I ever heard in the *Meistersinger*, the Viennese opera possessed the only singer capable since Mlle Isaac, who created them for Offenbach in Paris, of sustaining all the three women's parts in *The Tales of Hoffmann*. Yet the Opera shone less by the brilliancy of individual performers than by the perfection of its ensemble and the taste, no less than the dash, of its execution. Its orchestra was thought the best in existence. *The Tales of Hoffmann* had been the piece played twenty years before when the old opera house had been burnt to the ground. It was a ghastly tragedy in which scores of lives were lost. When Offenbach's opera was revived, there was for long a peculiar thrill in the audience : everyone in the house had known or known of some family that had lost a member or friends in the holocaust, and the emotion engendered by the memory enhanced the special pains lavished on the production. I have rarely seen a more beautiful spectacle than the Venetian scene in this opera as staged at Vienna, unless perhaps it were the Venusberg in *Tannhäuser*, where the beauties of the Imperial ballet posed, just as part of the background, in a *tableau vivant* of Botticelli's Primavera. The fire at the Hofoper had one curious result. Thereafter smoking behind the scenes was strictly forbidden. Now there came a time when Caruso was engaged to sing there. As is well known, he was an inveterate smoker. Either he or his manager had supposed that no such rule could apply to him. But when he arrived at the opera house, he was told to put out his cigar. Rather than break his habit, he declared he would break his contract ; in which case the Vienna Hofoper would have remained the only principal opera house where Caruso had never appeared. The deadlock was broken by a special relaxation of the rule : wherever he went within the precincts of the Hofoper, in the wings or dressing-rooms, Caruso was followed by a fireman carrying a bucket of water. In Caruso's biography this pleasing story is placed in Berlin, but the Viennese told it of themselves and its humour is surely more redolent of Vienna than of the rigid and arrogant Prussian capital. An earlier incident at the Opera well shows the difference between the simplicity of Viennese manners and the snobbishness of North German etiquette, and this despite the formalism of Austrian Court ceremonies. The German Crown Prince William, afterward William II, was visiting Vienna and went to the opera with the Archduke Rudolph. At the door of the Imperial box the old attendant, who had known Rudolf since his birth, said to him : " Der Herr Papa ist schon da "—" Your dad's gone in already." William, furious at so familiar a tone, burst out : " Ist der alte Bursch betrunken ? "— " Is the old fellow drunk ? " On which the attendant, imagining William's question to apply to the person of the Emperor, retorted indignantly : " No ! Certainly not, your Royal Highness ! His Majesty has never come drunk to the Opera ! " The Burgtheater, though it cost the Emperor less than the Opera, was conducted on the same lavish scale and with an equally fine result. The company was one of great strength in all departments and was used with real intelligence. It would be tiresome to give a list of names unknown to the English reader, but two of the actors were outstanding even in the first class. One was Hartmann, the best and the only really satisfying Falstaff I have ever seen ; the other Kainz, one of my five best Hamlets and superior even to Sir Frank Benson, better than all since him, in Richard II. Shakespeare, it will be observed, was a prime favourite at the Burgtheater ; all the German classics and many modern French as well as German plays were in the repertory too. Taken all round the Burgtheater was barely less good than the Comédie Française of the same period, and superior to any North German or Russian theatre, though my experience of the latter was still to come.

My arrival in Vienna synchronised with a visit of Donald Tovey, come to play with the principal Austrian quartet of the day. It was curious at the rehearsals, to which Donald invited me, to see how these renowned players fell under the spell of his already immense musical knowledge and judgment. At the piano Tovey with his disjointed limbs, swivelling neck, and roving, beady eye seemed like some strange bird on the look-out for unconsidered trifles ; but he soon got the hang of his surroundings and his concerts, given before the most critical audience in the world, were a pronounced success. This was something for a pianist to be able to boast about, for the darling of Vienna was Dohnyanyi (whose name by the way no one there like the B.B.C. today pronounced "Dochnyanyi", but just as it is written) still a young man and perhaps the finest pianist of the moment, short of Paderewski. Through Donald Tovey I came to know Mandyszewski, the head of the Vienna conservatoire, whom he described as "the most learned musician in Europe". Mandyszewski, who was soon to return the compliment, passed me on to a cousin of his, Frau von Lamprecht, the widow of a civil servant on the lookout for a lodger. So to Frau von Lamprecht I went and had a most comfortable room, the run of her small flat, two excellent meals, coffee and rolls in the morning and even an orange, then a rarity in Vienna, with them, all for 4s. 2d. a day. *O tempora, O prandium!* I rather think washing was extra. In theory I was working at the Vienna University, but in fact never went there more than occasionally to attend Professor Redlich's history *Seminar*. This institution, for those who know it not, is a sort of conversation class on a grand scale, with fifty or sixty students attending, and is a fruitful method of instruction. Redlich's *Seminar* attained such fame that, on my later saying I had been admitted to it, someone, perhaps inspired by the green-eyed monster, ejaculated : "Oh, everyone's been to Redlich's *Seminar*!" Just as, in after-years in Paris crowded with Russian refugees, a common jest was : "Tous les Russes ont tué Raspoutine!" My real job, however, was to study German. For nearly five months I took an hour's lesson a day with a University lecturer, read and wrote for several more, and in the evening went to the Opera (2s. in the front row of the upper circle!) or the Burgtheater, or to friends to whom other friends with marvellous generosity passed me on. Before my time was up I could prattle in almost any company and spoke German well enough to be taken in Vienna for a Reichsdeutscher, and in Germany for an Austrian : there is a wide difference of accent between German as spoken in various parts. If only I had been able to stay for a year I should have had a sound, solid knowledge of the language instead of by now having forgotten much of what I learned, which is the sad case. My worthy teacher had learned his accurate English from books. One day, translating to him, I read : " For breakfast the boy had . . ." and baulked at an unknown word. " Grit," said my teacher. Impossible, I cried : grit is hard dirt and uneatable. He got out his dictionary. There was the word, though in the plural, " grits " or " groats ". Worse and worse : a groat was a late mediæval coin. Our discussion ended by his promising to produce some next day. He did, and from the paper bag poured out a small heap of semolina. The *O.E.D.* gives " grits " or " groats " as meaning coarse, hulled grain, especially oats. But no one ever uses the words in that sense in ordinary life. Such are the pitfalls of learning from dictionaries.

The Viennese were immensely kind to me. This I realised not to be a personal matter so much as that a young Englishman was a totally strange animal to them. Violent anti-English feeling had been aroused in Vienna by the Boer War and there was much curiosity to see what one of our race of hateful oppressors was like. It would have paid handsome dividends for our Government to send a score like me to enlighten Austrians on the tyrannical British character. In a short time I was able to move in a number of different circles. Mandyszewski gave me an introduction to the Mautners, a Jewish banking family with wide musical connexions ; my father had been in correspondence with two women philosophers, the Fräulein Richter, sisters who turned out to be as charming as they were learned ; from Cambridge I had a letter to Robert Dunlop, the Irish historian, who had married a well-to-do Austrian lady and lived in a lovely flat on the Ring ; and all these passed me on to their friends. The Dunlops were an admirable couple. Frau Jo Dunlop—her full Christian name was Josepha, and by a pleasant custom in Austria married women were addressed by their own and not their husbands' Christian names—had Hapsburg features lit by a delicious smile, a perfect figure, and a very sensitive intelligence. Dunlop was a most handsome Ulsterman, of really noble presence, softened by the sweet charm of Vienna comforts. They had an extremely good-looking son, then a small boy. Since I have paid so many compliments to the Austrians, who thoroughly deserved them, I wish to tell here of the end of these friends. When war broke out in 1914, Dunlop, who had lived in Vienna for a quarter of a century, wholly at one with the country of his adoption, was arrested as a spy, then, when that senseless charge fell through, interned, though well over fifty, as an enemy. Frau Jo Dunlop was deserted by all their former friends, treated like a leper, and turned out of her home. Their boy, now of military age and wholly Austrian by breeding as well as nationality, was called up. Because his father was British, the poor lad was so abominably handled in his regiment that he tried to commit suicide, failed, and only succeeded in destroying his wits. Both parents died shortly after the war, having lost their fortune, their health, and their hopes ; Frau Jo Dunlop survived long enough to bury her son, in the end delivered from the misery of his life. Austrians gifted with so many and such rare qualities, yet lacked moderation, good sense, and justice. Perhaps that is why they plunged down the decline, the abyss at whose bottom destroyed their country.

In Vienna I came face to face with something the very existence of which I had not suspected. This was the Jewish problem. In London I was on calling terms at Jewish houses like the George Lewises. Jews like the Arthur Cohens and the Felix Schusters were often guests at my father's. Two of my friends at Eton were Jews ; I made more at Cambridge. It had never entered my head that there could be antagonism between modern, educated Jew and Gentile. Yet in Vienna society was divided into two sets—Jew and Gentile. Those who frequented the one were cut off from the other. I only learned this by degrees, on noticing the surprise expressed by Jews or by Gentiles on my saying that I had been seeing someone in the opposite camp. As a foreigner and a very young man such conduct was forgiven in me ; no Austrian could possibly have been allowed similar latitude. The one world in which over-lapping took place was that of music : there, so rigid an exclusion would have been impossible as was practised in every other walk of life, the university included. If you visited Gentiles, you were not received by Jews, and vice versa. When this mutual ostracism began and which side started it, I have no idea. That it was a fact there can be no doubt whatever. To me it came as a very curious experience, one moreover that later proved of serious value for the understanding of social problems I found in Russia. For the moment it seemed just extremely odd. It was only towards the end of my stay that good Frau von Lamprecht, my hostess, with whom I was discussing the subject, said to me : " I was so terrified when my cousin Mandyszewski wrote to me about you. I thought you must be a Jew ! Yes, I was terrified. But I did want the money so badly ! " " But what made you expect me to be a Jew ? " " Your name ! Don't you see ? " " I'm afraid not. My name's pure Scotch." " Pollak—I thought it was Pollak ! Oh, what a relief it was when I saw your nose ! " The same mistake has often been made since then by Continentals, Jew and Gentile. It has been encouraged by various persons of the name of Pollak—one of the commonest of Jewish surnames in Eastern Europe, by etymology meaning " the man from Poland ", where there were a great many Jews—adopting mine instead. Gordons and MacGregors are not the only sufferers from this insinuating Israelite practice. " Mr. Stanley, I presume ? " would have a very different meaning today from that in Dr. Livingstone's mind. When the American dramatist Channing Pollock came to London, my cousin Guy, then managing editor of the *Morning Post*, invited him to lunch, so as to ask him from what branch of the family he was descended, Channing Pollock answered with a poker face : " From the Pollocks of Jerusalem."

I have never been a traveller. Whatever foreign countries I have seen, I visited because work or desire to improve my mind on definite points took me there ; they amount to half a dozen or so. Your real traveller is moved by an urge to exploration, to discover what would be else unknown. He need not be driven by it to the Poles, North or South, or to Arabian deserts. Miss Edith Durham in the Balkans, Douglas Freshfield in the Caucasus, Arthur Morrison in unknown London, were on real exploration bent. And since only real travellers have things worth telling, whether of Cathay, Khartoum, or Canning Town, I shall not dilate on my own insignificant journeys. Yet

I had the luck to have a glimpse at Tangiers before it was civilised, and to see Greece before the tourist rush. Tangiers in the early 1890's was unchanged from its state of five hundred years before. It was a mediæval walled town, ruled by a Pasha in the Sultan's name. At night the gates were shut and no European was allowed within, but stayed, if he did, at the risk of his life. Outside the walls was a compound with the French and British consulates and a small hotel run by a Frenchman. Even by day Europeans were advised not to go about the narrow dirty streets of Tangiers, crowded with merchants and their donkeys and camels, unless accompanied by a guide known to the Moorish authorities. Communications by sea consisted, weather permitting, of a twice-weekly boat from Gibraltar that suggested a condemned penny steamboat from off the Thames. There was no harbour, jetty, or landing-place ; you were decanted from the steamer in the open water of the Straits into a small rowing-boat whence you scrambled on to the beach of burning sand. Three days before my father took me as a boy to Tangiers, the Pasha had ordered the extermination of all the stray dogs in the town. Their several hundred bodies, cast on the beach, lay there rotting under the African sun, and we visitors had to pick our way between them. A vivid contrast with the luxurious international resort of five-and-twenty years later.

Tangiers taught nothing not to be learnt from books. But no one could imagine Greece who has not seen it. My luck was to see it when, though safe from brigands who a generation earlier had made sightseeing precarious, there were still virtually no hotels outside Athens, and the traveller was put up by the local priests or by friends of his dragoman without whom it would have been extremely hard to manage a tour. Ours rejoiced in the name of Constantinos Ikonomides. Apart from carriages, horses, and sleeping accommodation, he also arranged for our feeding, on bread and honey for breakfast, and Greek honey is the most delicious in the world, and for the rest on lamb chops : " We call sips," Constantinos would proudly proclaim, the dragoman equivalent for " sheep ". The thing unimaginable in Greece is the savagery of its limitless beauty, like that to which Coleridge transports you in *Kubla Khan*. It hits you in the face, it takes your breath away, it makes you feel the very presence of the Great God Pan and all the host of Olympos. Not only does the violence of the blue in the sea and the sky of Greece, of the whiteness in its marble, of the mountain peaks cut as if with a knife, assail your senses and make your brain to reel, but there is withal in the siting of the ruins, the only material remains of those who founded Western civilisation, as well as in the detail of what survives, a harmony so potent that your soul, uplifted and thrilled, is purified into communion with the supreme nobility that the human mind has conceived. There are too, or were, in Greece singular concomitants that seem to carry you back over two thousand years at a step. The goatherd pipes as he piped when Cheiron was teaching Jason. One morning, coming down from an early walk up Mount Hymettos, I turned a corner in the track and there on a rock at my very elbow sat an immense coalblack raven that imperturbably watched me go by. In the gorge by sacred Delphi—shaken by an earth-tremor in the night—I saw hovering a perfectly snow-white hawk. And as I lay on the Acropolis at Athens four eagles overhead came floating in échelon from the south : there was not a flicker of their wings, but they passed over to the mountains in the north in less than twenty minutes while in my view, and the distance cannot have been under fifty or sixty miles. The grandeur of nature is very close to you in Greece. There is less grandeur in another memory of that same enchanted spot. Professor Goodwin of Harvard, noted for his Greek Grammar, was in Athens at the time. He obtained permission to go up on to the scaffolding in position at the Parthenon, where some repairs were in progress, and see close at hand the remains of the frieze, almost invisible from below : the ancient Greek sculptors worked " for the Gods ". Goodwin kindly took me with him. In the party also were an American painter, who with his wife was toting round Europe in the hope of awakening their souls to the call of beauty the two daughters of an almost illiterate mushroom millionaire in Boston. These two very pretty girls sat listlessly on a bench while Goodwin and the curator expatiated on the unique works of which they were having a privileged view. Not a spark of response. Finally Goodwin related how the frieze represented the noblest youths of Athens riding in the great Panathenaic festival that took place every five years, volunteer soldiers of their country about to take part in the noblest procession of antiquity. . . . At this point one of the sisters looked up and drawled to the other : " Why, Maisie, say, ain't that just like our Boston cadets ? "

If Greece was an unforgettable æsthetic experience, the United States provided me with another no less so, but of a social character. One of my father's pet wishes was that I should go to the Harvard Law School, as a preparation for the Chancery Bar. He probably never stopped to ask himself whether I should be suited to the latter, or if the Harvard Law School, admirable and famous though it is, made a good stepping stone to it. Harvard and Equity were two fixed stars in his legal heaven, the sun of which was the Common Law. Perhaps he thought the sun's rays over-strong for my weak wits. In any case, as applied to myself his ideas were much misconceived but to Harvard I went and stayed there for a year. I was full of youthful enthusiasms. I had won a Fellowship at Trinity and taken my M.A. degree. I had very little taste for law, but much for literature, life, and history and in particular American history, in which O. W. Holmes and other oversea visitors had aroused my interest. I doubt whether, even had it been otherwise, I or any other fairly intelligent Englishman could have settled down to study law in circumstances of such startling novelty as those I found surrounding me. In Mr. John Dickson Carr's *Life of Conan Doyle* are to be found many true remarks by that ebullient author about English misconceptions concerning Americans and vice versa. But Conan Doyle does not appear to me to have found, or perhaps sought, the *fons et origo* of ours. It took me a long time to discover ; yet it is quite simple. The reason why we make such grotesque errors about Americans is that owing to our common language we expect to find them very much like ourselves. When we are disappointed, we think it is their fault. Americans, noticing this without realising the cause, consider us haughty and anxious to show off. In reality Americans are just as different from English people as they are from other Europeans. Until the English visitor to America comprehends that he is in the midst of a civilisation totally different from anything he has known on our side of the Atlantic, he is exposed to countless shocks. Americans themselves often do not recognise this consciously : that they do unconsciously is testified by their common expression " the American way of life ". What makes this more puzzling to the inquirer is that the great difference is of fairly recent growth, say, of within the last seventy years. Anyone of my age can have known scores of Americans belonging to an elder generation whose way of life was essentially the way handed down to them through preceding generations from the original colonists of New England, Virginia, and the Carolinas ; and, for there seemed to be some sort of time-lag at work, they were more like eighteenth-century English ladies and gentlemen than anything to be found in England. Fifty years ago they were passing away. Now they are gone.

What then was the cause of this change ? I think the answer is fairly obvious. The cause was compounded of two elements : the Civil War and foreign immigration. The brilliant Russian-born English surgeon who writes under the name of George Sava was astounded, as he tells in *The Knife Heals Again,* by the many contrasts he found with English life on his first visit to America after the recent war. It should be made compulsory for any Englishman going there to read the American passages in this book and in Conan Doyle's Life. What had happened was that the Civil War cut through the roots of the earlier American civilisation inherited from the Colonial period. The United States then started on a fresh lap in the race of the nations, unhindered or unaided by the influence of the Southern States that had been preponderant in the formation of the Republic, and this at precisely the moment when the invasion, as it virtually was, of America by Germans, Poles, Irish, Swedes, Italians, and Jews was rising to its peak. These immigrants for the most part became perfectly good American citizens. The days of the German *Bund* and of feverish effort by Imperial and Nazi Germany to organise German-Americans in an anti-American drive were still far off. One friend I made at Harvard, a crack member of the University XV, was the grandson of a German immigrant. His family still often spoke German at home and had preserved many of the better German characteristics. But their attachment to Germany was purely sentimental. On New Year's Eve they would all stand on their chairs in the true old German style, and on the stroke of midnight jump off them, calling out *Glückliches Neujahr*! But politically, socially, and in their outlook on the future, they were typically American. They had lost their historical German background. Yet there was no other historical background for them to acquire, as George Sava (to cite him again) acquired in less than a generation the English background. America may develop a background; but it is not a thing that grows in seventy years. Europeans may sometimes live too much on their past: Americans live wholly on their future. An indication of this is seen in the common use of two words in America, one of which is never heard in Europe and the other in educated circles usually with an apology or a sneer, because we have both things and therefore need not talk of them. The words are "poise" and "culture". In the American sense "poise" means an assured attitude towards life: "culture" all that is implied in the anecdote of the Chicagoan who said: "Maybe we have not much culture, but when we do get it, you bet we make it hum!" The mass of Americans, unconsciously conscious of their lack of historic background, feel themselves more deficient in both than to my mind they really are. The novelty element in American civilisation has one perhaps unexpected result. That is, to give to the universities in the United States, as the most stable feature in the intellectual life of the country, an unusual prominence, and to professors in them a degree of general regard that does not attach in the popular mind to university professors in England.

One advantage of having no background has been to develop in Americans an openmindedness astonishing to Europeans. When accompanied by ignorance, this amounts to simplicity; yet it is prevalent among the most intellectual of Americans too, and doubtless has responsibility for the mental, and so often practical, hospitality accorded to strangers. A disadvantage is that it lays Americans more open than we are, or at least have been in the past, to assault from the herd instinct: once this gets a hold, whether in fashion, in literary taste, or in politics, it would seem to be irresistible. This explains the paradox that all American men and all American women dress alike, but that if anyone is bold enough to dress with a difference, millions will instantly follow his or her example.

Nobody can safely generalise about a nation the size of America, especially when it has no capital. Politically, Washington is the capital ; financially, New York ; industrially, Chicago and Detroit ; artistically—must we admit ?—Hollywood. But every little town with its Main Street stands on its own and feels itself the equal of these giants. The personal element in national impulses is thus very strong : witness the outstanding success of President Truman's whirlwind electoral campaign. One generalisation however I will make : it is an error to think that wealth is the lodestone of American life. Its acquisition is important, certainly : but that is because it is the main, often the only, criterion of success in a young country the development of whose resources is still in progress. Success and not " the almighty dollar " is what Americans worship. That the criterion is sometimes wrongly applied is only natural. I was once present at a Harvard professors' club when a caustic old chemist was severely criticising an historical novel then much in vogue. Finally the professor of English literature, whom the other enjoyed baiting, said with a hurt air : " Well, I know it sold twenty thousand copies, anyway ! "

Among the many friends I made at Harvard, the best were Professor Toy, of Hebrew and Assyrian repute, and his wife, and Robert M. Johnston and his. The Toys were Southerners and like many of their kind still had an aura of that older mental atmosphere whence the United States sprang. He was wise as well as learned ; she, a great reader of poetry, a perfect hostess, and a fine musician. Their house was a Mecca for the junior professors and for visiting artists : there, among many others, I met George Santayana, poet and philosopher. He wrote his exquisite series of sonnets as the result of a challenge from Mrs. Toy, who had maintained that Shakespeare could not have written his without having a living object in his mind. I had younger Southern friends too, and can bear witness that the Southern charm is no bar to intellectual energy and the solid character that Boston and Philadelphia too exclusively claimed. In the latter this claim was caricatured in the tale of the New Yorker who asked the Philadelphian : " Do you eat snails ? "

and received the slow answer : " No, we've never been able to catch any." The pretensions of New England were taken off by the New Englander who wrote :

> O Boston, the land of our fathers,
> O home of the bean and the cod,
> Where Lodges speak only to Cabots,
> And Cabots speak only to God.

Boston beans and brown bread was a famous regional dish, and the two families named among the oldest of the " modern Athens's " intelligentsia.

Johnston, when I first knew him, was looked at a little askance at Harvard, where he was Assistant Professor of history, as almost too much of a European. He was gay, he was witty, he was critical, he was poor. His wife was a fascinating little Englishwoman, a cousin of Lord Portarlington. He had been born in Paris, where his father was a dentist during the Second Empire, was educated there and at Pembroke, Cambridge, spoke French like a native and Italian almost as well, and had travelled in South Africa. There he had known some of the Jameson Raiders. One of them later admitted to him having received a telegram from Cecil Rhodes's headquarters containing an order to Dr. Jim to hold his hand. " What did you do ? " asked Johnston. " Oh," said the other, " I let her rip." Such, Johnston remarked, was the levity with which the Raid and the consequent Boer War were precipitated. Johnston's uncle, General Albert Sydney Johnston, had at the beginning of the American Civil War been among Robert E. Lee's most trusted army commanders ; unluckily for the Confederate cause he was killed in one of the early battles. From him R. M. J. inherited a taste for military science : he turned it to the Napoleonic era and wrote what is the standard book on *The Napoleonic Empire in Southern Italy*. This work revealed its author's powers not only by its research in a nearly untilled field and its admirable clarity, but in the following way. Johnston posted his MS. to the Oxford University Press. Assistant professors at Harvard were meagrely paid and to save expense Johnston did not have a copy made. The MS. was sent for an opinion to Professor York Powell, who promptly mislaid it among his mountains of papers : it was thought to be utterly lost. The Press apologised profusely and by way of amends paid Johnston £100. Johnston sat down and rewrote the book, which was published. Then York Powell died and the MS. came to light : it was almost word for word identical with the work as rewritten, one of the most astonishing feats of memory and accurate scholarship I know. Johnston wrote too the best short life of Napoleon in existence, of which Lord Rosebery, surely a good judge, wrote to him that it was among the books he kept constantly at his bedside, to mitigate the horrors of insomnia. Then one summer, to amuse himself, R. M. J. wrote another life of Napoleon, in diary form, made up of extracts from letters, reports, proclamations, and so forth. He was urged to publish it and did so under the title of *The Corsican*. The sequel could never have happened in England. *The Corsican* hit the fancy of the American reading public. It became a best seller. From its proceeds the author was able to buy a country house, keep a motorcar, and enjoy a life of ease. Also from being an almost unknown scholar he found himself a widely prized personality. He was appointed a full professor and when the United States entered the first World War was, for his reputation as a military student, invited to take a Staff appointment with the rank of Major. I have been told that he drew up the plans for some of the most successful American operations. This exacting labour strained a heart never strong and R. M. J. who, when I saw him in 1920 was worn to a shadow, died of its failure soon after, to be followed within a year by his wife, bereft of all will to live. In them I lost two of my dearest friends.

Opportunity is master of us all. In a life whose hours are too short often for even the daily task it is not possible to keep in contact with more than a few friends however valued whose paths do not cross one's own with fair regularity. If some of those Harvard and Boston friends who so very long ago made me welcome in every possible way, or their children, should chance to see these lines—the Lymans, the Merrimans, the Putnams, the John C. Grays, Maurice Darling, Catchings, Edgar Wells, that band of fine young people in the orbit of William James, philosopher and charmer, brother of Henry the novelist, and many others—I should like them to know that throughout the years they have ever had a warm place in my heart. Some of this flower of a then rising generation have passed from our world : one, the handsomest and most admired, William James the younger or, as Americans say, William James 2nd lives and works, a far too modest painter, in the lovely ancestral " James house ", an American term redolent of the old traditions, on—for " in " would be an Anglicism—Irving Street, Cambridge, Massachusetts. To one and all of them, greetings and heartfelt thanks.

CHAPTER XI

BOW BELLS

A PALPABLE sign of the openmindedness instinct in Americans came to me before I left Harvard in the shape of an invitation to accept a job on the staff of a Boston daily paper to which I had during my stay contributed one or two articles. I was too inexperienced to comprehend the significance of such an offer. Only when years afterwards it was repeated by two other American papers did this dawn on me. In the course of over twenty years as a practising journalist, but one similar proposal has ever reached me from a British daily or weekly. Monthly and quarterly reviews have commissioned work from me, but on the newspaper side of journalism I had, as John Lane at an early stage warned me I should, to fight every inch of the way. Yet American newspapers and their managements have a reputation for being " harder boiled " than our own. The explanation can only be that Americans are more keenly on the lookout for novelty than are our own people, more ready to believe not only, in the old prizering saying, that " youth will be served ", but also that youth can serve with advantage to others besides itself, and that they are more open to fresh impressions.

Each of these three opportunities however was dependent on residence in Boston, in New York, or in Washington. If an American editor had wanted me to work for him as correspondent in Europe, I should have jumped at it. But it has been London editors who wanted me abroad, while their Transatlantic brethren thought I might be useful in America. For the moment, though I paid another long visit to the States some years after leaving Harvard, I felt the latter opening impossible to accept. Bow Bells rang too insistently.

London of the early 1900's was a vastly different place from what it became after the 1914 war and today would be unrecognisable. Its main architectural beauty, that splendid sweep of

Regency design from Carlton House Terrace to the Regent's Park, has long since been blotted out ; the turn into Portland Place is damned past redemption by the B.B.C. monstrosity ; and its northern end round the Park has been left so bedraggled after Hitler's attentions that it can never recover its pristine charm. Similar ruin has befallen other quarters too. Bloomsbury's " Tory brick-built streets " have quite lost their cachet, so broken up are they by modern office buildings and flats. Alone almost among London squares, once the pride of our capital, Bedford Square and tiny Victoria Square still stand, frozen flowers of the past, amid a horrid spate of incongruous concrete. Over the miserable fate of Leicester and, worst of all, Berkeley Square let a veil be drawn. The process that has stolen away London's architectural character has at the same time robbed the town of its former special amenity. There was a spaciousness, a solid elegance, a quiet self-assurance about London life that inspired contentment. This was true of all classes. London was London then. It was, if you like, a thought provincial ; yet it was metropolitan too. It was, as German philosophy used the phrase, a *Ding an sich*—something in itself, of its own. London has lost this characteristic. It has stood up less well to the vast changes wrought by modern transport, the radio, and above all by the cinema than has Paris, which through everything has preserved her soul. London's has evolved into something totally different and sadly chaotic. Nor was the Cockney's mind contented alone. It was aspiring. When this century was young, no hopes seemed impossible. The world was free. Passports were held a badge of slavery : they existed but in Turkey and Russia. The world was on an upgrade that should brook no arrest. The present was good, the future looked better. London had its black spots : what city in what age has not ? Only interested hypocrites or sentimental idiots can maintain the possibility of complete perfectibility in human conditions. But progress was general. The London clerk, working man, or artisan, for this last class still existed, led a busy and on the whole cheerful life. Wages and salaries were low, but costs and prices were lower still. Entertainment was cheap, the quality of food and drink first rate. A spirit of greater self-reliance was noticeable in that age than now when the individual is coddled and chivvied by the State

from the cradle to the grave. Class hatred standardised by Karl
Marx, a German Jew, half a century earlier, was still a line of
political propaganda that had few genuine adherents. Does a
university professor hate a duke, or a violinist resent the existence
of a squire? Neither in those days did a working man resent
the existence of the middle-classes. The stigma of social inferiority
was not visible on the brow of doctor, lawyer, or merchant. The
man of independent means was not yet a pariah. Artists, actors,
and men of letters could exist on their own : they had not yet
been forced into trade unions, nor did they see the prospect of
work ceasing to come their way unless under the ægis of Government subsidies and regulated councils or vast corporations as
soulless as the Government offices whose manners they ape. A
few lawyers foresaw the menace of bureaucracy, but the minor
official had not yet come to his full stature. In a word, it was
an age of independence, of ambition, of hope. The old saying
was still true : " An Englishman loves a lord." Nor were great
ladies less popular favourites. Until the last century's knell had
rung, perhaps longer, there was a large shop window in Regent
Street filled with cabinet photographs of them. Marvellously
beautiful they were and fully held their own—the Princess of
Wales, Lady Dudley, Lady Londonderry, and Lady de Grey
queens among them—with the great " professional beauties ",
among whom Mrs. Langtry was still *facile princeps*, the " Jersey
lily " so rapturously lovely that my mother remembered leaping,
in company with dozens of other ladies, on to chairs to see her
come into a room at a private party. Then there were the four
superb beauties of the Gaiety Theatre—the original Big Four
whose title statesmen, Scotland Yard, and bankers afterwards
sneaked—Birdie Sutherland, Hetty Hamer, " ten thousand
pound " Miss Fortescue, and the fourth, was it Maud Hobson?
—all cast in a goddess-like mould long since broken.

It was in a way a small world. Down to the last war there
persisted in France *le tout-Paris*, that's to say, a crowd of people
whose activities formed " Society ". With us " all London " in
the same sense, *le tout-Londres*, vanished with the 1914 war. But
it existed till then and formed a spectacle as entrancing to the
audience as to the actors.

The Season was its high spot. Relatively few of course took

part in the Season. Yet Covent Garden, the Eton and Harrow Match, Ascot, the Derby, Goodwood, Henley, thrilled not only the happy few who frequented them, but far wider circles by report of their splendours. They formed a focus of attraction that was also a centre whence lines of light radiated to illumine every imaginable form of entertainment, sport, and art. It would be an error to imagine the motives of this brilliant social energy to have been snobbish. Most of those engaged in it were genuine enthusiasts. One Caruso night at Covent Garden, when even the gallery, my natural habitat, was full and I was glad to get standing-room at the side of the gallery where one leant against an iron railing to prevent one from falling headlong into the stalls, and whence the stage was virtually invisible, I found myself next Sir Claud Phillips, the curator of the Wallace Collection. Middle-aged, plethoric, fashionable, immaculate in evening clothes, white waistcoat, and patent leather shoes, corseted maybe, Phillips, having been disappointed of a seat in a box on the grand tier, had clambered up to the very top of the house and stood all the evening rather than miss the divine music of Caruso, Melba, Journet, and Scotti. This was real devotion. No such collection of voices can ever have been heard anywhere as in the early part of this century at Covent Garden. Only an immensely wealthy society could have afforded it ; it is to London's credit that money was spent in this way as well as in racing or yachting. A just criticism would be that Covent Garden in the season cared for little but the voices. Certainly there was small chance of a well acted opera when Caruso was on the stage. He rushed about it like one demented and it took the majesty of his incomparable, incommensurable voice to make one forget his earnest antics. That exquisite dramatic artist Scotti made a strange contrast with Caruso judged as an actor. Melba, almost Caruso's equal vocally, could not act and did not try to ; she just " stayed put "—dignified and statuesque. Whenever he was in London at the same time as Melba, Joachim the great violinist used to buy a stall and listen to her every night she sang, so exquisite was her singing. Yet judged by voice alone, Caruso was surely unique. The box-office was well aware of this. Covent Garden paid him £400 a night and he sang the whole season through. New York, lagging long behind London in appreciation, later paid Caruso £1000 for a single concert appearance, Havana £2,000 for one in opera.

Far more than the opera, the London theatre was my joy. For a considerable time I went to the play one night in every three. By comparison with later days there were then few theatres in London. The opera apart, there were perhaps a dozen or so that counted, plus a few outlying playhouses like the Court and the Kingsway that flourished under exceptional managements, lasting rarely beyond a year or two. One great difference between theatres then and now was that you knew within a fairly narrow margin what fare to expect at any of them. People up from the country would " go to the Haymarket ", or the Criterion, or the St. James's, according to their taste, without having to examine in detail by whom was the play they would see, or what was its subject, or who was in the cast. They were certain to get good value for their money. There was also the Stage Society, formed largely through the influence of Bernard Shaw and his friends, to produce plays that could not find an opening elsewhere. Amid important works such as G. B. S's own *Mrs. Warren's Profession*, Gogol's *Inspector-General*, Brieux's *Three Daughters of M. Dupont*, and Somerset Maugham's *A Man of Honour*, the Stage Society produced my first play, a one-acter, with Gertrude Kingston, an actress of the front rank who, if she had married an actor-manager, might well have stepped into the shoes vacated by the famous Mrs. Kendal. Austin Harrison, then dramatic critic of the *Daily Mail*, later founder and editor of the *English Review*, wrote that *The Invention of Dr. Metzler* was by " a dramatist, perhaps the dramatist, of the future ". Well, well . . . No doubt it all depends, as Professor Joad might have said in his palmy B.B.C. days, on what you mean by " a " and by " the " and, if it comes to that, by " dramatist ". The theatre in any case was as irresistible to me as Matthew Arnold said it was to the world at large. So soon as I could, I disengaged myself from the Bar, an opportunity given me by the invitation to write a chapter in the *Cambridge Modern History*, which meant between six and nine months' hard work, incompatible with Lincoln's Inn.

For the legal profession I have nothing but admiration. It is one that demands qualities of a high order and, if success is to be achieved, total devotion. It demands immensely hard work. Barristers in good practice often—or in my day they did so—get up very early in the morning, sometimes at four or five, in order to study their briefs, believing that this keeps the brain fresher than to sit up late at night. After that they work all day too. To be successful at this a man must take a deep interest in the subject of his work, in this case law in its scientific and scholarly aspects, or have a fierce determination to get on in the world. Also to win through competition as keen as in any imaginable profession, a man must have first-rate health. Many who start well in the race fall by the way, and anyone not gifted with a goodly share of one or other of the two motives required or of a mixture of them and with an iron constitution to boot is mad to try and make a career at the Bar. Strong man as was Austin Cartmell, under whom I worked, the Bar killed him in middle life. So among my own acquaintance it killed Dighton Pollock, "Bull" Hurst, and C. P. Sanger. My liveliest recollection of the Bar is a case in which I devilled for Cartmell. It was a complicated affair of share transactions in which Cartmell appeared for one music hall magnate who was suing two others. This was just down Cartmell's street, for he was held one of the cleverest financial lawyers of the day. For hours we had sweated over the shady juggling that had taken place. In the end we thought we had it all straight and could prove our client to have been swindled. The case came on, Cartmell opened well, but had difficulty in making the judge understand the points at issue, so involved were they. Of this, of course, the defence prepared to take full advantage, when, just as their principal witness was being examined, in blew Rufus Isaacs, who was "leading" Cartmell. Isaacs, one of the handsomest men and most brilliant barristers at Court work ever seen, had not even glanced at his brief. He sat down and while the witness's examination was going on hurriedly looked through it. Then he stood up to cross-examine. Now no living man in fifteen minutes could grapple with a puzzle it had taken Austen Cartmell days to master. Even with his gigantic experience of finance or with his lightning rapidity of mind Rufus Isaacs got the angles of the case wrong. Cartmell, and even I, were on hot bricks. But Isaacs had got hold of enough of the pith of the matter to be able to cross-examine with deadly effect. He seemed to know the way in which such minds as that in the witness box worked. The stout music hall " big shot " who was our chief opponent was reduced by Isaacs to a rag, and when Isaacs sat down for a moment before going on to another court, there maybe to repeat this astounding performance, we had won our case. Rufus Isaacs was as popular at the Bar and in its surrounding society as his brother Godfrey, who ran Marconi finance in England, was unpopular when he appeared at houses where Rufus was welcomed ; Rufus was always distinguished, courteous, friendly, and no more touched with arrogance after becoming ambassador, Viceroy, and Marquis of Reading, than when he was first emerging into prominence as an advocate.

Covent Garden was at its zenith forty-odd years ago, with Italian opera in the season and Richter's electric conducting of Wagner in the autumn. There were other inspiring centres of music in London. One, well known, was the Queen's Hall where Sir Henry Wood first taught us to appreciate the beauties of Russian music. Another, unsuspected by the multitude, radiated an influence that has lasted till today. Outside London, to be precise, for Edward Speyer's home was at Elstree, as yet untransformed by cinema studios from a large country village. Speyer, whom I have cited above as witness on developments in Germany, had prospered in his business. He did not, like his more dashing cousin, Sir Edgar Speyer, launch out into the fields of metropolitan and cosmopolitan finance, but devoted his fortune to the exaltation of his life's passion, chamber music. No one can have had a more extensive knowledge of all music, but it was the piano, the string quartet, the singing of *Lieder* that were his chief delight. He had built on to a comfortable country house capable of putting up a score of people a panelled music-room so spacious that two concert grands and a full-sized billiards table seemed to leave it empty. H. G. Plimmer, one of my friends at the Savile Club, had a music-room almost as good in his house at St. John's Wood. So too had the Alma Tademas in their miniature palace with its celebrated " golden staircase ", in reality resplendently polished brass, behind Lord's. But Plimmer's love was for the organ and for Wagner ; fine musician as he was, he exercised little or no influence on London's music. Plimmer was also notable for his appearance. He wore his hair long, a black sombrero hat, a brown velveteen jacket, and a red silk tie. Few would have spotted him as chief pathologist at St. Mary's Hospital, and Professor of Pathology at the Imperial College of Science and one of the leading European authorities on cancer. The Tademas' musical evenings, where if you were lucky you might hear Paderewski play and De Soria sing, were more social than artistic affairs ; Alma Tadema, a delightfully genial person and a great craftsman even if his painting has gone clean out of fashion, would take endless trouble to catch artists arriving in England and get them to perform on or accompanied by the marvellous gilt piano first autographed by Paderewski : *he* was in another category, and a close and lasting friend of the house.

Edward Speyer's aims and results belonged to a different order. His sole ambition was to have good chamber music well played in the best conditions so that by his example and help it might be better understood and loved in England. At that time the St. James's Hall in Regent Street was the finest imaginable place for chamber music : nothing comparable to it exists now. Every year Joachim, who from his earliest days had a devoted following in England, was engaged by the proprietors of the St. James's Hall to come over from Berlin and play ; but the terms offered did not enable him to bring his complete quartet, the most famous in the world. Speyer now intervened. With the aid of my father and of Hugh Godley, later Lord Kilbracken, he founded the Classical Concert Society, hired the St. James's Hall, and brought over the entire quartet, Joachim, Halir, Wirth, and Hausmann ; moreover, he rearranged the seating so that the quartet played not at one end but in the centre, this being the right place for chamber music to be heard all over the hall or room where a concert takes place. The stimulus thus given to chamber music in England was immense and enduring. Behind the scenes, and the centre of an influence even greater than the Classical Concert Society, was Ridgehurst, the Speyers' house. Mrs. Edward Speyer not only ran the constant parties and weekends held there like the perfect hostess she was, but ably seconded Speyer's musical inspiration. They were a couple of truly noble character, beloved by all that knew them. She was a sister of Maurice Kufferath, a noted director of La Monnaie, the Brussels opera house, and herself a pupil of Brahms and one of the finest *Lieder* singers of her time. To Ridgehurst came, and at Ridgehurst played and sang, much of the cream of European executants. The Joachim quartet, and Joachim alone, had a standing invitation and rehearsed all their concerts there. It was a joke relished by all happy enough to be guests at Ridgehurst to watch Joachim when the company had moved after lunch or dinner to the music-room ostensibly for coffee and billiards. No one ever suggested that he should play. First he stayed sitting quietly in a corner by the fire. Then he would begin to fidget and his fingers to drum on his knees. Finally he could bear it no longer and broke out : " Ach, wollen wir nicht ein wenig Musik machen ? "—" Ah, shan't we have a little music ? " And he would settle himself at the music-stand and play perhaps for an hour on end, accompanied by Leonard Borwick, the finest living British pianist, who used sadly to say that he was appreciated only in Germany, or by Fanny Davies, Frau Schumann's favourite pupil, or by other stringed instruments. F.P. once asked Speyer what Joachim thought of *Symphonia Domestica* by Richard Strauss. Speyer wrote back : " I don't know if Joachim has heard that work. But I feel sure his general opinion is :—If it is Richard, it should be Wagner ; if Strauss, it should be Johann." Frank Bridge, more admirable as a viola player than as the composer he afterwards became, was often at Ridgehurst. So was Elgar, who had not yet attained to his full fame, and some of his chamber music was first heard there. It is a painful memory that Elgar asked me at the Speyers' for a subject for a light opera. Alas, I had nothing to offer but a tragedy, my one-act play *Rosamond*, afterwards set to music by Napier Miles. There were singers too, among them von Wahrlich, the Baltic Russian whose father had been musical director at the Imperial Court, the most perfect of all Schubert singers. Wahrlich's vogue in London was unique. Once I asked my mother, to whom he was much attached, returning from a concert by him, if she had seen him to speak to. " No indeed," she answered tartly, " all the duchesses in town were crowded round the platform." Van Rooy, the great Dutch baritone, came down one Sunday morning to Ridgehurst. I had often heard Van Rooy at Bayreuth and at Covent Garden and once had the curious experience of hearing him practise, the whole of one morning, over and over again, the few notes that form the Wanderer's laugh in *Siegfried*. Now he was to sing at Covent Garden next day, and Speyer begged him to rest. Van Rooy insisted on singing and sang the afternoon through, then, deaf to all advice, went out into the garden : result, he caught cold and was out of the bill next day, and Speyer told with mixed amusement and despair how Van Rooy went about complaining that his weekend at Ridgehurst had cost him £200, his regular Covent Garden fee. It is a melancholy reflexion, in days when artistic patronage is in the hands of " cultural " associations dispensing government money often through cliques and egotistical thrusters, that, even did a man with Speyer's knowledge and genius for inspiration exist today, he could not conceivably exercise a similar beneficent influence : to do so a man would need to be richer than Crœsus. And any line of Crœsuses would nowadays be smashed out of existence by the death duties in two generations. Forty years ago moderately well-to-do people, who yet did not rank among the really rich, frequently gave musical parties where promising performers could be heard by critics and connoisseurs. Such delights, no less than encouragements, were given among many others, at the houses of Sydney Schiff, who earned distinction as a writer under the name of Stephen Hudson, at that of his handsome and brilliant sister Mrs. Morley, and at my mother's ; and on a larger scale at Lady Palmer's of Huntley & Palmer's and the Carl Meyers, who were very rich indeed. People would sometimes also rent a theatre for a season, in order to give opportunity to a particular actor or actress, or to the works of a foreign author. By such means Ibsen was mainly introduced to the London public. Now private artistic patronage, musical and theatrical, is dead.

" This man shall eat meat, or this man shall die " : so had proclaimed the medical profession. This man, as all the world knows, did not die : on the contrary he still lives over ninety years old. Bernard Shaw's defiance of the doctors, that blossomed later into the fun and braggadocio of *The Doctor's Dilemma*, coincided with my first acquaintance with him. He was at Hind Head, recruiting after the illness that failed to cut him untimely off. It was not long after his marriage. Mrs. Shaw, who had brought him £150,000 and saved him from the drudgery of journalism, was like a clever kitten, sweet, pretty, admirably intelligent, utterly adorable, as indeed she remained till her death. Rumour had it that G. B. S., still in the heyday of Jæger clothes, and she had driven to the registry office in a four-wheeler, and away from it in separate hansoms, just to show their view of the value of such ceremonies. They were a most united couple. At Hind Head they saw few people, but came several times to my father's. The only link I know between the two men was that F.P. too at that time wore Jæger boots, which had the merit for walking in bad weather that they let out the wet through a brass-bound hole in the heel intended to ventilate the sole. G. B. S., as again all the world knows, was a unique individual. It was a shock to find that his imperturbable kindness was totally devoid of any personal quality but was a mere basic element in his character. Sensing my serious interest in the theatre, he invited me to go with him, ostensibly as secretary, to the rehearsals of his plays at the forthcoming season of the Barker-Vedrenne management at the Court Theatre that so much enhanced his own and Granville Barker's reputation. I went from beginning to end through the rehearsals of *Candida*, *You Never Can Tell*, and *Man and Superman*. G. B. S. was there at his best, that is, his most serious. He, not Barker, was the producer of his plays and the organiser of the Court's victory. No detail escaped him. His system was based on the tone in which each line in the dialogue was delivered. It was a matter of intense interest to see how, as the rehearsals proceeded, he progressively instilled his intention into the actors, and how famous artists like Kate Rorke, Louis Calvert, and Sydney Fairbrother took from him precisely the tone he wanted. Many who afterwards rose into high repute, among them Lillah McCarthy, Edmund Gwenn, the unforgettable chauffeur in *Man and Superman*, Norman Page, to become famous as the Cat in Maeterlinck's *The Blue Bird*, and Lewis Casson, learned or perfected their art from G. B. S. So far as his own plays were concerned he was a practical master of the theatre. It was concentrated work, as is all serious work on the stage, in which his gift for repartee was of striking value. Once when Kate Rorke was objecting to an exit speech in her part and cried out : " Oh, but Mr. Shaw, isn't that terribly stagey ? " he answered like lightning : " You can't be too stagey on the stage." After which brilliant statement of a truth so obvious that it is often missed, there was nothing more to be said.

Some years later I came again into close contact with Bernard Shaw over the publication of Brieux's *Les Avariés*, which I had translated under the title of *Damaged Goods*. I had hoped the Stage Society might produce the play but on enquiry it was found that the mere suggestion would rend even that advanced body from top to bottom. Mrs. Shaw then proposed that *Damaged Goods* should be included in a volume of Brieux translations by herself and St. John Hankin, who had done *The Three Daughters of M. Dupont* into English, while she was responsible for *Maternité* in its first version. Brieux had written a second and very different version of this play and insisted on this being printed too, but Mrs. Shaw disliked and refused to touch it ; so I translated *Maternité* in Brieux's perfected form, which was produced at Daly's in 1934. St. John Hankin was a man of much charm and an original slant of mind. His unseasonable death robbed the English theatre of one of our real writers of comedy ; I still think his one-act play, *The Constant Lover*, among the best in the language. Mrs. Shaw most capably carried out all the business side of the venture. No publisher could be found bold enough to undertake so stormy a work and *Three Plays by Brieux* was published on commission with, I may add, material profit to all concerned ; none of the mournful prophecies of probable prosecution for obscenity on account of *Damaged Goods* came true. One who thus attempted to deter me from the project was Egerton Castle, great French scholar, brilliant swordsman, and second-rate but highly successful novelist, whose best work was a translation into French of Stevenson's *Prince Otto*, a truly remarkable feat for an Englishman, even one who had been educated in France. G. B. S. was to write, and did write in his finest manner, an introduction to *Three Plays*. This was a trump card. But, oh, the trouble I had to get him to play it correctly ! He had got into his head from some quasi-medical work, so quasi indeed that genuine experts dubbed it a piece of charlatanry, a theory on the subject of the disease of which Brieux's play treats that virtually knocked the bottom out of Brieux's subject. He had actually written this into a draft of the introduction. I had to persuade him to take it out. It would have ruined the book. Here all his traditional Irish obstinacy came out in Shaw. He simply would not be convinced. I brought Walter Morley Fletcher, who knew all the specialists in London, to G. B. S., and statements of the utmost authority were obtained on the subject, all to little avail. Meanwhile Mrs. Shaw smiled serenely ; St. John Hankin hovered anxiously in the offing. The situation seemed desperate. Suddenly I had a brainwave. I would get G. B. S. to meet H. G. Plimmer who, though the subject of *Damaged Goods* was not his speciality, was nonetheless a noted master of pathology. This did the trick. Plimmer's noble head, long hair, velveteen jacket, red tie and the fact that he too was a " perfect Wagnerite " won over Bernard Shaw. The introduction to *Three Plays* was amended. I breathed again.

Another debt I owe to G. B. S. I never ventured to avow to him. He saved me from being a Socialist. While reading political economy at Cambridge I had ploughed through Karl Marx. The success of *Das Kapital* I believed to be largely due, as indeed is the case with much German philosophy and even some modern English poetry, to its indigestibility. If a work is sufficiently obscure, it can always command attention : *omne ignotum pro magnifico*. Marx at all events worked on exactly the contrary of Boileau's maxim :

> Ce que l'on conçoit bien, s'énonce clairement ;
> Et les mots, pour le dire, arrivent aisément.

The Fabian Society had however succeeded in extracting a certain plausibility from the turgid stodginess of the German-Jewish revolutionary *Führer* and like many other young men I was no less anxious to be instructed than tempted by novelty. I attended Fabian meetings, read yards of Fabian pamphlets, and frequented the Sidney Webbs, archpriests of the Fabian Society. It is a shade ironic that the chief Socialist prophets in England, Shaw and Webb, should have married capitalist fortunes, while the London School of Economics, whence most of their followers and not a few Communists have issued, was endowed by a multimillionaire, Sir Ernest Cassel, by the way another German Jew. Sidney Webb had married one of the three beautiful, rich, and clever Miss Potters. The Webbs made on me an impression of pompous pretentiousness, and I concluded they had gone in for Socialism in order to be able to crow in their own backyard since they lacked the capacity to shine in the front garden. For some reason Mrs. Sidney Webb, undeniably handsome as she was, always looked dowdy. Possibly that was why she married a pedant like Webb. Dreary though the Socialist prospect looked when seen from the Webbs' windows, Bernard Shaw, himself in a maze made roseate by William Morris's idealistic communist dream of *News from Nowhere*, gave Socialism a tinge of will-o'-the-wisp allurement. The Socialist system, I had already convinced myself, was incapable of conferring on mankind the benefits it held out, like a carrot before the nose of an ass, except in a world that should be perfect ; and then it would be unnecessary. But the thing I wanted to find out was how, in Shaw's view, the artist would fit into the Socialist scheme and in what manner he would be recompensed for his effort that in a society not shackled by what has since euphemistically become known as planning but is really departmental despotism is paid for by competition in a free market. G. B. S. owed what was solid in his reputation to his artistry as a dramatist, without which all his jibes at the established order would have seemed very jejune, and not to his pose as a social philosopher that has since so tickled the groundlings. It seemed to me that, if there were a satisfactory answer to my question, that brilliant artist Shaw should be able to provide it. So I went to a lecture in which he was announced to deal with precisely this subject. Needless to say, Shaw was amusing, eloquent, paradoxical, the greatest fun out : he always was. But he propounded no answer at all to the question. The conclusion was unescapable that in a perfect Socialist society artists would be relegated to the position of the wretched authors in " the Hutches " under that princely publisher's place of business in *Mr. Meeson's Will*, Rider Haggard's satirical novel no less entertaining for being now hardly remembered. This indeed is what artists have become, and scientists with them, in the Soviet Union, which claims to have perfected Socialist doctrine and practice. On the spot then, emerging from G. B. S.'s lecture, I shed the last rags of my Socialist aspirations.

Pretentiousness, especially in the sphere of social philosophy, is unfortunately rife among Englishmen of letters. Pretentiousness of this sort completely ruined H. G. Wells and the touch of it in him may yet rob Bernard Shaw of the lasting place his lively genius entitles him to. Mr. J. B. Priestley is another deplorable instance. Save in this special respect among authors it is a vice not exclusively ours. Axel Munthe, whom I met in Rome at the flat of the American dentist philosopher Brewster, was badly infected by it. Whatever the truth about his scientific attainments it is clear from the account of him in the Grand Duchess Marie Pavlovna's *Education d'une Princesse* that he pushed them by pretentious puffery to the verge of hocus-pocus. Happily for the world he found his true realm in the delicious *Story of San Michele*. But when I met him he was very pretentious indeed. He wrote the following in my sister's autograph book : " The first great step forward taken by man was when by standing upright and by his consequent left frontal development he gained the power of speech. The second will be when he learns to control it." I do not know whether the habit persists of getting eminent persons to write epigrams in pocket books, on the principle of so-called " golden books " kept by hotels ; probably it has been swept away by the sheer clamour for unadulterated autographs. It was a habit widespread for over a century. When young English or American ladies were brought up to be introduced to him, the Italian tragedian Salvini began the conversation with : " Vere ees ze leetel boo-ook ? " in which when produced he would scribble a line from Shakespeare. It took a man of firm character to express his opinion of such pestering in the ferocious lines written by Pushkin in an importunate hostess's book:

Three Graces had been born—so said the ancients' lore.
Then born were you : still were there only three, not four.

It was in 1909 that Lydia Yavorska, the Russian actress, and her husband Prince Vladimir Bariatinsky came to London. Most people supposed that their coming was part of the invasion of the West by Russian art that began with the appearance of Karsavina at the Coliseum in 1907 or 8, followed by Pavlova's triumph at the Palace, and blossomed with the full ballets and operas staged by Diaghilev at Covent Garden. The Bariatinskys were Rurikovichi, that is to say, descendants of the Scandinavian hero Rurik who with his two brothers were summoned in the ninth century by Russian boyars in the famous prophetic message : " Great is our land and plenteous, but there is no order in it. Come thou and rule over us." The few families, like the Bariatinskys and the Kropotkins in White Russia, sprung from these three, whose deeds have been immortalised by the great Russian modern painters Repin and Roerich, were immensely proud of the fact and looked down on the Romanovs who, until they were elected to the throne in another age of anarchy, were of secondary importance. This did not prevent the Romanovs from producing Russia's brilliant and tremendous emperor Peter the Great, the most constructive and far-seeing statesman of his age, and in the nineteenth century three more of first-rate capacities : had they been followed by a fourth of equal character and that fourth not married an hysterical degenerate, the Russian revolution would never have taken place and the world would have been spared the horrors of Bolshevism. A Bariatinsky had been among the conspirators against the Emperor Paul and helped to set Alexander I on the throne, and another held high office at the Court of Alexander III and was his personal friend. The eldest son of this prince, Alexander (Sasha) Bariatinsky, astonished Paris in the 1890's by his reckless expenditure : it was he who launched the beautiful operatic artist Lina Cavalieri on an admiring world and later married the no less beautiful morganatic daughter of Alexander II. The old prince though immensely wealthy kept his sons very short of cash. Prince Vladimir, Sasha's younger brother, had no resources save a moderate allowance from his father. When this was exhausted, he would wire in French to the old prince for more. Presently he would receive a laconic answer : " Refus absolu." Then he would send another wire : " Refuse de croire à ton refus." And so on until the old man would weary of the struggle and a further remittance was forthcoming.

The Bariatinskys came to England for a reason more compelling than artistic ambition. This was that Lydia Yavorska had been prohibited from appearing on the stage in Russia, where she was the leading actress outside the Imperial theatres of Moscow and St. Petersburg. Among her greatest successes were *Madame Sans Gêne*, *La Dame aux Camélias*, and *L'Aiglon*, and her

husband's own satirical comedies which were extremely amusing.
C. F. Keary, a good judge, said that he had " a truly Gogol-ish
wit ". Outside the theatre they both had marked liberal
tendencies, and it was this that brought them into conflict with
authority. He had founded and edited a paper that was sup-
pressed : the news of its suppression came when he was staying
with Tolstoy at Yasnaya Polya and was read to him by that
mighty figure in a telegram Tolstoy had received. His wife's
views or at all events acts were more extreme. She was intimate
with many of the prominent revolutionaries of the period and
had helped some of them to escape from Russia. Prince Peter
Kropotkin, the naturalist philosopher who began life as a page
to Alexander II and became first anarchist and then Social
Revolutionary and had long lived in exile at Brighton, was a
fast friend. Another was Wesselitsky, the veteran correspondent
in London of the *Novoe Vremya*, for all that their political opinions
were poles apart. Wesselitsky was a mine of diplomatic history.
He had known both Bismarck and Napoleon III, and was so
highly valued in England that, when the *Novoe Vremya* ceased
to exist after the revolution, a post was created for him as con-
sulting adviser on Russian affairs at the Foreign Office. He died
in London in the late 1920's, his amazing intelligence vivid to
the end, at the age of ninety-five. Kropotkin used to call
Yavorska " Lydia Svobodnitza ", that is, Lydia, daughter of
Freedom, instead of " Borisovna ", her true patronymic, from
her father General Boris de Hubbenet, who had been governor
of Kiev, Russia's third capital, and an honorary ataman of the
Orenburg Cossacks. The de Hubbenets, or in Russian style von
Giubbenets, were of French Huguenot stock, the real name being
Hubigny de la Motte-les-Rouvray, and had emigrated from
France after the Revocation of the Edict of Nantes, passing
through Austria, where they received a title of nobility from the
Emperor Joseph II, into Russia, where they were again ennobled
under Alexander I. General de Hubbenet had been noted for
his clemency as governor of Kiev, and it is not surprising that his
daughter, who pushed his liberalism so much further, and her
husband, whose views and whose marriage to an actress profoundly shocked his family, found their activity in Russia brought
to a full stop.

Perhaps Valy, as his intimates called him, or the Prince as he became simply known in England, would have temporised, being the possessor, besides his engaging sense of humour and genuine literary talent, of a typically Russian slothful disposition. I never saw a man more averse to exertion. Apart from endless talk with friends over slowly consumed light beer and innumerable cigarettes, his chief pleasure was in long walks so slow that it was difficult to keep pace with him, and cooking, an art at which he excelled. He was an admirable lecturer and gave several first-rate historical and literary lectures at private houses in London until he was, as he conceived, insulted by being asked to undertake a professional lecture tour on very remunerative terms, when he stopped them abruptly, and this though the money would have been welcome : another truly Russian trait. " The bills ! The bills ! " he would shriek, parodying Irving's celebrated cry in *The Bells*, as he watched the mounting pile of unpaid accounts on his desk. Lydia Yavorska, on the other hand, was ever driven on by a dæmon of energy that barely gave her time to sleep or to eat. She had absolutely no sense of time and invariably tried to crowd into twenty-four hours the normal activity of a week. Only great mutual devotion could have kept such a couple together, buttressed by the defensive armour of the Prince's lethargy ; his motto might have been : not " Bien " but " Rien faire et laisser dire." In the end the bond broke, to the Princess's for long inconsolable grief. Certainly it was Yavorska's determination that on Russia becoming a closed book to them led the Bariatinskys to the West. First, with a somewhat scratch company of actors, they played for a season in Russian in Vienna. Then they repeated this in Paris, where the great Mounet Sully himself toasted Lydia Yavorska as " Princesse dans la vie, Reine au théâtre ". Next year she was engaged to appear in French at the Théâtre Michel by two authors, now both dead. One had demanded her for the principal part, the other had as strongly objected. " You either adore her or you can't bear her," said the Prince of his wife. I was sitting next to him at one of the rehearsals when a storm between the two authors beat up so violently that Michel Mortier the manager finally apostrophised the objector with : " Do you say that this is the fault of the actors in my company ? " The author replied :

LYDIA YAVORSKA IN " FOR RUSSIA ! ", COLISEUM, 1914

PRINCE AND PRINCESS BARIATINSKY WITH HENRY JAMES IN HIS GARDEN AT RYE

From a photograph by Sir John Pollock

[208]

" Of a certain actress, rather." On which Bariatinsky called out from the stalls in a trenchant voice : " Or of a certain black-guard (*goujat*)." The author leaped to his feet with a challenge on his lips, then funked it and sat down, and ten minutes later got up and went quietly away, saying that he could not stay in a theatre where he was insulted.

Frederick Whelen, whom I knew as secretary of the Stage Society, had become secretary to Beerbohm Tree, then at the zenith of his career at His Majesty's Theatre. Whelen persuaded Tree to start the Afternoon Theatre, at His Majesty's, with a series of interesting and original matinée productions. Among them Lydia Yavorska's Russian company played with such success that the project was mooted of her appearing in English, and this took place at the Little Theatre, a lovely playhouse started by Gertrude Kingston, now destroyed by the blitz, in my *Rosamond* and in one act from Bariatinsky's *The Career of Noblotsky* which I did into English as *The Great Young Man*. The Prince was a fine linguist ; Yavorska, though fluent in French and German, had much difficulty with the pronunciation of English. Kate Rorke, however, took her in hand with such success that within two years of her first appearance people at the theatre were often heard to say of her while playing the part of a foreigner —to which parts of course her accent restricted her—" Oh, isn't it wonderful how she puts that accent on ? " The matinée at the Little Theatre was followed by a triumphant season in Ibsen's *The Doll's House*, by a brilliant *succès d'estime* in Henry Becque's *La Parisienne* at the Royalty, in an English version done by me, and by Yavorska's astonishing production of Maxim Gorki's *The Lower Depths* translated by Lawrence Irving, that marked an epoch in London stage production. Nothing like it had ever been seen. Frank Collins, afterwards Sir Charles Cochran's stage director, and I acted as Yavorska's assistants, but the whole design of the production down to the smallest details was hers. Sir Charles (then C. B.) Cochran now offered Yavorska the lead in his production of Reinhardt's *The Miracle* at Olympia, but she was under contract to play at Glasgow in *The Lower Depths* and could not accept. Yavorska had an electric gift for inspiring those who worked with her to touch the highest they were capable of. Like all actors of the first rank she was a tireless worker,

driving herself as hard as she drove others, and invariably with
the aim of making a success for the play and the whole company
and not for herself alone. It was this that made her beloved
by her company, despite occasional irritation at what seemed to
them her erratic ways and, being sensed by the public, added
to her personal genius in creating the greatest success a foreigner
had had playing in English since the days of Modjeska, the
beautiful and talented Polish actress with whom Forbes Robertson
when young had played the lead.

Yavorska's success was no less striking " on the halls ".
Through the agency of Eric Wollheim, a clever Polish Jew who
brought Sarah Bernhardt to the Coliseum and later Diaghilev
to the Alhambra, she was engaged by Sir Oswald Stoll to present
Lolotte, the famous one-acter of Meilhac and Halévy, adapted by
me. If I seem often to refer to myself in this connexion, I am
afraid the reason is simply that the Russians thought better of
my work than most of my compatriots seemed to do. Zinaida
Vengerova, a leading St. Petersburg dramatic and literary critic,
compared my *Rosamond* with Oscar Wilde's *Salome* ; Prince
Bariatinsky translated it into Russian, and this as well as another
of my one-acters, *Mlle Diana*, in which Petrovsky the best character
actor at the Imperial Theatre in Moscow had played for a charity
matinée, were down for production there when the revolution
smashed all such plans into dust. *Lolotte* was a riotous success
for three weeks at the Coliseum and thereafter at all the No. 1
music-halls throughout England and Scotland. It certainly
needed outstanding qualities for an unknown foreign actress in
a foreign play to sweep audiences of two and three thousand
Britons off their feet. This progress, chequered by one or two
setbacks in London due to faulty judgment, led up to what had
been Yavorska's great ambition in coming to England, namely,
to stage a dramatisation of Tolstoy's *Anna Karenina* and play the
name part in it. There were, said the Russians, six-and-thirty
Russian versions extant, all mediocre, and there was known to
be a successful French play taken from the novel ; but they
wanted an English dramatisation, and commissioned me to do
it. I may say without vanity that my effort bore fruit, for *Anna
Karenina* ran for nearly a year at the Ambassadors and Scala
Theatres, followed by a triumphant tour, and was only prevented

from resumption in London by the course of the first World War.
Tolstoy's tragic heroine, torn between her lover and her child,
provided the top notch of Yavorska's English career. Among
others the Grand Duke Michael, the Emperor's brother and heir
presumptive to the throne, then in exile in England owing to
the morganatic marriage he had contracted, was consulted about
the production. The picture given of life in Moscow and St.
Petersburg was as masterly as it was original. One difficulty
was the scene at the races at Peterhof that precipitates a crisis
in the story. How was a brilliant scene at a race course, where
the hero's horse falls at a fence and breaks his back, to be enacted
on the stage of a very small theatre? At the Ambassadors—
named, by the way, by Lydia Yavorska, in response to the request
of Herbert Jay, who built the theatre, " the Ambassadors of Art,"
she said—there could be no question of a grand spectacle such
as might have been possible at Drury Lane. I solved the problem
by setting the scene in the interior of a box in the grandstand, the
backs of its occupants being turned towards the footlights while
all that passed on the course was seen by them but invisible to
the audience. The trick was perfectly successful and the result
far more agonising to the public than the direct spectacle of
Vronsky's race proved to be in any of the films made from
Tolstoy's book. One actor who in the part of Prince Oblonsky,
Anna's brother, had revealed himself as an artist of real class,
Scott Craven, volunteered for the army at the first possible
moment in 1914 and was killed in one of the earliest engagements.
At the end of the run at the Ambassadors in that summer
Yavorska who, like most Russians, enjoyed doing things in a
crowd was taking a holiday at Lulworth Cove in company with
Professor and Mrs. Forsyth, Dr. Nodel, a Russian exile who had
built up a practice as dentist in the East End, Yavorska's insepar-
able companion Elizaveta Blagoveshchenskaya, known for short
to English friends as Miss Blago, the similarly exiled editor of a
Tiflis paper, and myself. The public news was disturbing. One
morning we were all standing on a cliff and looking out to sea,
when before our eyes the British Fleet that had been at Portland
for dispersal after manœuvres steamed back up-Channel. So
we knew, Russians and British, that war with Germany was
upon us.

The Prince had already gone back to St. Petersburg, save for short visits. Life in England began to bore him. He yearned for Romanov's, the oyster shop in the Nevsky Prospect, whither he could stroll, there over a dozen of them and a bottle of champagne to write another witty scene in a new comedy. For he had made up his quarrel with authority. He had a play, by no means his best, produced at the Imperial Theatre. He had taken a new flat and formed new connexions with a distinctly anti-British flavour. The war caused the revocation of decrees against Russians in exile from the Grand Duke Michael downwards and they flocked back to Russia, the Emperor's brother receiving the command of the famous " wild division " of Caucasian cavalry. Yavorska too returned, in an aura of pro-British enthusiasm, to find that her husband refused to see her. It was a still greater blow when he tried to divorce her. In decent Russian society divorce by consent was admitted as a normal readjustment, but a divorce action against an unwilling spouse held to be almost the ultimate human baseness. Prince Bariatinsky's action failed flagrantly. Yet that was not the end. One further shock was in store. Rasputin was there. To compass the end of this and of another marriage obnoxious to the pro-German elements of the Court, Rasputin had the Over Procurator of the Holy Synod, an honest man, dismissed and replaced by a venal tool of his own who in flat contradiction of the law pronounced both marriages to be dissolved. Lydia Yavorska's indignation and sorrow were tragic. It was not until four years later after her return to England that she overcame them and consented to marry me. But she had brought back from Russia the seeds of illness, aggravated by her indomitable efforts against the Bolsheviks. In the course of these on one occasion she bearded the chief of the Cheka, the ill-omened Uritsky, in his very headquarters to obtain the release of a former member of the Duma : a barely imaginable feat of courage and persuasiveness. Only a few months had passed in England when she died at Brighton, a place that for the sake of Prince Kropotkin, who like her had returned in joy to Russia, to die there disillusioned and like her loathing the Bolsheviks, she always held in affection. They were two great souls.

CHAPTER XII

THE RUSSIAN SCENE

C.F. (" CHARLIE ") KEARY whom I have mentioned more than once was the first man to turn my mind to Russia. Like Horace Greeley and his celebrated " Go West, young man ! " Keary told me to look East. I was still up at Cambridge and looking Paris- and Vienna-wards when he said that if he were beginning life again he should go to Russia. What interested him beyond Russian literature and art was the Russian character, still a vast question mark for western Europeans, one might almost say for Europeans without any qualification, so far across Russia did certain aspects of Asia seem to stretch out. Elder men often influence their juniors more than they think by such remarks. Just so Lord Justice Kennedy inculcated in me when still at school a lasting prejudice against the Civil Service by saying : " Never go into red tape, Jack ! Never go into red tape ! " Keary's advice, though I did not dream of taking it at the time, stuck in my mind and fermented. But not till I met Russians so as to be able to see them at close quarters in their daily occupations—without which it is impossible to get to know anybody—did the value of it become plain to me. The Russian empire formed an eighth part of the globe's whole habitable surface. Its population was then some hundred and twenty million, almost a third of that vast conglomeration known as China and nearly double that of Great Britain and France put together. Russia had produced gigantic figures in political life, in music, and in literature. Asiatic as she looked from some angles, from others she was seen highly susceptible to Western influence. Without Byron, Russia's two greatest poets, Pushkin and Lermontov, would not have written as they did. The bulk of Russia's people were of the same ultimate stock as ourselves, and the Russian language, when its initial difficulties were overcome, was found to be full of roots and words that cropped up in other European tongues. Thus, to take a few simple instances, the Russian for house is *dom*, the Latin *domus* ; *adin*, *dva*, *tree*, one, two, three, are virtually the same as English ; *stul*, a chair or stool and *sadit*, to seat, are again all but the English words ; *vino*, wine, is the same in Latin languages, English and German. It followed not only that it was important for anyone desirous of understanding the world we live in to become acquainted with Russia and Russians, but also that there existed links which must make acquaintance easier than was commonly suspected. There is no such barrier between Russians and other Europeans as there is between the latter and the Chinese, Japanese, Negroes, Mongols, and Semites. With all these we can be friends ; we can admire them. But they are different from us. Even without taking into account the infusion of Western ideas through the Baltic Germans, a small but vital element in Russian life, and the deliberate importation into Russia of Western values by Peter the Great and Catherine the Great, the average Russian at the beginning of this century had the same fundamental attitude towards life and its problems as his brother of similar station in the rest of the Indo-European world. When you came to live among them, you found them very easy to understand, and very easy to like. English people had the advantage over other foreigners of getting quickly on terms with the Russian language. It is less hard to master than German and its pronunciation is simple to us, who swallow half our syllables just as do the Russians ; the French pronounce every syllable clean cut, which makes Russian barely intelligible, and Italians have great trouble in not introducing into it their own heavy tonic accent that has nearly the same effect. For myself, I learned Russian as a baby learns to speak, without any regular lessons, and I learned in about the same time, for after living three years in Russia I could go about everywhere without my nationality being suspected. Which turned out to be just as well, since after the Bolshevik revolution my life depended on it.

It is a truism that Russia has been cut off from the rest of the world for thirty years. But this is generally taken to mean that Russians no longer have any knowledge of what is outside their country. What is equally serious is that, save for the diminishing number of those who knew the older Russia, Westerners have become steadily more ignorant not so much of what is passing in Russia today as of what Russia represented down to the date when " the veil in Moscow ", as I called it at the time, now more appropriately notorious as " the iron curtain ", was dropped and clamped down in front of our noses. Especially since the last war it has become evident to me that the younger generation in England has barely the foggiest idea of what pre-revolutionary Russia was like, and this despite their keen desire to know. Thus it is possible for the wildest notions and sometimes the most impudent fictions to prevail, as when Mr. Emmanuel Shinwell in 1948 publicly ascribed the present miseries of the Russian people to the " barbarism " of the Imperial regime.

Russia was the result of her history. " Oh," I hear some say, " he's going to talk history at us ! That's what comes of having read history at Cambridge and of writing scraps of it. Let's get on with the future ! " To this objection there can be no answer except a flat affirmation. The future, the present, and the past alike grow out of history. All that we are is history ; all history is in us. Anyone trying to get an idea about Russia or Russians without attending to their history is a dunce doomed to failure. I apologise for stating a truth so self-evident. But re-statement is needed where sketchy and incorrect imaginings, often the result of lying propaganda, hold sway in place of real knowledge of facts. And facts are history. Geography too, which is history's twin sister.

Russia is a country of plains. The steppes, that to foreigners appear an unconscionable stretch of nearly flat land for hundreds of miles in every direction, are dear to the Russian heart.

ЧОРТЗ ВАСЗ ВАЗМИ СТЕПЬИ, КАКЗ ВУІ ХОРОШИИ !

or, transposed for English lips,

Chort vass vazmee, styaipee, kak vui harashee !
The dickens take you, steppes, how good you are to see !

So wrote Gogol. With the perversity of ignorance Seton Merriman in a book otherwise not devoid of merit laid the scene of its action near Tver between Moscow and St. Petersburg, with an impressive description of the steppes there. Now Tver happens to be virtually the only district blessed with hills between the Baltic and the Caucasus. The rest is plains.

These plains then, immeasurable before the era of railways, made Russian history. The plains and the absence of sea coast. Sea Russia had none until Peter the Great " opened an eye " on to Europe with his wonderful city, until 1917 the most lovely monument extant of eighteenth-century town planning. The Black Sea, hemmed in to the west and south by the Turks, its exit blocked by Constantinople, was no more than a lake. Therefore the Russians rarely developed those qualities of individual enterprise and hardihood, and the habit of taking a long distance view that are bred by proximity to sea and mountain. On these plains too are few defensible positions save rivers which though broad are seldom swift and present little obstacle to invaders, as German and Polish and Swedish successes bore frequent testimony. But the greatest invasion of all was that which besides her geographical situation stamped an indelible influence on Russian history—the invasion of the Tartars. In the middle of the fifteenth century a traveller wrote : " If Moscow is not in Asia, it is certainly on the very edge of Europe, and very close to Asia." This Asiatic complexion was given to Moscow and to all Russia, partly by the Orthodox Church which derived from the Eastern Roman Empire at Constantinople, but mainly by the Tartars who dominated the country for nearly three centuries and, though their power was broken at the end of the fifteenth, remained for long after a potent influence that did not sensibly diminish till Peter the Great at the beginning of the eighteenth forced his subjects to abandon long Asiatic skirts and long beards, and to allow freedom to women who had been habitually kept in quarters called the *terem*, somewhat analogous to the Oriental harem. Thus it came about that the organisation of society in Russia was four centuries behind that in Europe proper and that at the end of the nineteenth century the Russian peasant, that is, ninety per cent of the population, was not far removed from the condition of his Western brother in the fifteenth.

For Russia as a whole to have changed from the sluggish semi-Oriental country it was down to Peter the Great into the urgently progressive nation it had become before the first World War is a proof of the ludicrous falsity of the charge that the Imperial regime was a bloodthirsty and reactionary despotism stifling the people's legitimate aspirations. In fact it was exactly suited to the needs of the Russian people, far too undeveloped to profit by anything save autocracy. Tyranny there was, and brutality there was ; but it was chiefly spent on the small number of intellectuals who, having drunk the heady wine of Western liberalism, conceived the introduction of parliamentary method into Russia as a doorway to Slav millennium. There was also abysmal stupidity on the part of the last emperor, Nicolas II, who resembled our own Charles I as much by his incompetent obtuseness as by his virtues as a family man. The error of the sincere revolutionaries was confessed after the revolution with horrified contrition by patriots like Plehanov the Socialist leader, Burtsev, the Social Revolutionary who unmasked the double agent Azev, convincingly portrayed by Joseph Conrad in *The Secret Agent*, by Kropotkin, and by Yavorska. " I see now," Plehanov said to me, " that Peter the Great was right : the Russians are only good for anything ' under the stick ' "—one of Peter's famous sayings. The eyes of such ardent, often inspired and self-sacrificing idealists were blinded by generous hopes the blasting of which by self-seeking adventurers, mostly not of Russian blood, who ran the Bolshevik party was the prelude to the unparalleled tyranny that the world has witnessed but that the world, save for a small minority, has only just begun to comprehend. The truth is that no country had made strides forward in the nineteenth century comparable with those in Russia effected by the reforms of Alexander II, who abolished serfdom, developed local self-government, established independent lawcourts and, when he was assassinated by revolutionaries incapable of judging reality, was on the point of presenting Russia with a constitution. Alexander II was with truth named " The Liberator ". Nor was the progress political only. The land reforms of Stolypin, Nicolas II's prime minister murdered by reactionaries who armed the killer, a crazy student stuffed with revolutionary ideals, enabled the peasants to buy the land they tilled, so that by 1914 a considerable percentage of the land in Russia was owned by peasant farmers, who thus learned the taste of what Arthur Young called " the magic of property ". A decade later this invaluable class was to be annihilated by the Bolsheviks under the derisive title of *kulaki* or " fists ",

meaning " closefisted fellows ", who were the most formidable
obstacle to the institution of Communist tyranny. Stolypin, it
is worth noting, was also responsible for the introduction of a
reasonable degree of sanitation into St. Petersburg. At the
same time the commercial and industrial advance in Russia was
amazing. The finest cloth in the world was made in the mills
at Schlüsselburg, some of the best perfume and soap in Moscow,
and the rubber factories of St. Petersburg produced two of the
best-known motor tyres, the Treugolnik and the Provodnik,
besides a host of domestic articles like rubber sponges, of a quality
not seen anywhere since then. The best tinned vegetables and
fish in the world came from Odessa. Of Russian leather and
agricultural produce it is unnecessary to speak : one-eighth of
the entire wheat consumption of the British Isles came from the
Ukraine, then better known as Little Russia. The fertility of
the " black " earth in that vast region whose centre is Kiev
was celebrated. Kiev was the most beautiful of Russian cities,
and by nature the most beautiful I have ever seen except Rome.
Life in Little Russia touched a peak of comfort and ease.
According to the Little Russian's traditional dream, he was
lying under a cherry tree and into his open mouth dropped—
not cherries, but *vareniki*, little round balls of the finest floury
dough, filled with cherry jam.

In the four years I spent in Russia it was obviously impossible
to see more than a small part of the country and of the nation.
One might say " nations ", for it should not be forgotten that
the Tsar was Emperor not of Russia but " of all the Russias "
and that his subjects came from a dozen different nations and
races. Yet there was a power of assimilation in the Russian
character instilling into them all, Great and Little and White
Russians, Tartars, Armenians, Jews, and Germans, a subtle
unison that despite centrifugal forces as yet untamed forged
from this immense conglomerate a recognisable whole, solid
against the world outside. Except for the Tartars, who had
become very quiet folk, sober, well educated, busily commercial
and in the main monogamous although still devoutly Mahom-
medan, I saw much of the other elements, and made friends
among them all. Over all, a symbol of Russia, hung the idea
of God and the Tsar.

German armies invading Russian Poland in 1914 adopted the same policy they practised in Belgium and with complete success in France in 1940—driving before them the helpless civilians to block the roads and litter the enemy's lines of communication. From a military point of view the Russians did not suffer much. They simply let, indeed urged, the refugees through, only taking care to keep the roads and railways clear. But the wretched civilians suffered greatly. Princess Kropotkin in far-away England, where these events went unreported, bestirred herself. She was a strong-minded woman and took up the cause of the Polish refugees with the cry of " Poland is the Belgium of the East ". Princess Bariatinsky's sympathy was instantly engaged and the two stumped the country in favour of a movement they called " Great Britain to Poland and Galicia ". Galicia had to be thrown in because friends at the Russian embassy (who maintained amicable relations with many of the exiles, such are the mysterious ways of the Russian mind) pointed out that no relief movement would be admitted by the Russian Government which implied Galicia, where the distress was not less than further north, to be part of Poland. When I got there I discovered that in fact at least sixty per cent of the Galician refugees were not Poles but Ruthenians, who are Russian at one remove. However, Poland and the Poles formed the main object. Things always turn out differently from what mortals expect them to be. The committee's small delegation to Warsaw to give effect to the sympathy thus aroused in Great Britain, and to expend the money generously subscribed in English and Scottish cities, fondly thought to return in a few weeks' time. At its outset the war was expected to last not more than six months. When Kitchener was asked by his neighbour at a dinner-party how long he would give the war and answered " Three years," it was thought the best joke in the world ; only long afterwards did it become known that he had made contracts for the British army in France for precisely that length of time. It would be hard to parallel Kitchener's reputation and authority. On his becoming Secretary for War, Mrs. Asquith, afterward Lady Oxford, told a friend of my sister : " My dear, the whole Cabinet trembles before him and, as for Herbert, he might as well be a black man ! " I was above serving age ; when I was ultimately due to be called up I was immersed in work that the British ambassador in St. Petersburg, or Petrograd as it had become, thought of sufficient importance for it to be continued, and I received an order from the G.O.C. London district not to return but to carry on in Russia.

The duration of the war was one error made by the Great Britain to Poland committee in common with everybody else. Another was that the relief work it undertook would help to build mutual understanding and confidence between Britons and Poles. Quite the contrary happened. The Polish Central Citizens Committee, a body established for war purposes with the consent of the Russian Government and of the Grand Duke Nicholas the Russian generalissimo, whose mistress was a Pole, when they learned that the money subscribed in Great Britain was not to be handed over to them in a lump but to be expended under British supervision, took an instant aversion to the delegation's doings, the more so when it was revealed that Polish Jewish refugees too and not Catholic Poles alone were to benefit from it, a matter on which I had strict orders from home. The goodwill created by " Great Britain to Poland " was solely among the Russians, who thought this little private effort a touching manifestation of the newborn friendship between the British lion and the Russian bear. However small the scope of the work, this was a perfectly definite point of value. So definite indeed that from an early date those engaged in it were pursued by the hostility of pro-German and reactionary elements in Russia : the terms were identical. The stories of the Emperor and Empress's unpatriotic leanings, current for a while in England, were later shown to be a legend propagated by the Germans themselves. But there was plenty of German spying and fifth-column work, largely radiating from Rasputin and his circle. Now Rasputin's chief liaison with the Court during his frequent absences was Mme Vyrubova, lady-in-waiting to the Empress. This person's brother-in-law had obtained the post of head in Warsaw of the Zemsky Soyus, or Union of Zemstvos, an association of county councils (or something like them) that carried in it the germ of a constitution for Russia far more fertile than that contained in the talkative and unpractical Duma. The Zemsky Soyus did Trojan work throughout the war in supplying comforts to the troops at the front and running supply and munition factories in the rear. At Vyrubov's instigation or at least with his knowledge, and certainly with the object of discrediting me, a Polish officer took me on a tour, ostensibly to inspect the need for relief work, into a prohibited military district. The German lines, be it noted, were but forty-odd miles west of Warsaw. I was naturally arrested and, though on investigation I was quickly released, I received a prohibition from ever re-entering the zone of the Western Front, that was the central zone of the whole Russian front from the Baltic to the Carpathians, divided into the Northern, Western, and Southwestern Fronts, each under a separate C.-in-C. with a completely separate organisation of its own. Actually the Western Front soon ceased to interest my work. Warsaw its then H.Q. fell, and all Poland proper with it passed into enemy hands in the summer of 1915 and relief work there ceased. The refugees from the Warsaw zone were drafted to Moscow and tended by the committee of the highly efficient British colony I was lucky enough to help set up there. But I was determined not to rest under the stigma put on me by Vyrubov or his agents. It took me fifteen months to achieve a reversal of that galling prohibition and I succeeded only after a personal appeal to General Alexeiev, the C.I.G.S., who after hearing my case sent me to General Ebert, C.-in-C. Western Front, with a strong recommendation that did the trick. I already held rank in the Russian army. The Great Britain to Poland Fund had been taken into the Russian Red Cross organisation and I found myself an International Red Cross Commissioner with the rank of a Russian ensign, Russian uniform and sword complete. Rather than buy a sword at a military outfitters, I obtained a beautiful Caucasian blade of the finest steel welded at Vladikavkaz, where the daggers made had as a final test to pierce two silver rouble pieces—about the size and thickness of a florin—one on top of the other without the point being blunted. Like all my other possessions there, it never left Russia.

The reason for the fusion with the Russian Red Cross was that in the course of 1915 it became increasingly difficult for anyone out of uniform to travel and work in or near the army zone. It was a great privilege to be accorded to so small an outfit. I have little doubt this privilege and perhaps the success of my appeal to General Alexeiev, even my obtaining an interview with him, were due to a distant but potent influence that I felt, more strongly looking back than at the time, to have held out a protecting hand over this volunteer British relief group. I never had the honour to approach the Empress Marie Fedorovna, widow of Alexander III and sister of our own Queen Alexandra. I had but one occasion of personal touch with her and that extremely sad. After the war she learned that I had been in 1918 in contact with the Grand Duke Michael, her second son, the younger brother of the murdered Nicolas II, and thought that I might give her hope of his being still alive. It was true I had been in communication with the Grand Duke. I knew that he had not, as generally surmised, been killed together with the rest of the Imperial family near Perm, but had been rescued from the Bolsheviks by a trick of a party of friends. This trick was more than once successfully played during the German occupation of France in the late war to rescue French patriots from the Gestapo. The person to be rescued is in prison. He shams ill or induces illness and is removed to the prison infirmary, always less carefully guarded than the prison itself. Actually the Grand Duke Michael was suffering from gastric trouble. Then late one evening a party perfectly disguised as Gestapo officers or, in the Grand Duke's case, Bolshevik Commissars and their minions arrives to carry him off to instant execution. He learns the truth only when they are speeding away together. The Grand Duke Michael then had escaped. This was in the middle of June 1918. He was with his friends somewhere in the district of Ufa, on a tributary of the Volga that comes down from the Ural Mountains. Thence his A.D.C., Captain Johnston, a Russian of old Scottish descent, came in the summer of 1918 to Moscow with a message for Captain Miloradovich and for me if he should find me to invite us to return with Johnston, join the Grand Duke in the Urals and try to break through to Admiral Kolchak in Siberia. Miloradovich was a nephew of the President of the first Duma, and a noted swordsman. The prospect was tempting. I was close penned up in Russia, living under a false name, and had failed to find any way out. I should undoubtedly have accepted, for I was very friendly with Miloradovich and had complete confidence in Johnston's sincerity. As to his ability, it was he who organised the Grand Duke's escape. He was a small, very quiet man. But I could not go with him within the limit of time assigned for his return. I was in the process of getting the Bolsheviks to take over the refugee children's orphanage under my charge in Moscow, without letting them know that they were negotiating the affair with a British proscript. Otherwise the wretched mites would have been flung on to the streets. In the end I had the satisfaction, all unsuspected in the next room, of hearing Krupskaya, Lenin's " wife ", magniloquently claim for the Bolshevik administration the credit of so well conducted an orphanage. So I did not go with Johnston and Miloradovich to join the Grand Duke Michael, and so I did not die with them. For they were never heard of again. Obviously then they did not get through to Kolchak. Obviously too they did not remain hidden in the Urals, for in the autumn Kolchak's forces overran the district as far as Perm, where compelling evidence of the massacre of the remaining Grand Dukes and their families was found (except the four murdered in the fortress of St. Peter and St. Paul in Petrograd in February 1919), as may be read in Robert Wilton's authoritative *The Last Days of the Romanovs*.[1] The Grand Duke and his friends must have fallen in with a detachment of Bolshevik marauders and been killed to the last man without the Grand Duke's identity being revealed. Had he been recognised, alive or dead, the fact would have certainly been made known. One can only hope they gave a good account of themselves before being wiped out. Having known three of these men, I think it likely.

To the Empress Marie Fedorovna then, who had escaped the common Imperial fate by being out of the country, I had the melancholy duty of writing what I knew. Her eye was quietly upon the work under my charge till the end and, since she is dead, I may express my gratitude openly. I owed to her too, on the very eve of the revolution, a Russian decoration that I

---

[1] Authoritative, that is, as far as the actual evidence open to Wilton went. Wilton, ignorant of my later contact with the Grand Duke Michael, concluded that he had been murdered at Perm with the rest of the Imperial family.

highly prize, St. Anne with Swords, that can rarely have been bestowed on a non-combatant. It was also from her, through her private secretary, that I received the details, not entirely accurate, of Rasputin's death. My account of this event, necessarily anonymous, was smuggled to England and created a sensation when published in *The New Europe*. The complete and true facts, afterwards published by the deputy Purishkevich and by Prince Yusupov, two of the assassins, were so sedulously concealed at the moment that even the Dowager Empress, who was well placed for finding out, did not get them quite right. But for this minor error, my account of Rasputin even today requires little correction.

Like everything else in wartime, refugee work grew. Not that after 1915 there were many fresh refugees. But those of 1914 and 1915, mostly Polish peasants, elderly, ill and many small children, required unremitting attention. This they got in Petrograd and Moscow from the daily work of the British committees and in Kiev, where there was no English colony, from a Russian committee I got started. The British colonies in the two capitals were admirable. They were formed of residents of long standing engaged in businesses stretching back in Russia for two or more generations. They had a high standard of interests and education and combined strong British characteristics with a very pleasant softening of comfortable Russian traits. They knew Russia far better than the British embassy circle. A saying of one of their principal members Mr. Arthur Woodhouse, the British Consul-General, achieved celebrity and has since been ascribed to other more prominent people. Woodhouse was wont to say : " There are only two people in Russia who count—the Emperor and the man he is talking to." Woodhouse became keenly and justly alarmed in 1917 for the safety of the British colony in Petrograd, about three thousand strong, and wanted to get them evacuated. Knowing that I had good railway connexions he sent for me and propounded his idea. I went to the chief engineer of the Nicolas Railway. He was a Russian Pole, a colonel, extremely pro-British and extremely capable. It was he who in 1915 gave me the land close to the railway on which was built the canteen for feeding the Polish refugees. Now he went into Woodhouse's scheme with enthusiasm. Most Russian railwaymen, the highest type of organised labour in the country, were strongly anti-Bolshevik, and their chief easily enlisted their assistance. Earlier in the summer a Bolshevik outbreak had nearly succeeded. Everyone knew that, short of decisive measures being taken by the Kerensky Government, it would be repeated ; and no one believed such measures would be taken. The Colonel, who in October when the Bolsheviks' successful *coup d'état* did take place was one of the first people to be murdered by them, sounded five of his engine drivers. They all accepted. The plan was simple. Five trains and their engines with steam up were to be ready for departure at a moment's notice. The British colony should arrive at a zero hour to be fixed by the Consul-General, their progress to the Nicolas Station being covered by the six British armoured cars then in Petrograd, on their way back from the Southwestern Front where they had made an effective token appearance ; without this protection so large an exodus could not fail to evoke obstruction and armed attack from Bolshevik gangs. The British civilians should entrain and be whisked round on the loop-line south of Petrograd to the Finland Station whence it was less than an hour's straight run to the frontier and security. This well thought out and perfectly feasible plan of the Consul's was vetoed by the British Ambassador who feared diplomatic complications, with the result that the next year, as only a few individuals among the British had left Russia, most of them were flung into prison by the Bolsheviks, and many died either there or subsequently of illness and the effects of harsh treatment.

Sir George Buchanan was a thoroughly high-minded and in any ordinary circumstances a first-rate Ambassador. But he did not know Russia outside the small Court and diplomatic coterie of Petrograd. The Embassy had had in its Counsellor, O'Beirne, one man who did know Russia and Russian well ; but he was unfortunately sent to Sofia in a vain attempt to prevent Bulgaria from joining in the war as Germany's ally and after that happened no one apparently thought of sending him back to Russia where his knowledge would have been of outstanding value, till he was attached to Kitchener's mission to Petrograd in 1916 and was torpedoed and drowned on the way together with that great man. No one could persuade intelligent

Russians that the date of Kitchener's departure had not been
given away to the Germans by Stürmer, who had been made
Russian prime minister by Rasputin's machinations and was one
of the few men from whom it could not be concealed. A single
example will show the limitations that circumstance imposed on
Sir George Buchanan. In the early summer of 1915 he sent
for me. I had just come back from the front. Could I give
him some information? Iszrael Zangwill was creating a rumpus
at home about atrocities he alleged were being practised by the
Russian troops on Jews in the army zone, amounting to veritable
pogroms. Pro-Russian feeling in England was in danger of
cooling off. Ugly articles had appeared in the press. Meetings
were being organized. The Foreign Office had applied to
Buchanan for information, and the Ambassador in turn to
Sazonov, the Russian Foreign Minister. Despite repeated
requests, nothing came from Sazonov. The F.O. was wiring
more and more insistently. What could he, Buchanan, do?
He had no means of getting at the facts. Could I help him?
I said that I had seen and heard nothing which could suggest
ill-treatment of Jews by the army, but would make inquiries.
Leaving the Embassy, I went straight to Baron Günzburg, the
banker and head of the Jewish community in Petrograd.
Günzburg received me courteously and listened with gravity. He
would have inquiries made, he said, and let me know the result.
Five days later I had from him a memorandum compiled from
Jewish sources on all the fronts. I took it instantly to Buchanan
who as instantly wired it to London. There had been no anti-
Jewish manifestations at all in the Russian army. The whole
story was a piece of German propaganda. The Zangwill anti-
Russian campaign collapsed like a pricked bubble.

I had gone out to Russia with orders to work for civilian
refugees alone. In time, however, these orders had to be
modified. It was found necessary, so as to maintain the status of
the work in the eyes of Russians, who, small though it was, took
it very seriously, to extend it to work, when occasion offered, for
the wounded too. In 1916 the outfit was greatly strengthened
by the arrival of Miss Moberly, afterwards well known as Head
of an Oxford College, with two women surgeons and six highly
trained nurses. By arrangement made in England Miss Moberly

and I worked together. She represented, if I am not mistaken, an association sprung from the Votes for Women movement : in any case it had a name incomprehensible to Russians and I rebaptised it the Union of British Women, a name that, like their work, had instant success. Here I may remark that this insignificant bit of relief work in the 1914 war was the first occasion on which Russians had ever heard of Great Britain or of things British. Before, it had always been " England " and " English ". Apart from this being inaccurate and against the grain with me, it would have been most unfair to label as " English " work more than fifty per cent of the funds for which were subscribed in Scotland. So the " Great British "—one word in Russian—Committee and the Union of British Women joined forces. Besides the canteens or "feeding-points" as they were called in Russian, at Petrograd, Moscow, Kiev, and in Galicia, where about eleven thousand people were fed daily and attention paid to hygiene and to small children's education, there were now under the committee three orphanages, two children's hospitals, a home for Polish intellectuals at Kiev, and a military hospital with ninety beds at Zaleshchiki in Galicia. Before taking over the last we had worked at the Kiev station receiving wounded, mainly Austrian prisoners, from Brusilov's successful push on the Southwestern Front. Over 60,000 were received in one week, and of these we had our fair share. Miss Moberly's management of her team was perfect and their work beyond praise both in itself and for its propaganda value. I am not sure that they ever had proper recognition. After the war when the accounts were wound up the Great Britain to Poland movement received the seal of official approval and thanks from the Charity Commissioners. But the Union of British Women deserved a special word of gratitude. To my great relief they went back to England shortly before the revolution. It would have been too bad had they been swirled into that mælstrom.

My position as a Red Cross commissioner in however humble a capacity enabled me to see more of the Russian " sanitary ", as they were called, that is medical and ancillary army services than was open to most foreigners outside the superb and spotless hospitals run in Petrograd under the patronage of the Empress and various Grand Duchesses. My friend Herman Norman, who had served in the Embassy at St. Petersburg [1] and was later British Minister at Teheran, once said to me : " If you want anything done in Russia, you must get a German, a Jew, or a Pole to do it." This is a pretty epigram and like most epigrams true only in part. Russians have certainly a great taste for doing nothing. This is exemplified in their inordinate delight in talk which for them takes the place of getting something accomplished. Until foreigners recognise this they are always being upset by finding that, to Russians, talking about a decision taken is equivalent to its execution and that therefore you can have the fun of beginning to discuss it all over again, and so *ad infinitum* or very nearly. A friend of mine, Captain Perfiliev, of a crack cavalry regiment, who afterwards became a successful painter in America remarked : " People say drink is the national failing of Russia. That's bosh ! Our national failing is talk." Nonetheless when strung up by an emergency such as a patriotic war, Russians are capable of startling and prolonged energy. Their natural affability, to use an old-fashioned but apposite word, and their inclination towards ecstatic enthusiasm combine to make a formidable power machine. They possess uncommon physical resistance, partly derived from an affinity to other animals that Westerners have lost if they ever possessed it ; thus Russians can go to sleep whenever they want and sleep for hours at almost any moment, to wake and be ready to go without sleep and without fatigue for perhaps a day and a night. Also they can eat prodigious quantities of food at a sitting and then fast for twenty-four hours without feeling it. The sum of these, to us, strange faculties enables them, when they apply themselves to organisation, to produce results of striking value. However badly the Russian army was equipped at the outset, within a year it was dowered with a medical service that would be hard to surpass, while the organisation of the base and the supply services steadily improved till nearly the end of 1916. The urgency for the Germans to create a revolution lay in the fact that by the end of that year the Russian army under the impulse given by General Alexeiev was almost completely equipped and would have been ready in the spring of 1917 to advance in an irresistible mass. This was the reason why

[1] Changed to Petrograd in the war.

Protopopov, Rasputin's Minister of the Interior, created artificial famine in Petrograd, followed by riot, then revolt, which was quickly turned by powerful fifth-column slogans into revolution. And it was for this that General Hofmann, C.-in-C. on the German Eastern Front, had Lenin and his fellows in readiness to rush through Germany in sealed railway carriages to Petrograd, there to achieve the dissolution of Russia with the aid of German gold provided through Swedish banks. Hofmann, when I met him in Berlin in 1923, made no secret of this. Hofmann had a further scheme that did not come off, too long to be more than mentioned here ; I described this at length in *The Fortnightly Review* in November 1920.[1] What Alexeiev, working to rebuild the Russian army, did not allow for, was the danger to his troops of remaining idle and without fighting for months on end, a state of things that led to a disastrous decline in morale : the same error was made in France in 1939–40 when M. Daladier and General Gamelin staked all on a defensive war and drew back the troops after their brilliant advance in the Sarre.

The medical service and that of supplying comforts to the troops had far outstripped the rest of the army organisation and barely flagged even during its epic retreat in 1915. Part of every company's equipment was a set of Russian, that is hot air, baths built of wood and carried in carts when dismantled. When men came out of the firing line they had a bath and their hair was cut short (many officers shaved their heads), while at the same time their clothes were cleaned and disinfected ; and every man going into battle was given a clean linen shirt, thus lessening the risk of blood-poisoning after wounds. Supply trains with tea, sugar, and fresh clothes circulated as near the front as possible ; one waggon would be completely filled with boot-soles to be distributed. On my asking what was the good of soles apart from the boots, I was told with a laugh that every Russian village has a cobbler and no company would be at a loss to fit them. The result of this care was a high level of health among the troops. Surgeon-General de Hubbenet, head of the medical services on the Western Front, told me that until the revolution there was hardly a case of syphilis and not one of typhus among the armies under him, and no outbreak of typhoid ;

[1] " Why the Tsar was murdered."

boiling water was always on hand in unlimited quantities for making tea, the national Russian drink. After the revolution, with the relaxation of discipline, disease of every sort was rampant.

Relief work was not my sole object in going to Russia. I was also correspondent of the *Standard*. But apart from the difficulties of getting news out of Russia, far more formidable than any of the correspondents there had imagined beforehand, the *Standard* proceeded within a few months to give up the ghost. I was too busy to try to fix up with another daily paper, and indeed there was little to be hoped from the attempt. One of the most brilliant and experienced journalists in the world, Hamilton Fyfe, representing the *Daily Mail*, was fuming in Petrograd at being unable to get to the front. So was Robert Wilton, the accomplished *Times* correspondent. Bernard Pares whom *The Times* had got leave to send to the front was despatching what is technically known to journalists as " tripe ". He had no experience or aptitude for the work and was soon withdrawn. Even had Wilton, who knew Russian and Russia far better and had several years in the St. Petersburg office to his credit, then been at the front the result might not have been more fruitful. The Russians had an incurable distrust of journalists and their censorship let through hardly anything of interest. Thus four of the best English correspondents—Fyfe of the *Daily Mail*, Wilton of *The Times*, E. H. Wilcox of the *Daily Telegraph*, and Guy Beringer of Reuters—kicked their heels in Petrograd with little to do save send and comment, when comment was allowed, on official communiqués, eked out by what is known as " frill stuff ". Wilcox, who had been the *Telegraph*'s star in Berlin before and was again after the war, characteristically set himself to a thorough study of the Russian language. He adored life in Russia and said to me once : " Both the Russians and the Germans are children. The difference between them is that the Russians are lovable children, while the Germans are hateful." To remedy this stalemate Marlowe, the editor of the *Daily Mail*, who afterwards engaged me as special correspondent during Yudenich's ill-starred push for Petrograd in 1919, sent out Ferdinand Tuohy, one of his youngest lights, in the hope that he might gatecrash where Hamilton Fyfe's solid claims had failed. Tuohy got as far as Warsaw, where I met

him and at once conceived an affection for this typical Irish
" bhoy ", handsome, quick tempered, truthful, bubbling with
dash and charm. Like Fyfe, Tuohy was fuming. He could not
get to the front, and what he wrote from the base at Warsaw
did not get through. I managed to attach him to my party
going to Galicia. There we were at the front. We were, I
believe, the first foreign civilians to get into Perimyshl—to conserve
the Russian spelling of the famous fortress—a few weeks after
its capture by the Russians, and saw much of interest, including
the beginning of the Austro-German counter-offensive under
Mackensen that smashed through the Russians, retook most of
Galicia, and by cutting their lines of communication forced the
Russian army to concede all Poland. A mere scratch kept me
on my back in hospital in Perimyshl while the big German guns
thundered closer and closer in the distance. We got out in
time, just before the Russian commander, the heroic General
Radko Dmitriev, retreated in person. But from a news point
of view it was a hopeless job. Tuohy gave up and went back
to England, to be followed by Hamilton Fyfe. My affection for
Tuohy has lasted till this day, tinged with keen admiration, for
he became one of the brightest of all *Daily Mail* special correspondents and the articles on foreign affairs he still writes in a
weekly illustrated are of far more value than most. I did not
start writing again till Rasputin's death and the revolution, when
the *New Europe* and the *Nineteenth Century* took all the articles I
could get by devious ways out of Russia.

Whoever wants to learn the truth about the Russian revolution, has only to read *Red Hell* by the Belgian Joseph Ameel,
my own *The Bolshevik Adventure*, and the Grand Duchess Marie
Pavlovna's *Education d'une Princesse* ; while its results have been
made sufficiently plain to all by Victor Kravchenko's *I Chose
Freedom.* I shall not reiterate these facts here. I have said
enough to show my view that many notions prevailing about
Russia were false : among the most outrageously false was the
belief prevalent in England that the Bolshevik revolution was a
progressive step forward taken by the Russian nation. Actually
it was the very reverse. The Russian educated classes were
socially the freest in the world. Their ideal was self-expression.
Except in the matter of politics no one attempted to force his

opinion on anyone else. Life was cheap, Russian beds were good, Russian cooking delicious, literature, learning and art respected and flourishing. The peasants lived a simple life and were infinitely cleaner than any other peasantry or labouring men, for it was almost a tenet of the Orthodox religion that all should take a bath once a week. Now a Russian hot air bath was as effective as its Turkish steam variant. If the peasants did not often eat meat, they made up for its lack by endlessly munching sunflower seeds, rich in proteids. Their needs were few : leather for their boots, paraffin for their lamps, linen for their underclothes, cloth for their trousers and jackets, sheepskins for their coats and hats, cotton for their women's dresses, needles and thread. All these, except the needles, were products of their own soil. Increasing peasant ownership of the land meant a rapid growth in intelligence and the demand for education, which was also being satisfied by many landowning squires. I had a friend, a serving A.B. in the Baltic fleet, the son of a well-to-do peasant farmer from near Moscow, with whom no one would have been ashamed to discuss any serious subject under the sun. There can be no doubt at all that Russia was heading for rapid intellectual and social development in the second quarter of this century. This prospect was swept away and the road to it blocked for thirty years by Lenin, Trotsky, Stalin and the other Communist dictators in the Kremlin. For how much longer, who shall say? There was a common jest among Russians : " We had the Tartars for three hundred years. We had the Romanovs for three hundred years. And we shall have the Bolsheviks for three hundred years." A friend of mine, one of the old-school exiles in London, told me that he had once put up Lenin on a visit from Switzerland. He had not known Lenin before and was absolutely horrified by him. All Lenin thought and spoke of, my friend said, was personal power.

I owed my escape from Russia to luck and a woman. On a night in the summer of 1918 I travelled from Petrograd to Moscow. Railway travel in Russia, by the way, was inexpensive and the trains far more comfortable than those anywhere else, America included. On arriving in the morning at the Moscow terminus I was met by one of my young assistants, an extremely

THE AUTHOR

From a drawing by Neville Lytton (3rd Earl of Lytton)

intelligent Russian high-school boy of fifteen, who said : " Don't go back to your hotel. The Red Guards are looking for you." This lad, like almost all the educated Russian middle-class strongly liberal and pro-British, terms virtually synonymous in Russia, had the same name as a young man who some twelve years later assassinated one of the chief Bolshevik tyrants in the old capital. I have often wondered if it was he. The news he now brought me was the beginning of a new existence. That night all the British and French still in Russia had been arrested ; three years were to pass before the remains of them could be extricated from jail and repatriated. I was saved by my night in the train. I had been unable to leave my work in the air while the going was still good ; besides there seemed a certain fitness in seeing my Russian avatar through to the end. After the Bolshevik revolution exit from Russia became very difficult indeed : now it was impossible. So I disappeared, took a new name, obtained a false passport and spent six months more liquidating homes, hospitals, canteens, generally tidying up, and under the guise of a Lettish refugee recently returned from America seeing a great deal of the Bolsheviks' doings. All went tranquilly till a spy got on my track. I had made contact with a man who for £300 per person arranged for fugitives from Bolshevisia or Sovdepia, as Russians in derision called their now wretched country, to get across the frontier into Finland. My spy denouced this man who, it turned out, was already being hunted from a different quarter : he and his wife and a dozen others were arrested. I will call him Ivan Petrovich. I had slipped through the net flung out, but fell into a trap laid for me at Ivan Petrovich's flat. Thence I was carted to the headquarters of the Cheka for serious grilling, which of course implied torture in one or more forms, perhaps long imprisonment under revolting conditions, certain death at the end. I had committed no crime or even offence beyond being an Englishman, but this would be enough for me to be condemned out of hand as a spy, saboteur, and counter-revolutionary. At the Cheka I found Ivan Petrovich's wife, partner, and man-servant also under arrest. He had already been shot. We were taken through a maze of corridors and sat down on a bench outside the room of Antonov, the assistant chief of the whole

Bolshevik inquisition. The room had a large number on the door : 36. For some reason, perhaps simply their morning cup of " char " (in Russian, *chai*), our guard was now changed. This was my first bit of luck, for I had determined to try and escape before an examination and fate the prospect of which I thoroughly disliked. Presently a clerk came up to say that Antonov could not, probably for the same reason, take us yet. The two guards who being new did not know us by sight called out to follow them. Now came my second bit of luck : I was sitting at the far end of the bench. Instead of following, I stayed sitting. Then I got up and walked out of the place. This was not quite so simple as it sounds. I had to dodge guards and find my way through the maze of the huge building, once the Prefecture of St. Petersburg. Luckily, I have a good bump of topography. Luckily too I was dressed like any Bolshevik ruffian in a soldier's dirty fur coat and sheepskin hat and wore a heavy Cossack-like beard. I found my way to the kitchen on the third floor, passed through, and went down the backstairs to the courtyard, a good thirty yards in width. Across this I strolled to the gate. " Your pass ? " sang out the guard. I called over my shoulder without stopping : " From room 36." Room 36 was an " Open, Sesame." I strolled on, fighting temptation to run, and was free. I hopped a tram.

Freedom is a relative term. I was free for the moment, free on the icy streets of Petrograd, without money, food, or a roof over my head. But I had friends. They risked their lives in helping me. Yet such help is not endless. It was impossible to stop long in one place. The hunt was up. No prisoner had ever before escaped from the Cheka H.Q. Petrograd was being combed for me and I narrowly escaped capture more than once. Friends' flats were searched after I had left. So a week passed. I was nearly at the end of my tether, when I remembered having been told : " If ever you are in trouble, go to Mme R." I did so, to find instant sympathy and schemes for escape. My luck had held. This admirable woman, the middle-aged daughter of a deceased general, was devoting herself to help people get out of Russia. This was never an easy mission. Now since Ivan Petrovich's mishap the frontier guards were doubled and large sums of blood money offered. Things looked black when forty-eight hours later an ex-naval officer blew in to Mme R's. He was in touch with Finnish smugglers who had brought in sledges over the ice of the gulf of Petrograd filled with butter and sugar, articles unknown for months in the city, and for a stiff consideration would take back with them four fugitives. I jumped at the offer of a place and that same night, after missing one last hunt for me, set out across the frozen sea in the bottom of a smuggler's sledge, drawn by a tough Finnish pony. I was so tired that I slept most of the way, jerks from the rough ice notwithstanding, only waking for an alarm of a Red patrol that caused the Finns to dash off at a tangent. At midnight we had started ; at eight in the morning the two sledges ran up the shingle at Terioki in Finland, free till it succumbed a score of years later to the brute force of Red aggression. I felt I had paid to know the taste of real freedom.

CHAPTER XIII

A NEWSPAPERMAN IN PARIS

"NEWSPAPERMAN" is good American, but bad English. We say "journalist". Why then do I give a transatlantic slant to a period of some twelve years in my life? Journalism is a bigger thing than the papers. It comprises not only the daily press but weekly and monthly reviews. These last are ignored, if not despised, by Fleet Street, which however often pays them the compliment of appropriating and retailing views expressed in them, it may be months later and naturally without acknowledgment. I started in journalism by writing in weekly and monthly reviews, went on to do about a column a week in the literary page in the *Morning Post*, and when the war of 1914 broke on us, joined the *Standard* as foreign correspondent. Except during the revolution in Russia, when I was able to smuggle articles out of the country and into the *Nineteenth Century*, I did little journalism for the next fifteen years save as foreign correspondent.

A foreign correspondent is emphatically a newspaperman and nothing else. His business is to get news to his paper and get it, if he can, quicker, fresher, livelier than anyone else into another paper. Not political news alone : sport, art, science, society, all is grist to his mill. If he is successful on some important matter, this is called a "scoop". If they do not come by sheer luck, the technique of scoops is usually simple. An American friend of mine scooped the news of Sarah Bernhardt's death for his agency. He disguised himself as a French plumber, bribed his way into the dying actress's house, and sat there in a corner for over twenty hours till Sarah passed away. Then he only had to slip out, call his office, which flashed the news to New York, and it was on the streets a few minutes later. It took me less than five minutes to get an exclusive bit of news on to the streets in London. Lord Beaverbrook had a fancy to run an afternoon edition of the *Sunday Express* carrying the result of the Grand Prix. There was no opposition but speed was the object. In London the edition was fully printed beforehand, leaving only the Stop Press blank. In Paris where I was given a free hand to make arrangements I booked a twenty-minute phone call to London, to cover the time when the race should be run. While my assistant in the Boulevard des Italiens sat waiting and to fill in time chatted with the news desk at the *Express* in Fleet Street, I was at Longchamps. The instant the numbers went up I darted to the taxi I had waiting, drove to the restaurant of La Cascade in the Bois de Boulogne and thence phoned the news to my office on a line I had paid to have at my sole service for the afternoon. My assistant, taking the message on our second line, had only to conclude his talk with London by saying, " Grand Prix result first Untel, second Qui lo sa, third, Nitchevo." The Stop Press was filled in and the paper was almost simultaneously on the streets. The technique was simple, but there is a certain amount of nervous strain about such an operation. I knew I could not phone from Longchamps where punters, touts, and pressmen would be fighting for the booths. La Cascade was just the thing. But plans might go wrong. My taxi despite a royal retainer might be pinched by someone else. The restaurant might break faith with me. Their line might go out of order. In the Paris office my assistant was racked by doubt, would I come through within the twenty minutes booked for our London call? If not it would mean two, five or ten minutes' delay getting another call. Translate such doubts and fears into a really important business when twenty correspondents are trying, first, to get the facts, second, to beat the others with them, and you have an idea what a foreign correspondent's nerves, and nerve, must be like. By use of the latter I once got a small scoop. This was at Versailles when M. Doumergue was elected President of the Republic. Etiquette has it that the newly elected president should make no statement to the Press and give no interview. But he receives and exchanges bows with all and sundry who choose to pass before him and thus do homage to his office. I took my place with the others and in time came before this smiling Southerner with a head like a later Roman emperor. Now I knew M. Doumergue to be a Protestant, the first Pro-

testant to be elected President. So as I bowed I said rapidly:
"Monsieur le Président, permettez moi de vous féliciter au nom
de tous les Protestants anglais." The result was what I had
banked on. Etiquette or none, M. Doumergue felt like saying
something, and he did say most graciously: "Remerciez-les
en mon nom, je vous prie." There was my interview with the
new President of France, exclusive to the *Daily Express*. This
little incident had an unexpected and regrettable sequel. Reporters never walked in the line before the new president,
knowing it to be pure waste of time. So an American agency
man who had seen me get into the line suspected I was on to
something and followed me. But he knew nothing about
Protestants or presidents, his French was none too fluent, he
just bowed and was bowed to. Next day when my "interview"
came out, the unhappy wretch nearly got the sack and was in
fact soon recalled to America. Afterwards President Doumergue
remembered my "cheek" and was always particularly nice to
me in consequence. I have made it a practice to share news,
except with rivals for it, and consider this much more effective
than swopping drinks and blue stories in bars as many journalists
do. For instance Leland Stowe, a brilliant American correspondent, later well known in the U.S. as lecturer and com-
mentator, and I constantly shared news and hunted it together.
In newspaper parlance, news is a "story" or "the dope";
what you write is "stuff". On that occasion at Versailles I
could not share my story. I barely knew the agency man in
question; besides, my tiny scoop was really exclusive.

To Harvard I doubtless owed the fact that I saw more of
American correspondents in Paris than most of my British
colleagues did. The majority of them were very good fellows,
and capable newsgetters; some, of real distinction. English
and Americans often understood one another badly. I was
fortunate in being safe from this mutual want of comprehension
and, when in my turn I became President of the Anglo-American
Press Association of Paris, worked in perfect harmony with the
U.S. correspondents. The only criticism I would venture to
make is one not of them, but of American editors, who appear
imperfectly to recognise the value of education in newspaper
work. George Steevens, most famous of all special correspond-

ents, had been a scholar of Balliol. In my time the best Paris jobs on the London press were held by a former scholar of King's, Cambridge, a scholar of Wellington and New College, a scholar of Marlborough and sometime Eton master, a Wykhamist and scholar of Brasenose, and a Fellow of Trinity, Cambridge. None of the Americans were of the same level in the fields of history, economics, literature, general knowledge, and of course European background, and I have more than once seen the best of them stumped for an understanding of what was A B C to us. Two of the most important American jobs in Paris were indeed held by Englishmen, so that some people in New York newspaper offices did have a glimmering of the notion that education pays. The R.101 disaster was "covered", i.e. reported, by a first-rate man from the most important American agency. He learned, like the rest of us who were early on the ground at Beauvais that fearful morning, that a girl's shoe had been found in the wreckage. Want of educational background made him assume the presence on the tragic airship of a clandestine female passenger, whereas any Englishman could have told him the shoe was a mascot. The American thought he had a scoop and flashed the story of a girl stowaway to New York. Violent reaction followed. Our Air Ministry protested. The correspondent was sacked.

I once wrote a line in a play, never acted : " You judges see politics as bankers do finance. You are at the centre of everything without being concerned in anything." The judge who inspired this was Lord Sumner, whose sagacity and penetration were unluckily turned to the field of politics too late to enable our country to reap their fruits. Lord Acton had said that Napoleon would have made Sir Henry Maine prime minister. Half a century later Lord Sumner would certainly have been his choice. My line, I have come to think, was not true of His Majesty's judges in general and later I applied the phrase to foreign correspondents, of whom, if they have their wits about them, it is absolutely true. Had warnings given by the Berlin correspondents of *The Times* and the *Daily Telegraph*, for instance, between the two world wars been taken seriously, we should have been spared the second. But people in London always think they know better. It is exasperating to a foreign correspondent who knows his job to see his predictions come true when time and again his despatches on which they were based have been mutilated or " killed ", i.e. not printed at all, because their contents ran counter to received opinion. This was the fate of a series I sent to the *Morning Post* on dates between 1928 and 1932 containing evidence of the rearmament of Germany. I had obtained it from contacts made in Germany when I was Berlin correspondent of the *Daily Express* in 1923 ; but because I would not reveal the identity of my sources (who, had their names been even suspected, would have been executed or more simply " done in ") my editor refused to print them. An equally galling moment was when, working for the *Daily Express*, I got an interview with Clemenceau on the American debt question, a thing no other British or American correspondent had succeeded in doing ; but because Clemenceau's views did not support those of the paper, my interview with him was killed.

Few foreign correspondents work throughout their career for the same paper. Those who do may be the best ; to use an American expression, I would not know. In my time I worked for the *Standard*, the *Daily Express*, the *Daily Mail* and *The Times*, the *Express* again, and then the *Morning Post* : Russia, Finland, Germany, and France were the countries I worked in. There was an extremely brief interlude during the Russian revolution when the *Manchester Guardian* desired my services ; but the facts I sent from Petrograd were too unpalatable for a Liberal paper when all Liberals (and most other people too) were bent on seeing the revolution as the dawn of liberty, democracy, and prosperity in Russia, whereas conscientious observers on the spot were becoming clearer daily that the exact opposite of these desiderata was on the way. So that ended abruptly. Like most correspondents and most diplomats as well I thought of Paris as my Mecca : not so much because I yearned after its brilliant charms, lodestar though they are to all of good taste, but because I already knew France and French fairly well and wanted to know them better. My first acquaintance with Paris had been made at the age of two. My parents were taking my sister and me with them to Switzerland before the days of through trains, breaking the journey in Paris. The morning after our arrival Jessie Shiach in almost complete undress was horrified by the floor-waiter flinging open her bedroom door. On her violently protesting, the man—as Jessie told it to my mother—pointed behind her, and said " Pettitt ongfong ! Pettitt ongfong ! " The *pettitt onfong* was me, with my finger firmly pressed on the button of the electric bell, a new joy to the infant mind. A further commotion was caused when, as the family was just about to start for the station, the same *pettitt onfong* sat heavily down, with all his clothes on, in the hip-bath, this being before the era of separate bathrooms. This stirring beginning to my Paris experience had no sequel till I was fourteen or fifteen years old, an interval not inflicted as a punishment for infantile misdeeds but occurring, as Dolores Gray sang in *Annie Get Your Gun* " naturally ! " There seem, by the way, not to be many people now alive in England who saw the real Little Annie Oakley and can testify, as I can, that she did trick shooting as amazing as that supposed to be done on the stage by Miss Gray : some even better, for she shot down coloured glass balls thrown into the air while standing on her head. Meantime I was made to work fairly hard at French and when I went back to France was reasonably comfortable in it. I have known but one Englishman who never made mistakes in French ; this was Herman Norman, of the Diplomatic Service. French is a harder language than most realise, and I once heard a bad blunder made by an Englishman who had been educated at a French *lycée* or high school and had spent most of his life in the country. After my first return to France my visits were frequent and often prolonged, and I made there endless friends, among the best being that brilliant being Robert d'Humières who was killed in the 1914 war, translator of Kipling and founder of the Théâtre des Arts.

The job of foreign correspondent is prized as one in which a man has great freedom of action. Its disadvantage is that he runs the risk of being completely forgotten in his own land. The one dominating rule of a foreign correspondent's life is that he must get the news and get it accurate. Subject to that he can work what hours he pleases. The only rules laid down for me by a very experienced editor, and in this order, were : loyalty to your paper, loyalty to your country, loyalty to the country you are working in. Scandalous conduct of course is not tolerated. I knew one outstanding man who ruined his career at Geneva by hitting over the head with a bedside lamp a Foreign Minister he found in the bed with his lady—unfortunately not his wife, or the incident might have been condoned. A foreign correspondent in a good post is well paid—French journalists used to talk with envy of our " ambassadorial salaries "—and has sufficient latitude in the matter of expenses. Since the last war and the imposition of high taxes on profits, I am told this item has sensibly increased. Also he meets and if he has the wit can profit from contact with virtually all and any men eminent in every walk of life, statesmen, lawyers, artists, doctors, dancers, scientists, authors, athletes, comedians, ambassadors. Few of this final, very important category know how to use the press, though most statesmen have by now been thoroughly broken in. Thus M. Edouard Herriot showed no annoyance but only apparent pleasure when I waylaid him during a complicated piece of cabinet-making and got an interview he had managed to withhold for three days from British and American correspondents. I got it by discovering where he was going to have lunch and catching him as he came out. Naturally M. Herriot gave nothing away. But he did give me the interview. The one ambassador in my experience perfect in this respect was Lord D'Abernon in Berlin. He knew that I disliked his policy and knew that I knew he knew it. Nevertheless, the British embassy was always open to me when I chose to ask for half an hour's chat ; I was frequently invited there ; and I never left Lord D'Abernon without learning something. He kept his secrets of course ; outside them he was wise enough to realise that the more enlightenment that was given to even a hostile observer the better it was for everybody, himself included. But Lord D'Abernon had not been Sir Edgar Vincent for nothing. As Sir Frank Schiff, among the most striking financiers of his day, once said : " You would have to get up very early in the morning to take Edgar Vincent in."

If one of the main objects of an ambassador, as it must be, is to please the country to which he is accredited, no one should be ranked above Lord Crewe in Paris. A distinguished appearance, tact grown perfect by long handling of affairs of state, wide knowledge of French literature and thought, noble manners, imperturbable calm, combined to give him exceptional standing with the French ; and this was enhanced by his deserved reputation of keeping the best table in Paris. Lord Crewe had a peculiarity of which Mrs. W. K. Clifford had told me years before : she had known, as she knew all literary London, Lord Crewe's father, Lord Houghton, one of the wittiest and one of the ugliest men of his age. Lord Crewe would never sit at meals for longer than an hour. The first time I dined at the Embassy I was on the lookout for this. It was a very large, very grand party. I looked at my watch as we sat down. Sure enough on the tick of the sixtieth minute Lord Crewe rose from the table. Those who had not known what to expect had to leave their fruit and wine unfinished. I have never eaten better dinners or seen one better served than Lord Crewe's.

Among statesmen and politicians during those years I saw and talked with every prominent minister and parliamentarian from Clemenceau to Léon Blum who, more than any single man, was responsible for the decline in French national morale and thus for France's catastrophe in 1940. Also many visitors like Benes, of whose judgment I formed a very poor opinion, and Ramsay MacDonald, whom I forced at a press conference to admit, by his refusing to deny it, that he was prepared to give up the right of search at sea. Aristide Briand was for long one of the figures in Paris most adulated by foreigners, ourselves included. I judged him a windbag and an insincere climber and his celebrated " cavernous " voice a mere part of the professional orator's technique. A timely death saved his reputation from being shattered in the fall of his card-castle schemes. Pierre Laval formed another interesting subject for study. The epithet " corrupt " was later flung at him ; yet if he was so, it was in the sense not of taking bribes but, like Sir Robert Walpole, of giving them. There is, I submit, a distinction. Laval had no need to take bribes. He had a genius for making money : first, as a highly successful corporation lawyer, by settling big cases out of court ; then by speculation on Wall Street, acting on tips given him by American financiers ; and, thirdly, as a farmer in Normandy and a local newspaper proprietor in his native Auvergne. His failing was lack of education. Success in arranging lawsuits privately made him believe the same method applicable to affairs of State. The Hoare-Laval agreement would have been an eminently statesmanlike move, if it had been practicable. Unfortunately it was not, and when the scheme was thrown down by Baldwin and broke into little pieces, Laval turned his back on England. He thought that sheer adroitness could suffice to iron out differences between France and Germany the secular depth of which he was incapable of appreciating. He was confident of being able to manage Germany as he had managed lawyers, clients, and parliament and as he did manage Marshal Pétain after setting him up on the unhallowed altar of Vichy. Therein lay his mistake and the cause of his downfall and miserable end. He knew humanity perhaps, but he never knew men.

The most intelligent of all men I met in Paris during those years was André Tardieu, thrice Prime Minister of France, the most purely intelligent indeed of all men I ever met. His two weaknesses were that he could not conceal his luminous mental superiority, nor yet would trouble to assume the staid and outward, if seldom more than skin deep, decorum that the French elector likes to see in cabinet ministers when on public view. The most colourful was Marshal Lyautey, who gave Morocco to France. This magnificent soldier-administrator, whose services to the French colonial empire were inestimable, ended his career by organising, still, at the age of seventy-six, as straight as an arrow and as active as a goat, the great Colonial Exhibition of 1931 in Paris that gave the French and foreign visitors an ocular demonstration of the extent and varied interest of France's oversea activity. The exhibition, almost incredibly beautiful, took place during my term of office as president of the Anglo-American Press Association which I therefore had to represent at numerous functions, inventing a fresh speech to make on precisely the same theme at nine or ten different banquets, and in the end at the closing banquet to reply to the toast of the foreign press as a whole.[1] I was thus for ever meeting Marshal Lyautey, as High Commissioner of the Exhibition, and having to address him. On one of the earlier occasions I had to present the members of my association to the Marshal. There was some slight delay and, to hurry up the file of correspondents

[1] See Appendix B.

waiting, I murmured, " Allons ! Allons, mes enfants ! " Lyautey turned his penetrating eyes on me and said with approval : " Ah, you talk to them just as I used to talk to my soldiers ! " This tiny incident appeared to win his sympathy which further increased when in the course of a long luncheon our conversation turned on Royalism and the Bourbons. I remarked that the last chance Royalism had had in France was ruined when the Comte de Chambord in 1873 refused, should he be restored to the throne, to recognise the tricolour flag as the national standard. With an odd trick he had the Marshal slewed round on his chair to face me full. " Ah," he said, " now that's a very intelligent thing for an Englishman to say ! " Clearly some knowledge of modern French history was the last thing he expected from one of us. In the end my relations with Lyautey at these functions became so cordial that I plucked up courage to ask him a question in many people's minds. National morale under the Third Republic had so far declined, though with spasmodic efforts at recovery, from 1924 onward that the question was often mooted by serious minded men whether recovery in face of the German military revival could be achieved without a change of regime. Among those touching whom the question was put had been General Mangin, one of the most successful army commanders in the war of 1914. Mangin's sudden death had put a stop to these speculations, which in any event were off the mark in his case, since I had earlier obtained reliable information that Mangin had been approached to lead such a movement and had refused. I need hardly say I had kept this knowledge under my hat. A foreign correspondent must know how to hold his tongue. But later speculation became attached to the person of Marshal Lyautey. The Government had behaved towards him with signal ingratitude. He had been solemnly received, after a long period outside it, into the fold of the Catholic Church. He was known in private as a trenchant critic of the regime. The supposition did not seem improbable. But no one knew. At one of these interminable banquets then I was sitting on Marshal Lyautey's right hand. Opposite him was an influential colonial Governor-General. At one end of the table was a Cabinet Minister. Two junior members of the Government and numerous official

personages were scattered about among the pressmen to whom
the feast was given. A great buzz of conversation filled the
room. Under cover of the noise I said as quietly as I could
into Lyautey's ear : " Monsieur le Maréchal, I should so much
like to know—not of course for publication—why you did not
make a revolution when you came back from Morocco ? " I
need hardly explain that I expected some humorous reprimand
for my audacity or ironical retort that would give me for my
own satisfaction an inkling of the true state of affairs. But the
Marshal was not having it this way at all. First he swung
round and fixed me with his commanding, searching eyes. Then
he brought into play another trick he had worked on me before.
When he wanted particularly to impress on you what he was
going to say, he would catch your arm as in a vice with his
elbow, dragging you close to him. This he did now. These
manœuvres naturally attracted the attention of others sitting
round. The hum of talk died down. Then Marshal Lyautey
in his high, harsh voice barking out every syllable at almost
parade ground pitch, said : " Ah ! you want to know why I
did not make a revolution when I came back from Morocco ? "
Sudden and complete silence throughout the banqueting hall.
" Well, I'll tell you why I didn't make a revolution when I
came back from Morocco. I didn't make a revolution, first,
because I was really very ill at the time ; and, secondly, because
I found I could not count on the support on which I had thought
I could count." As suddenly as the previous silence had fallen,
so now did a violent cackle break out round the table, every
official, governor and minister displaying the vastest interest in
food, the weather, sport, anything and everything to pretend
that he had not caught or understood a word of what the chairman of the feast had shouted. Lyautey leaned back in his
chair and inscrutably surveyed the results of his bombshell.
Neither he nor anyone else ever made any allusion to this episode.
He did not need to. The Government side did not dare. It
was natural to Lyautey's resolute spirit, rapidity to seize an
opening, and the semi-oriental subtlety polished in him by years
spent in Indo-China, Madagascar, and Africa, that he should
snatch at a chance to tell the republican bigwigs what he thought
of them, well knowing that, short of wrecking the whole Colonial

ALIX L'ESTOM SOUBIRAN (LADY POLLOCK)

From a painting by René Tapissier,

" The Union of Scotland and Gascony "

Exhibition, they could not say a word in reply. He was a fascinating character, combining grand breadth of view with a delight in clever tricks. In short, a thoroughly wily old bird.

The earthly paradise is one of our great illusions. Mankind's perfectibility can never attain perfection. But if ever a distant approach was made to that land with milk and honey blest it was in France in the first half-generation between the two world wars. Never can so great a proportion of any nation have achieved such prosperity, comfort, and opportunity for education, enjoyment, and broad, simple happiness as in France during those fifteen years or so. Much has been written in England about our neighbours across the Channel ; [1] we all think we know them, all, that is, except those who know that we can never know them fully. Yet it is doubtful whether most of us realise what an admirable standard of life had generally been touched in France. A land so blessed by nature has evident advantages. Where can be found another soil so rich in the production of the main necessities of life, wheat, fruit, and meat ; the best and most plentiful wine ; the best butter, the most varied cheese ? What country, save France, so combines the benefits of northern and southern climates, the joys of sea, river, plain, mountain, and forest ? Or offers, through long cultivation of the arts and crafts dating back to the Roman conquest, such artistic impulse, such widespread wealth of architectural beauty ? These are things that affect the mass of mankind unconsciously but affect it nonetheless. Again, whether owing to Roman influence on the astonishing mixture of blood in France—Greek, Gaulish, Frankish, Celtic, Scandinavian, Iberian, even Moorish, or to the impress longer than on us of the Catholic Church with the brilliant intellectual level of its prelates, or to the impulse given to universal education by the French Revolution, the average level of intelligence is higher among the French than in any other of the nations known to me. Intelligence is far from being the only quality needed by a nation for success ; but it is one of those needed, and in the French it is very marked.

[1] Among others by myself in *Paris and Parisians* (Geoffrey Bles), and in a score of full-length articles that appeared between 1942 and 1950 in the *Quarterly* and *Contemporary Reviews*, the *Hibbert Journal* and the *Nineteenth Century*.

Not one class alone in France was touched by these benefits coming almost, so it seemed, to fruition in the years from 1920 onwards, but all classes. What really happened was that the growth of prosperity and especially the advent of cheap motoring brought them within the reach of all. Thousands of good workmen owned small cars, bought second-hand of course but still thoroughly efficient ; thousands owned their own houses in the suburbs of a city or in the country. At least forty per cent of the nation, its agricultural population, made money very fast by supplying the nation's needs at moderate prices, and used the wealth so got to support the nation's finances. There is no question at all but that freedom and happiness were general. Even since the last war and the havoc wrought by it on France, the causes that led to this desirable state have reasserted themselves. Despite innumerable drawbacks the French, within five years of the war's ending, were brighter, more active, better fed than ourselves and had rewon much of their former ascendancy in thought and in taste. It was a noble tribute to them paid on the fifth anniversary of the landing in Normandy by Field-Marshal Montgomery when he claimed to be as much a French as a British soldier and wished, did he die in battle in another war, to be buried in France. English people were long in comprehending the fact, but it is a fact that for over fifty years our own safety has been bound up with that of France. If France were to succumb before an onslaught from the East, Great Britain would go down with her. And more than Great Britain. In such a catastrophe the whole of Western civilization would collapse. " The auld alliance " between France and Scotland has taken on a new extension and become an essential link in the chain binding Great Britain and all her Commonwealth to the community of Latin and Christian Europe.

CHAPTER XIV

PRONTI! PARTENZA!

AS Maurice Chevalier once said, when a man reaches the Psalmist's age of threescore and ten, it is high time for him to pack his suitcase and begin preparing himself for the great journey. So too of old did the traveller in Italy make ready to swing himself on to the train when the guard shouted " All ready! We're off! " waiting only for the shrill blast of the whistle to say that the departure announced was a fact. What we can take with us on the journey is doubtful. But what a man can do by way of preparation is to clear his ideas and make up his mind what he thinks of the world he has lived in. Plainly you should not wait till the last moment, as the old phrase has it, to " make your peace with God " ; for if you have not done it by then, there must, I think, come on a man a sense of futility and frustration that might appal the strongest. There is a vivid glimpse of this in the relation of the death of George Villiers, Pope's " Great Villiers ", the second Duke of Buckingham.[1] Spinoza says that a wise man thinks of nothing less than of death ; but Spinoza's whole life and work is proof that the wise man's mind should be prepared for it. This truth was perhaps brought nearest home to me, as it must be to everyone in time of war, by those days during the revolution in Russia when no man could feel sure of being alive on the morrow and when in fact few people in England, except my father with his unshakable optimism, thought of me as still being in the land of the living.

I make no apology for touching on these grave subjects. I am neither philosopher nor divine. But the problems of philosophy and theology touch every man, not only their professions, and I conceive that every man has the right, perhaps the duty, to consider them and express himself on them. Just in the same way every man may form and speak out an opinion on

[1] See Hester W. Chapman's admirable study *Great Villiers*.

249

music, which so many professional critics and musicians would like to keep as a private sanctum. This is true of the other arts too but is peculiarly important to be remembered about music as the most technical and ethereal of all the arts and therefore affording the easiest ground for the specialist to despise the common herd that forms the listening public. Theologians and metaphysicians have often tried by obscurity of thought and the use of incomprehensible terms to choke ordinary mortals off from considering their lofty subjects. Yet human curiosity has in the end always been too much for the obscurantists, however many men and women have been condemned, browbeaten, tormented, and even burnt at the stake for their obstinacy in telling the truth as they saw it. Not all theologians are tarred with this brush. One of the most famous and in his day most influential, Bossuet, " the Eagle of Meaux ", wrote : " The beginning of madness is the wish to see things other than as they are." With Bossuet then we may take our stand in trying to see things as they are rather than as others would have us see them.

Religion is the expression of man's aspiration towards the highest of which his nature is capable. That is why religion is not a fixed thing but changes according to man's time and place and developing knowledge, since knowledge must be considered as part of his total mental make-up, that is his nature. Man feels himself superior to other animals owing to his reasoning power. Without that it would be hard to distinguish him from them except by difference of habits. In both domestic and wild animals, just as in man, some are brave, others cowardly ; you find among them sycophants, gluttons, devoted friends, tormentors, the faithful, the treacherous, simpletons, cunning fellows, altruists, not often, egoists by the million, leaders, parasites, even heroes ; man is no better than they are, perhaps less good than some, for with him it is rare to find the complete sexual fidelity shewn among the greater birds. Man towers by his reasoning power alone, and by its practical results. Professor Jacques Duclaux, in his recent remarkable book *L'Homme devant l'Univers*, has shown with extraordinary brilliance how man, by his reasoning power and by its combination with the curiosity that inspires certain individuals among the species, has become dependent for everything he does and for the whole scheme of his life on that combination which we call scientific research. In that process, the most striking part of which is of extremely modern growth, men have become no wiser than they were before, for all that their species is known as *homo sapiens*. " It is doubtful ", writes Professor Duclaux, " whether they wish to be wise ; in any case they do not know how to set about it." What they have done is, by force of the reasoning power they have developed through a million years, to create physical conditions for themselves differing totally from those of other animals and even of the primitive humans surviving to our day, such as the Bushmen of Australia. Side by side with the growth in knowledge that has rendered possible man's control of the physical powers contained in the world about him, has grown also curiosity among a relatively small number of his species to know the truth about the ultimate nature of that world. Knowledge divorced from reason is a void ; governed by reason it leads to belief.

Bossuet's " See things as they are " is a command harder of application than appears at the first blush. Man, since the earliest records of him, has always tried to explain the known by the unknown. We see this from the carvings of the cavemen through myriad generations down to the latest attempts to pierce the veil of experience by the planchette and spiritualist mediums. Midway between the two comes the asseveration that God made man in his image which provoked Voltaire's ferocious retort : " Depuis, l'homme le lui a bien rendu." It can hardly be denied that men have paid God out by attributing to the deity almost every cruelty and callousness characterising the human race.

Just as reason leads to belief, belief ministers to reason. Once you begin to use your reason you cannot stop except on pain of wholly frustrating your reasoning faculty. If you start trying to see things as they are, you must go on to wherever the dictates of reason take you. This it is that has led to the religious crisis of the present day in which want of belief struggles with a longing to believe. The crisis mainly affects Protestant countries. To be sure, those in which the Catholic Church is predominant are the scene of conflict between the religious and the antireligious, the latter class owing its existence to a number of causes more historical, social, and personal than intellectual, that for my purpose need not be considered here. The religious crisis so noticeable in England arises from the fact that at the Reformation the Protestant Churches made use of reason to cast off allegiance to Rome. Reason told Protestants that the basis of the Christian religion was the Bible, that book of the Holy Word which had only just been brought by translation within the reach of the common man. By trusting to the Bible the common man felt sure of seeing things as they were : he was in direct communion with God. Nobody, except perhaps a very few, so few as not to matter, thought of the Bible as anything but an authentic and complete revelation of God's will. But now comes the trouble. Criticism, that is, the application of reason to the growth of knowledge, has shown the Bible to be a collection of works of differing age and origin, of immense value to the student of history, poetry, and folklore, but full of fantasy, subject to the severest caution when offered as a repository of fact, and certainly not a whole and solid block inspired by the divine afflatus. What then becomes of religion based on the Bible ? Besides, there are other difficulties. If reason is called into play, as Protestantism has called it, it is quite impossible to reconcile the postulated existence of an all-powerful, omniscient, eternal and beneficent God with that of sin, pain, misery, and injustice : unless indeed some form is admitted of Manicheism, in which the divine and the evil spirits are co-existent and of equal stature. But Manicheism is condemned by Christianity, Catholic, Orthodox, and Protestant. It is also impossible by the light of reason to find an answer to the question debated by Flaubert and Turgenev, viz. What did God do before he created the world ? Wider historical knowledge than that possessed by our forebears has revealed the doctrines of the Divine sacrifice, of the Trinity, and of the Resurrection to be by no means peculiar to the Christian religion. Further, we know now that the universe does not, as all Christians conceived down to the sixteenth century and most till a much later date, consist of our earth, a fixed point surrounded by some odd lights hung in the sky, mankind being thus the most important part of creation ; but that the earth is a minor planet of a minor star which we call the sun, that uncountable billions of greater suns exist so far from us that their light may take over 500 million years to reach our puny globe, and that each of them may have planets which in turn may maintain forms of life perhaps similar to our own, perhaps different from and perhaps vastly superior to anything we can conceive. So that man, far from being " the lord of creation " and of special interest to the Creator, is a miserable animalcule crawling on the surface of a minute body rushing through space and, if there is a superior intelligence to watch him, of perhaps far less interest with his poor history of a mere million years than reptiles who can boast of ancestry at least two hundred and fifty times as old.

These doubts and difficulties do not trouble members of the Catholic Church. Those born into it, as well as those received into it in later life, are its children by an act not of reason but of faith. By that act of faith the Church is to them the repository of true religion and they have not to bother their heads about its doctrines. This is not to say that Catholics renounce the use of reason. They do not apply it to religious dogma, that is all. And just because they do not apply reason to it, they are free to treat religious dogma in the privacy of their minds in a variety of other ways, mystical, allegorical, symbolical, or transcendental. The advance of science then, historical, physical, mathematical, contains nothing that need shock or confuse them : if necessary, it may require a fresh interpretation of some point of doctrine and this will be forthcoming from the Church's authority, doubtless after delay, perhaps after obstruction, yet in the end it will come. This at all events is the construction given me by a brilliant Catholic surgeon, scientist, and anthropologist, still under middle age.

Clearly the path is far easier to tread for one born and bred in the Catholic Church than for a later convert. Such a one, it is hard not to think, must have to swallow pretty hard before that act of faith which will place him under the Church's jurisdiction as well as within her protection, especially if his national and historical background should have been opposed to both. Even in the case of one whose ancestors down to the last two generations were fervent Catholics, the way back into the fold may be long and hard. This was the case of Ernest Psichari, the grandson of Renan, and the story of his conversion, told by himself and his intimates, is of deep interest for the consideration of such matters. Yet once the act of faith or, to put it another way, the abnegation of reason as applied to religion is achieved, the Catholic can look on the world, physical and metaphysical, with untroubled eyes. It is in fact a matter of common observation that such conversion does bring peace to perturbed spirits.

Not so with your Protestant. He has appealed to Cæsar : his reason. By Cæsar's judgment then he must abide. For him it is vain to treat religious dogma symbolically or in what other way you will. If he does, his reason is abdicating and he ceases to be a Protestant. He may become a sceptic. But if he does that he ceases to be able to partake in the consolations of religion. Men placed in this dilemma doubtless often avoid it by simply refusing to apply their reason to a particular point. When I was rejecting confirmation into the Anglican Church, I asked my tutor at Eton, Henry Luxmoore, a man, as I have said, of great intelligence and of the highest principles, on what he based *belief* in a future life as expressed in the Athanasian creed. As a Protestant, it was not open to him to say that he had been taught it by the Church. Luxmoore answered that he could not bear not to believe it. Yet this was obviously not belief : it was faith, or, more vulgarly, wishful thinking. The same would seem to be the true interpretation of the reported answer by Jowett, Master of Balliol, to a young lady who brought her religious doubts to him : " We must believe in God, dear child, in spite of what the clergy tell us."

Spiritually the world was a far more comfortable place when reasoning was a luxury for a few highly educated men and the majority of mankind accepted without question the doctrines and consolations of religion. It is not without significance that *consolamentum* was the name given to acceptance into salvation by the sect of the Cathares, whose heresy disrupted Christendom in the middle ages for over a hundred years and was finally exterminated under the Sainted King Louis IX of France, and that this acceptance was consummated only on the point of release by death from a world whose visible and sensible elements were taught by priests of this widespread sect to be so utterly wicked that mankind as a whole could be saved only by men ceasing to propagate their species. One of the early Bolshevik slogans was : " Religion is opium for the people." So, if its ideal aspiration be subtracted from religion, it may be, and if by " the people " is meant ninety per cent of humanity. Yet, properly regarded, and even on so far lower a level, this is not a condemnation of religion. Narcotics are a very good thing for those in pain and most of humanity, if not in active pain, lies in fear of it and of misery, poverty, grief, and wretchedness. That elegant poet, Arthur Clough, in his confutation of atheism wrote :

But those who live beneath the shadow of the steeple,
The parson, and the parson's wife, and mostly married people,
And every man when grief, old age, or illness comes to strike him,
These do believe there is a God—or something very like him.

For the ills of life religion, whether Christian, Buddhist, Mahometan, or even Jewish—I say, even, because the Jewish religion is the harshest and least consoling of all—affords succour and relief. To hope is good and religion brings hope beyond the sorrows of this life. The opium of religion, if it were admitted to be opium, would yet be more wholesome food than the arsenic of materialism.

Existentialists, the latest and still among the most fashionable of philosophers, maintain that existence comes before essence, developing from that initial point a complete philosophy of pessimism. The sense in which this is true is obvious. Bare existence is the first necessity of man. Everything else is a subsequent refinement. Anyone who has undergone famine, danger and uncertainty whether his life may last till the morrow, and especially anyone who has had to confront these disagreeables without the sensation of an army or an organisation at his back or solid ground beneath his feet, will I think agree that the primary needs of man are a shelter over his head, enough food to support life, and clothing to protect his body. The order in which these should be put must vary according to circumstance and especially climate. But, whatever the order, these are the basic requirements of man. Is this to say that life has no more to offer than their fulfilment or that all effort else must end in the dustbin? Surely not. Whether or no we find an answer to satisfy our curiosity about ultimate reality and about the object of the universe, supposing it to have an object ; no matter how much or how little good it would do us to know, if we could ; nonetheless the values in the world of our own experience remain. About the existence of these, in whatsoever form they present themselves, there can be no doubt. Good, Beauty, and Truth inform all we have, all we appreciate with our senses, all we do. Or if they do not, we are very quickly and unpleasantly conscious of their negation. They do not make life, but they make life worth living. To give the aweful name of God to the motive force, supposing there to be one, behind these values or responsible for the form of energy that we call life, may be entirely appropriate. But it should not imply identity with the fierce tribal God of the Old Testament, nor yet with the far loftier but still personal conception to be drawn from the New, to say nothing of the debased divinities of Hindu theology, or the anthropomorphic gods of Greece and Rome and of Asgard. This may be said to be a formless religion. It is certainly one devoid of dogma. But dogma in itself has no merit. It may be a hypothesis that has outlived its usefulness. It once was possible, but I find it now impossible for a reasoning man to believe in a personal life beyond the grave of any kind that we in this life could recognise. There is certainly no reason for such a belief ; some reason against it is afforded by the almost unimaginable difficulties postulated in the sort of life in heaven pictured by William Blake and by many lesser men. Nor do I see why the universe must necessarily have an object or be created by a mind having some intention. If there is one, it is certainly an intention we are incapable of grasping. Paley's celebrated example of a watch found going, from which a man to wind it must be deduced, is patently absurd. We know that watches are made by men, but have not the beginning of comprehension of a mind capable of creating the universe as known to us today ; we therefore have no reason to deduce such a mind's existence. The origin and nature of organic life is a physical, not a metaphysical problem. We know that life exists, that we live. *Cogito, ergo sum.* We are for the time being here. What then is important to us is not really why we are here, but what we do so long as we are here. The three great values are our guide and our hope. This may seem a singularly trite conclusion. Yet I think it is that implied in the great Lord Halifax's answer to an indiscreet inquirer : " Pray, what is your religion ? " " Wise men," said Halifax, " have but one religion." " And what is that ? " went on the other, " Wise men never tell," answered Halifax. Surely it is not a religion of despair. It was Clifford who, summing up his own views, and rejecting the imperative doctrines of revealed religion, said : " Do I seem to you to say, Let us eat and drink, for tomorrow we die ? No, rather I say to you, Let us join hands and work, for this day we are alive together."

APPENDIX A

THE SEED OF FULBERT

THE seal with the wild boar crest was used about the year 1204 by Robert de Pollok on a charter of gift to Paisley Abbey. This may have been earlier or later in date than the assumption of arms by the Polloks or the grant of arms to them, which arms by the end of the Middle Ages had become fixed, the chief features in the Pollok coat-of-arms, to avoid technical heraldic terms, being a saltire or St. Andrew's Cross with three hunting horns. The earliest authentic grant of arms in England is thought to have been the case of Gilbert de Clare, in 1138, but there is a story that King Henry I granted arms to Geoffrey le Beau, Count of Anjou, some ten years before. It seems reasonable to suppose that the use of arms became general among noble families in Scotland about the same time as in England. John Pollok, the first of his line to drop the French particle " de " made use of the arms described above, together with his seal, in a document preserved in the archives of St. Salvator's College at St. Andrews and dated April 21, 1453.[1]

In the same century an event took place which was to revive the French connexion in a family now completely Scottish for over three centuries. Louis XI, as all readers of *Quentin Durward* know, maintained a trusted guard of Scottish archers about his person. Why they were or were called archers does not seem clear. Your mediæval Scot was a notoriously poor performer with the longbow. Nor does the crossbow seem to have been notably his weapon, although it was most expertly used by companies of French archers in the fourteenth and fifteenth centuries. Perhaps the word *archer* had already become stylised, as meaning one serving in the royal guard, just as later, in the seventeenth and eighteenth centuries it came to have an entirely conventional significance when applied to the force at the disposal of the French King's *Lieutenant de Police* who certainly did not use bows and arrows of any description. The fighting Scots in France were celebrated for skill with the cold steel that has ever made Scottish infantry a terror to enemies on the field of battle. Even if they ever

---

[1] Both here and in many other passages I am indebted for heraldic and genealogical points to my cousin, Mr. Edward Langslow Cock, who, after a distinguished career as civil engineer in East Africa and Malaya, devoted himself to elucidating the many ramifications of the Pollock family history. He is, however, in no way responsible for inferences I have drawn from the facts.

carried bows, it is unlikely that the Scottish archers in France made serious use of them. " Les archers écossais ", however, was the title of Louis XI's bodyguard, a picked body of gentlemen adventurers, all Scots, resembling the famous regiment of Musqueteers under Louis XIII. The astute and persistent monarch to whose patient endeavours France owed much of her subsequent greatness did not invent *les archers écossais*, as Sir Walter Scott's novel suggests. Scott had the merit of apprehending, by a process of his prodigious imagination, that historical ages differ from one another. Readers of Gibbon, unquestionably one of the world's greatest historians, get the impression (if they reflect on the matter at all) that men of all centuries from the first to the fourteenth felt and thought in approximately the same way. This is not merely another way of saying that Gibbon knew the truth of the dictum of Professor Toy of Harvard University, in his day one of the most profound students of ancient civilisations, that mankind had not improved by one iota since the days of Hammurabi : nothing, he said, had changed, save the organisation of society. Gibbon, so far as we can judge, was unaware that the question so much as existed. To the sceptical eighteenth-century philosopher all mankind came from the same mould : the same reactions could always be predicated of the genus homo, just as Pavlov has shown that mice, treated to the same conditioning, will be subject to the same complexes. Fortunately or perhaps unfortunately for us, men do differ from mice or from ants, even more slaves to their environment, and it was left to Sir Walter Scott to make the great discovery that men of one age are no more identical with those of another than Frenchmen with Flemings or, if it comes to that, than Americans with Englishmen.

The author of Waverley took great pains to achieve historical accuracy in his novels and, if he did not succeed, he is less to be blamed than the degree of historical knowledge available to a novelist in the early part of the nineteenth century. It therefore came about that, although doing his best with the material ready to his hand, Scott's lapses from exactitude in dealing with ages other than his own were frequent and have become notorious. Among these was his treatment of Louis XI, the characterisation of whom by Scott was so far from that drawn by Commines, Louis's contemporary, that the shock of the discovery turned the youthful Von Ranke from his natural bent for poetry and patriotic effort and filled him with a resolution to devote his life to the study of historical truth. So it is to Sir Walter Scott that we owe one of the most influential historians in the nineteenth century in addition to his own epoch-making, if unconscious, apprehension of the barriers erected between men merely by the passage of time. Since Scott, it has been impossible for novelists or historians to ignore this. A far less striking error in *Quentin*

Durward was Scott's notion that the Scottish Archers in France had been formed by Louis XI. It was in fact recruited by his father Charles VII, " Charles le Victorieux ", who owed the inspiration of the victories that gave him a title to that name to Joan of Arc, and who so very badly defended that glorious saint of France. Scott's error has been repeated by at least one recent French historian, so Sir Walter's admirers need not blush for him.[1] It may be that Charles VII did not himself have the idea. But he had the merit of taking advantage of it. The captain of his Scottish archers was Sir John Stewart of Darnly or Darnley, ancestor of the Earls of Darnley, including Mary Stuart's luckless husband, and of the first line of the Dukes of Lennox. So well did Sir John Stewart fight for France that Charles VII created him Comte d'Aubigny, a title remaining in the family till the seventeeth century, and granted to him the right to use as his personal arms the three royal lilies in the blazon of France. Stuart d'Aubigny, as he was known in the land of his election, left a son or perhaps grandson who was later to be one of Louis XII's generals in his invasion of Italy. The lilies of France remained in the arms of the Stewarts of Darnley and the Dukes of Lennox until the latter became extinct in the seventeenth century, when Charles II of England revived the title in favour of his son by Louise de Kéroualle, Duchess of Portsmouth. The d'Aubigny title too with a duchy attached to it was revived by Louis XIV in favour of the same lady. Yet the lilies of France did not for that disappear from a legitimate Scottish blazon. For a descendant of Sir John Stewart, Dorothea, daughter of James Stewart of Cardonald, in the sixteenth century married John Pollok of Pollok who by consecrated usage quartered the Pollok arms with the d'Aubigny lilies and there they remain to this day.

Between the date of Fulbert's settling in Scotland and that when by this chain of circumstance the lilies of the royal house of Fulbert's native country became emblazoned on the shield of his descendants, great changes had befallen the family. The wheel of fortune had spun high for them, and again it had spun low. George Crawfurd, the Scottish chronicler, in his General Description of the Shire of Renfrew, published in 1710, remarks that the family, " without question ", he says, " among the most ancient in Scotland ", probably owned the barony of Mearns besides the lands of Pollok (" anciently ", adds Crawfurd, " called Pulloc "). This, Crawfurd inferred from the fact that records of donations by Polloks of Mearns lands were found by him in the cartulary of Paisley Abbey. Mearns Castle, according

[1] M. Jean de la Varende in his brilliant study *Anne d'Autriche*, published 1938, writes : " six beaux gardes écossais à la manière des anciennes troupes formées par le bon roi Louis XI ".

to Crawfurd, had seven hundred acres, and Crawfurd notes five other properties in Mearns parish as having belonged to James, Robert, John, Thomas, and another Robert Pollok respectively. " The great estate of Upper Pollok " was larger than that of Mearns. There was besides that of Nether Pollok. The family property was therefore considerable. Robert de Pollok (Pulloc or again, according to some, Polloc) was noted as a " companion ", that is to say, companion-in-arms, of Walter FitzAlan, the Sheriff of Shropshire who threw in his lot with Matilda, niece of King David I of Scotland, in the latter's invasion of England to support her in her struggle against the most despised and detested King to whom the latter country was ever subject, Stephen. It was King David " the Lion " who at Carlisle gave the accolade of Knighthood to Henry Plantagenet, afterwards Henry II of England. The misrule, civil war, and misery that bedevilled Stephen's reign lasted for nineteen years and, although it is not to be supposed that the Scots King's move was dictated by more than dynastic reasons, it may be that a Scottish victory would have ended a period of oppression and anarchy unparalleled in our history. David I, however, was beaten out of England. With him went north Walter FitzAlan, a knight of Breton origin, one of those doughty bastards whose deeds spangle the history of the Middle Ages, doubtless for the very good reason that his head was forfeit should he stay in the south, to receive noble rewards from David and the title of Hereditary High Steward of Scotland, whence came the name of the royal family of Stuart or Stewart. And with Walter FitzAlan returned to Scotland Robert de Pollok, that faithful " companion ". A suggestion has indeed been made that this was the first appearance of a Pollok in Scotland and that Fulbert, father of the line, had settled in England. This would seem improbable for two reasons. First the stream of donations, to Paisley and other churches, begins almost too soon to make it plausible. Second it is barely credible that, if Fulbert had settled in England before his sons became prominent in Scotland, no more should be known of him. He must at least have been known as " Fulbert de . . . " some place or other, whereas his name appears simply in connexion with his sons, as " Petrus de Pollock, filius Fulberti ". The anonymity of this description could only arise if Fulbert were so important a person that nothing more was needed to identify him, which was obviously not the case ; or if, as intimated above, he had fled from pressing danger and had no desire to be more fully identified.

By the beginning of the thirteenth century, then, it is clear that the de Pollok family, later to become Pollok of that ilk, had waxed powerful and prosperous. They held a barony and were therefore, Scottish barons, a title less considered than that of the English barons who mastered King John ; nevertheless, one honourable and puissant. But soon came the great change. Edward I of England was one of our strongest and most far-seeing sovereigns. An administrator of pre-eminently just mind, the union that he effected between England and Wales by giving to the Welsh the heir to the crown of England as Wales's own particular prince was a piece of statesmanship of the first order. Edward I's strength as king was largely due to or at least closely connected with his legalistic bent. A similar bent can be observed in the only other English king whose success is comparable to that of Edward I, namely Henry VIII. It is visible also in the most solid, as well as spectacular, of Mongol conquerors, Genghis Khan. We may therefore fairly conclude a legalistic turn of mind to be a powerful adjunct to a ruler.

Legal precision, however, may sometimes work inimically to the intentions of its owner. Such was the effect of this particular psychology in a notorious case in our own lifetime. No question of personal rule was there concerned, but the principle was the same. In 1923, Germany having defaulted on the war reparations accepted by her, France, as she had the right to do under the Treaty of Versailles, occupied the Ruhr. The operation was bloodless and despite the passive resistance employed by a recalcitrant and dishonest German Government, was on the point of complete success. It is now widely known, though less so at the time, that German industry and the German Government, which latter expression was only another name for the same thing, was ready to give in. It did in fact unofficially capitulate. It signified to the French Government that it would call off the passive resistance, which had proved an expensive failure, and asked the French to state their terms. I was made aware of this at the very moment of its taking place by the Secretary-General—in plainer English we should say the general manager—of the all-powerful industrial trust of which the Krupps and the Thyssens were prominent members. I was at the time Berlin correspondent of the *Daily Express* and I had, after much difficulty, obtained an interview with this important official. Accustomed, as were all British correspondents, to flatteries of ourselves as fulsome as objurgations of the French, from whom the Germans from Stresemann downwards aspired to detach us, were blatant, I was astonished to hear that the struggle for the Ruhr was over and that the German industrialists had caved in. They threw in their hand and awaited the verdict. But to the still more intense surprise of the Germans, Poincaré, the French Prime Minister, refused to state French terms separately. He was a lawyer and his legalistic mind insisted that Germany should not quietly yield to France but make public obeissance to the Reparations Commission, the international organisation of all the Allies.

This was too much for the Germans, or perhaps they swiftly spied a chance to snatch *in extremis* at the victory they had been convinced was denied to them. They managed to procrastinate still further, a new international conference was called with American influence preponderant, the Dawes Plan was born, and Germany mastered her lesson how to bamboozle the Allies. Had Poincaré been less addicted to the letter of the law and more of an opportunist, it is possible that Germany might never have got her tail up and that the second World War might have been averted.

There may not seem to have been much in common between the noblest of Plantagenet monarchs and the straitlaced, democratic barrister-statesman of the French Third Republic ; but Edward I made a mistake with regard to Scotland similar to that made by Poincaré with regard to Germany. It did not lead, as in the case of Poincaré, within twenty years to a disastrous defeat of Edward's country—and it must be emphasised that this error of Poincaré's was but one of many avoidable errors made by many Frenchmen and by many Englishman too that produced 1940 and may yet produce God knows what—yet, had it been avoided, centuries of warfare and bitterness between England and Scotland might have been avoided, and the whole course of European history been changed. For Edward I had a thoroughly admirable desire to unite Scotland with England as he had united Wales with her. There is no overwhelming reason why union should not have been achieved, given a retention by Scotland of real autonomy and a recognition of her honourable independence. But Edward's legal mind jibbed at this. In the matter of practical autonomy it seems probable that he was prepared to go all the way : further, some Scots may think, than the road actually trodden since the Union. But he would not retreat by an inch from his claim of feudal paramountcy. And this was a claim that Scottish national sentiment would not admit. So the two countries went to the arbitrament of arms. The clash of them never abated until three hundred years later, when a Scots king sat on the English throne, and it did not really die away for another century and a half. In his appeal to arms Edward I was defeated. The " auld alliance " was born. For five centuries and a half Scots fought on French soil against England, and at every crisis in her history England, instead of having a staunch ally at her back, had to be prepared to defend herself on a second front and against a skilful, relentless foe. Such may be the results of sticking to the letter of the law.

Edward I was not without support for his idea in Scotland. His candidate for the Scottish crown was John Baliol, and among the Scots barons who took Baliol's part and in 1296 swore to Edward the allegiance he craved as overlord of Scotland was John de Pollock, the name already being so spelt by one of the older writers : there is nothing peculiar about these variations, the spelling of names in both Great Britain and France being quite haphazard until well into the seventeenth century. Edward's plan for Scotland crashed to hopeless failure at Bannockburn, and very naturally the Scottish barons and lairds who had sided with Baliol paid the price.

It is idle to speculate on the motives of persons in the past where no definite evidence exists, but it cannot be said that adherence to Edward I and to Baliol affords proof of disloyalty to his country in a Scot of that date. It may be thought curious, as revealing a persistent trait in the family, that Sir Robert Pollock, the first baronet of the name, was among the Scottish Commissioners at the time of the Union under Queen Anne and went to England as one of the Scots members to the Parliament at Westminster. Probably the worthy Sir Robert had no notion that he was fulfilling destiny as an agent in the cause unsuccessfully championed by his remote ancestor, John de Pollock.

Robert de Bruce, now King of Scotland by might and by right, behaved with commendable leniency towards brother Scots who had taken sides against him. Robert de Bruce was of course like almost all the Scottish barons, and like his rival Baliol, of French descent. Not for nothing did he become called " the good King Robert ". Instead of chopping off the heads of John de Pollock and others of his family implicated in Baliol's collapse, Bruce lopped off their lands. The downfall of the Pollocks spelled the rise of the Maxwells, neighbours if not dependants. A large part of their estates were, says the chronicler, " ravished from the Pollocks of that ilk, and seized by the Maxwells. At the same time, about 1310, Robert de Pollok, son of John, was forced to make a grant of his movable goods—presumably gold and jewels—to the Abbey of Arbroath. Thus the lands that were to become part of the city of Glasgow, Pollok Shaws and Pollok Shields, passed out of the hands of that family and the Maxwells took the name of Maxwell of Pollok and Lord of the Mearns.

This " ravishment " was obviously carried out on the orders of Robert Bruce. Further proof of the Scots king's intention to master his former enemies by means milder and probably more effective than by shedding their blood is afforded by the marriage of Robert de Pollok with Agnes daughter of John Maxwell of Mearns. It is clear that such a union between a former rebel and the child of the man to whom part of that rebel's lands had been transferred could only have been made by royal command. Before ever the famous Hapsburg motto existed, Robert Bruce had evidently learned that marriage is often a stronger instrument of policy than war.

Happy nations, it is said, have no history ; so it may be presumed that families too without history are happy. In this case the Pollok family, after their frantic upset caused by the unsuccess of Edward I's plan for Scottish union, must have been pre-eminently happy. Save for a series of births, wivings, and deaths, nothing is recorded of them worth the slightest note for a very long time. Johns, Roberts, Davids, Charles's succeed one another through the fourteenth, fifteenth, and sixteenth centuries with a monotony almost of a meteorological chronicle, broken, towards the end of the last, by one solitary incident showing something of the fierce blood of Fulbert's earlier descendants. John Pollock, that same John who married Dorothea Stewart of Cardonald and quartered the Pollock cross of St. Andrew and hunting horns with the three lilies of France, took part, we are told by Crawfurd, in " the conflict of Lockerbie, anno 1593, assisting the Lord Maxwel (his cousin) against the Laird of Johnstoun, and was there slain ". It would seem that the marriage between Robert de Pollock and Agnes Maxwell in the fourteenth century had led to a lasting union between the two families, so justifying Robert Bruce's pacific policy. In 1486 moreover Charles Pollok had obtained from Robert Lord Maxwell a charter to the Pollok lands and, as he married Margaret Stewart, daughter of Lord Minto, and their grandson a daughter of Lord Sempill, plainly the family had climbed a fair way out of the abyss into which taking up arms for Edward of England had thrown them. The seventeenth century is again a long tale of nothingness. One Pollok, at least, went into business and became " a wealthy merchant of the city of Glasgow " : he was Alexander Pollock and dealt in leather, a predilection to be intensified later in the family. Another went into the Church (although which of the several Churches in Scotland is not specified) ; and by doing so both acted as prototypes for many of their descendants in the nineteenth and twentieth centuries. Three generations passed without brilliance and without catastrophe at Upper Pollok, " a stately mansion embossomed among its own full grown timber, situated on an eminence that overlooks the whole country ". But it is not until we come to another Robert Pollok that there is again a flash of the old Fulbert blood. This Robert, the date of whose birth appears uncertain but who died in 1736, carried on family tradition by his two marriages, first to the daughter of Sir George Maxwell, the then owner of Nether Pollok, second to Annabella Stewart, daughter of Stewart of Pardovan. Stewart and Maxwell and, later, Macnaghten form secondary threads in the pattern running through the carpet of the centuries.

The surprising events in which Robert was concerned deserve to be recorded in the words of their original chronicler, the noble strain and pathos of whose recital it would be vain for any modern to emulate. We read :

" He was, by Her Majesty Queen Anne, created a Baronet of Nova Scotia, 30th November 1703, to him and to the heirs male of his body ; it proceeds [*sic*] upon a recital of the antiquity and flourishing condition of the ancient family of Pollock of that ilk, for 600 years then by-past since the reigns of David and William, Kings of Scotland ; also, upon a recital of the many illustrous and faithful services of the said Robert, now Sir Robert of that ilk, the representative without interruption of that ancient family. As also," and here we touch the note of deeply pathetic quality, " his faithful and zealous services in defending the reformed religion at the time of the Revolution, and that, when bearing the King's commission, he had been taken and confined in the most barbarous and uncivilized parts of the Highlands during the space of nine months, because he would not renounce his allegiance to King William."

Torment of spirit and bodily privation inflicted on this staunch Protestant and Whig by savage and Catholic Highlanders must have been a sore trial indeed. The reward was great too. Honours, a title as yet by no means commonplace, and a seat in Parliament must have seemed to Sir Robert almost a transfiguration from the comfortable routine of life in that " stately mansion " in Renfrewshire. Few members of Parliament could feel they had bought their seats with coin of such value. And titles were titles then. No one in the eighteenth century could have said as my father did : " The chief use of being a baronet is that it makes it impossible for a man to be knighted."

The title and male descendants of Sir Robert Pollok died out in the nineteenth century, without any of them aspiring to do more than carry on the name. His last surviving granddaughter, Robina, married Sir Hew Crawfurd Bart., and their grandson born in 1794 added the name of Pollok to his own, having through his grandmother inherited the Pollok estates which thus, for a second time, passed into the hands of another family. The second and last Sir Hew Crawfurd-Pollok died in 1885 and this baronetcy too, which dated from 1628, became extinct like that of Sir Robert Pollok.

As demonstrated by the celebrated example of the " Worm " in Wagner's *Siegfried*, comfortably reposing on wealth would not seem conducive to a display of energy in humans any more than in dragons. Which of course was the moral Wagner wanted drawn from his ingenuous tale. A case in point is the elder line of the Pollock family. One generation after another inhabited that " stately mansion " without leaving a record of anything more noteworthy than their mere names. Who knows, had not the " barbarous and uncivilized " Highlanders spurred him into action by kidnapping and sequestrating him, whether Sir Robert himself would have displayed any greater energy ? To show that the spirit of adventure was not dead which had turned Fulbert's sons from Frenchmen into Scots was left to younger branches of the old tree. For them the seventeenth century was prolific of exploit. At least three split off to try the great adventure of their day : emigration to the New World. One settled in South Carolina, where in the last century a Colonel Pollock was a well-known sportsman, patron of the turf and the ring : engravings of his protégés, human and equine, can even now be found in some English inns. Another, probably of more serious bent, in Pennsylvania, and their descendant in our day, Professor James J. Pollock, who holds the chair of Political Science in the University of Iowa, is among the best qualified authorities in America on post-war Germany. A third in North Carolina, and these contracted their name to Polk and gave birth to James K. Polk, eleventh President of the United States. Another branch of the family about the same time went to Ulster and in our day gave a Cabinet Minister to Northern Ireland. But that which most spread and flourished was the branch sprung from John Pollock who early in the seventeenth century founded a separate, cadet line of his family at Balgray or Balguerrie, four miles southwest of Pollokshaws and seven from Glasgow proper, marrying his cousin, daughter of Robert Pollock of that ilk (that is to say, of Pollock), and became in time the ancestor of my great-great-grandfather, the Saddler. The Saddler was thus, perhaps without knowing it, Pollock of Balgray.[1] The senior line, Pollock of Pollock, otherwise Pollock of that ilk, has died out. The Lord Chief Baron, the Saddler's son, was born, however distantly, Pollock of Balgray, but founded another cadet branch and became Pollock of Hatton.

[1] Definite evidence proving the descent of the Saddler from John Pollock of Balgray was obtained by the efforts of Mr. Edward Langslow Cock, a grandson of the Lord Chief Baron, only in 1948–9, when it was accepted by Lord Lyon, King of Arms, the head of the Scottish heralds' office, and the arms of Pollock of Hatton rematriculated in consequence. The lateness of the above date is the reason why the descent of the Saddler from Fulbert did not figure in the post-war edition of *Burke's Peerage*.

LE BANQUET DONNE EN L'HONNEUR DE LA PRESSE FRANÇAISE ET ÉTRANGÈRE

(VERBATIM REPORT BY A FRENCH NEWS AGENCY)

D ISCOURS de M. Pollock :
Monsieur le Maréchal, Monsieur le Gouverneur Général, Messieurs et Chers Confrères,

C'est avec une sincère émotion que je me lève pour répondre au " toast " porté en des termes si généreux à la Presse, je ne dirai pas " Étrangère " ainsi que vous me l'avez demandé, M. le Maréchal Lyautey.

Il faudrait posséder une éloquence bien loin hélas, d'être la mienne, il faudrait en effet posséder l'éloquence de M. le Maréchal lui-même pour savoir exprimer notre gratitude, notre admiration au Grand Inspirateur de cette belle œuvre qui touche à sa fin, ainsi qu'à ses aides dévoués.

Notre gratitude pour la parfaite courtoisie vraiment française, la bienveillance éclairée qu'ils ont manifestée à la Presse Étrangère pendant ces longs mois, où le Maréchal et tout son remarquable État Major du Commissariat de l'Exposition, ont été surchargés de travail.

Notre admiration pour la grandeur des résultats positifs que ce travail a atteints.

L'Exposition Coloniale se meurt. J'ose dire que chacun de nous a l'impression de perdre un ami, tellement l'été, puis l'automne passés ont été dominés par le gigantesque monument de beauté construit à Vincennes. (*Applaudissements.*) Pourtant je ne partage pas entièrement les regrets—très naturels, très respectables—de ceux qui voudraient voir, coûte que coûte, prolonger l'Exposition Coloniale.

Il existe de telles perfections, tels efforts humains, qui, semblables à une étoile filante ou à quelque exquis coucher de soleil, sont encore plus attachants en raison même de leur brièveté. Ce n'est qu'un instant (*applaudissements*), mais dans ce court passage quelque chose est entré dans les fibres de notre existence, une chose dont l'impression sera ineffaçable. (*Applaudissements.*) Elle se meurt, la belle Exposition, aux allées charmeuses, aux perpectives hallucinantes, aux éclairages éblouissants dans ce coin ravissant du Bois de Vincennes. Mais jamais l'Exposition Coloniale ne sera morte.

Non, au delà des constructions étincelantes, des objets d'art sans prix, de cette adorable reconstitution de pays lointains, se projette l'ombre d'une grande idée, et cette idée est grande parce qu'elle émane de la vérité.

Il est bon quelque fois, Messieurs, dans un âge de conceptions faciles, d'être appelé à la contemplation de la vérité, à l'examen de la destinée des hommes et de leur tâche.

Ce que l'Exposition Coloniale aura accompli, le voici : elle aura gravé—peut être à leur insu—dans le cerveau des millions de ses visiteurs une meilleure compréhension de l'idée coloniale, l'idée du développement même de l'humanité, l'idée que toutes les intelligences sous différents climats ne sont pas au même niveau, que tous les peuples n'ont pas au même degré la capacité de diriger leur sort, mais qu'il y a encore une tâche pour les plus doués, les plus expérimentés en aidant dans l'intérêt commun les faibles, les retardatuires (*applaudissements*).

Déblayer les forêts, traverser les déserts, faire fructifier la terre, apporter l'ordre et la justice, détruire l'esclavage, combattre l'ignorance, la maladie, la haine, les préjugés, voilà l'œuvre des nations qui, tour à tour, se sont attelées au char de l'idée coloniale. Cette tâche est loin d'être terminée.

Maintenant la France, avec son immense progrès en Afrique et en Asie, tient la tête dans cette course au flambeau, que les nations d'élite se passent à travers les âges. Il est donc juste que le plus grand monument à l'idée coloniale ait été conçu dans la métropole française (*applaudissements*). Pourtant la conception n'est pas tout. Il y a aussi l'exécution. Il est rare, Messieurs, que les grands peuples soient trahis par leur histoire (*applaudissements*).

Dans la Révolution française germait Napoléon. L'effort français en Afrique arrivant à sa plus belle floraison a produit le Napoléon de l'idée coloniale : le Maréchal Lyautey (*applaudissements*).

En ce moment, on parle beaucoup de la paix : M. le Maréchal a fait mieux, il a créé la paix, il l'a fortement organisée, et, avec cette organisation, a donné un empire non seulement à la France, mais à la civilisation tout entière (*applaudissements*).

Aucun autre mot ne peut mieux lui exprimer notre admiration pour l'Exposition de Vincennes, qui couronne son œuvre, en répand et en fixe l'esprit. Aussi, c'est le propre du génie de se créer des aides brillants. Tout comme César, un Napoléon, un Cecil Rhodes, groupant autour d'eux les talents les plus complets, le Maréchal Lyautey a su trouver des lieutenants de premier ordre.

A eux, aussi bien qu'à leur grand chef, je lève mon verre au nom de la Presse Étrangère, avec le souhait que rien n'obscurcira désormais la grandeur spirituelle de leur œuvre. (*Applaudissements très chaleureux.*)

INDEX OF PROPER NAMES

INDEX OF PROPER NAMES